T0243631

We Are Free to Change the World

We Are
Free to
Change
the World

HANNAH ARENDT'S
LESSONS IN LOVE
AND DISOBEDIENCE

Lyndsey Stonebridge

HOGARTH
London/New York

Published in the United States by Hogarth, an imprint of Random House,
a division of Penguin Random House LLC, New York.

HOGARTH is a trademark of the Random House Group Limited, and the
H colophon is a trademark of Penguin Random House LLC.

Grateful acknowledgment is made to Farrar, Straus and Giroux for permission to reprint
an excerpt from "The Man-Moth" from *Poems* by Elizabeth Bishop, copyright © 2011
by The Alice H. Methfessel Trust. Publisher's note and compilation copyright © 2011 by
Farrar, Straus & Giroux; excerpt and facsimile of "Pigeons (For Hannah Arendt)" by
Rainier Maria Rilke, translated by Robert Lowell from *Collected Poems* by Robert Lowell,
copyright © 2003 by Harriet Lowell and Sheridan Lowell. Reprinted by permission of
Farrar, Straus and Giroux. All rights reserved.

Library of Congress Cataloging-in-Publication Data
Names: Stonebridge, Lyndsey, author.
Title: We are free to change the world: Hannah Arendt's lessons in love and
disobedience / by Lyndsey Stonebridge.
Description: New York: Hogarth, 2024. | Includes bibliographical references.
Identifiers: LCCN 2023020820 (print) | LCCN 2023020821 (ebook) |
ISBN 9780593229736 (hardcover) | ISBN 9780593229743 (ebook)
Subjects: LCSH: Arendt, Hannah, 1906–1975—Criticism and interpretation. |
Arendt, Hannah, 1906–1975. Origins of totalitarianism. | Totalitarianism. |
World politics—21st century.
Classification: LCC JC251.A74 S78 2024 (print) | LCC JC251.A74 (ebook) |
DDC 320.53—dc23/eng/20231101
LC record available at https://lccn.loc.gov/2023020820
LC ebook record available at https://lccn.loc.gov/2023020821

Printed in the United States of America on acid-free paper

randomhousebooks.com

9 8 7 6 5 4 3 2 1

First Edition

Book design by Debbie Glasserman

For SHH
after twenty-five years,
and for the love of our world

One of these days—when? It doesn't matter when, let's say at some point—I will be able to describe the actual domain of political life, because no one is better at marking the borders of a terrain than the person who walks around it from the outside.

—HANNAH ARENDT

Contents

Abbreviations

Illustrations

A Note on Imagination

Hannah Arendt was committed to what Immanuel Kant called "an enlarged mentality" which she believed to be the grounding for good judgment. This type of critical imagination is not creative, and nor is it necessarily empathetic. *You think your own thoughts but in the place of somebody else,*[*] she instructed her students. In this book I have tried to think my own thoughts in the place of Hannah Arendt. All direct quotations from her writing are in italics and referenced. I have imagined plausible scenarios in her life only where the evidence permits. Despite these precautions, there may be moments in what follows when Hannah Arendt also thinks her thoughts in my place.

---

[*] Teaching notes, "Political Experience in the Twentieth Century," The New School, 1968.

We Are Free to Change the World

Thinking What We Are Doing

In the months following Donald's Trump's election in 2016, Hannah Arendt's *The Origins of Totalitarianism* crashed onto the Amazon US bestseller lists. In the first year of his presidency, overall sales of the book increased by over 1,000 percent. Tweet-sized quotations from her writing began to flutter through the internet, and regular Arendt-themed opinion pieces started to appear in the press. A politics of the absurd and grotesque, the cruel, mendacious, and downright incredible had returned, and Arendt seemed to have something to say about it.

First published in 1951, *The Origins of Totalitarianism* described how historical conditions in Europe conspired to give evil a shockingly modern political formation in the twentieth century. Hate and fear dominated everything in totalitarian regimes, she argued. Political lies had triumphed over facts. All that remained were power, violence, and ideology. *What happened? Why did it happen? How could it have happened?* (OT 387) Arendt asked. The old political and historical narratives no longer gave plausible answers.

Arendt also warned that while the totalitarian regimes of her time would invariably fall, the contexts and thinking that permitted them might well linger into the future, taking on new forms in response to new circumstances, certainly, but building on a political and cultural rot that had taken hold sometime earlier.

There were few marching jackboots on the streets of America when Trump took the presidency, political dissidents did not start disappearing into torture cells at 3 A.M in the morning, although in Aleppo, Syria; Maidan, Ukraine; and elsewhere, there were already both boots and terror. Twentieth-century-style totalitarian regimes hadn't returned. But as commentators noted then and since, many of the elements Arendt first identified with totalitarian thinking have crept back into our political culture.

A cynical disenchantment with politics characterizes our time as it did Arendt's, as does an inchoate hate ready to be directed at anything and anyone. Conspiracy theories flourish. Self-censorship is back. Many of us are lonely. We have now added the reality of the climate apocalypse to the threat of total nuclear apocalypse. The tacit acceptance that there are certain categories of people—refugees, migrants, the uprooted, the occupied, the incarcerated, the permanently poor—whose lives are essentially superfluous has not changed much since the Second World War. The camps and ghettos have changed their locations, names, and appearances, but the misery remains, as does the thoughtlessly cruel administration of human beings as though they were little more than freight.

Hannah Arendt is a creative and complex thinker; she writes about power and terror, war and revolution, exile and love, and, above all, about freedom. Reading her is never just an intellectual exercise, it is an experience. I have been reading Arendt for over thirty years, first discovering her when I was a graduate student in the late 1980s, just as the Cold War was ending. I liked her style, her boldness and directness, her confident irony and worldly wit. She came from a past close enough to touch (she died in 1975, ten years after my birth), but spoke with a voice so utterly her own, and in such lucid prose, that she also seemed to come from out of nowhere.

But it was not until I sat down to work out why we should be reading her now, in the age of Donald Trump and Vladimir Putin, that I realized it was the stubborn humanity of her fierce and complex creativity that I had most to learn from.

Arendt is best known for her analysis of politically dark times, but her abiding question is one that is again being asked in a series of defiant, creative, and extraordinarily courageous responses to contemporary terror, occupation, and ideology: *What is freedom?*

For Hannah Arendt that question was neither abstract nor simply theoretical. She loved the human condition for what it was: terrible, beautiful, perplexing, amazing, and above all, exquisitely precious. And she never stopped believing in a politics that might be true to that condition. Her writing has much to tell us about how we got to this point in our history, about the madness of modern politics and about the awful, empty thoughtlessness of contemporary political violence. But she also teaches that it is when the experience of powerlessness is at its most acute, when history seems at its most bleak, that the determination to think like a human being, creatively, courageously, and complicatedly, matters the most.

Because she had lived in a post-truth era, Arendt saw what it meant when people no longer share the same basic sense of the world they inhabit together. We need her now because she understood, as few political thinkers have done since, what we have to lose when we allow our politics to become inhuman. The last few years have again shown us both how destructive and vulnerable the human condition is. Arendt teaches that if you really love the world (and she did) you must have the courage to protect it—to disobey.

For Arendt we can only be free so long as we have free minds. What follows is a story about how Hannah Arendt came to think about her own times, told in an effort to think more defiantly and creatively about our own. It is also a conversation, sometimes combative, between the present and her past. Arendt never told her readers *what* to think. There are no quick fixes for defeating autocracy, combating populism, and jump-starting social democracy to be gleaned from her work. Sometimes, especially when she wrote about race, her own thinking failed. What she offers instead is a model of *how* to think when politics and history are tearing up all the conventional safety rails, as they did in her time and as they have again in the early twenty-first century.

Having a free mind in Arendt's sense means turning away from dogma, political certainties, theoretical comfort zones, and satisfying ideologies. It means learning instead to cultivate the art of staying true to the hazards, vulnerabilities, mysteries, and perplexities of reality, because ultimately that is our best chance of remaining human.

She belonged to a generation of writers and thinkers born in the first decade of the twentieth century, just before it lurched into political and economic chaos, war, fascism, totalitarianism, and nuclear horror. This was a generation well practiced in appalled surprise at historical events, and Hannah Arendt, a refugee and outsider, was more practiced than most. She was the smart young Jewish woman who escaped from the black heart of fascist Europe and its crumbling nation states, made a new life for herself in America, the republic of new beginnings, and became one of its most influential public intellectuals.

Like Arendt's life, this book includes many journeys. Today, Königsberg, the bustling Prussian port where she grew up and learned how to think, renamed Kaliningrad in 1945, is a Russian exclave on the borders of the European Union. Authoritarianism has reclaimed Russia and a new generation of Eastern Europeans have begun reading *The Origins of Totalitarianism*—this time as a survival guide.[1] Her legacy is also present in places she never went, at least not directly. She refused to visit the Jim Crow South of the United States out of principle, for example, but this did not stop her from writing a controversial essay on desegregation that now echoes painfully in an America that is reckoning (or refusing to reckon) with its violently racist history. Meanwhile, in Beirut, Lebanon, Palestine, and elsewhere in the Middle East, activists in parallel, woefully under-recognized, struggles for a new politics of plurality and self-determination, critically and creatively read Arendt on revolution.

Thinking alongside Hannah Arendt today means asking the questions that first preoccupied her from our own precarious position in history. She described totalitarianism as a political attack on human experience. It followed for her that anti-totalitarian thinking began not with brushing that experience aside, but with really looking at it again. Fundamental questions about the human condition are not beside the point in dire political times; they *are* the point. How can we think straight amidst cynicism and mendacity? What is there left to love, to cherish, to fight for? How can we act to best secure it? What fences and bridges do we need to build to protect freedom and which walls do we need to destroy?

She liked distinctions in her answers because they gave clarity to what otherwise risked remaining dangerously obscure. She particularly liked categorizing things in threes. Anti-semitism, imperialism, and totalitarianism were the three modern political evils (*The Origins of Totalitarianism*). Labor, work, and action are what we do in the world, and the private, social, and public realms are where we do them (*The Human Condition,* 1958). Thinking, willing, and judging are what we do in our heads while this other activity is going on (*The Life of the Mind,* 1979). For all this symmetry, she was not a philosophical system builder. *Who would dare reconcile himself with the reality of extermination camps or play the game of thesis-antithesis-synthesis until his dialectics have discovered "meaning" in slave labor?* she once asked.[2] Her starting point was more straightforward: *What I propose, therefore, is very simple: it is nothing more than to think what we are doing,* she wrote in *The Human Condition* (*HC* 5).

Thinking was her first defense against the tyranny of the one-size-fits-all answer. A teacher as much as a theorist, her trick is to make us look again carefully at what is already there. More of a conservationist than conservative, she traveled back into the traditions of political and philosophical thought in search of new creative pathways to the present.[3] Her intellectual companions are straight from the white male European canon: Socrates, Saint Augustine, Niccolò Machiavelli, Immanuel Kant, Søren Kierkegaard, Friedrich Nietzsche, Karl Marx, and her philosophy teachers in Germany, Martin Heidegger (also her lover) and Karl Jaspers (her lifelong friend and mentor). But she read and interpreted these men to preserve what was most radical in their thought and often against their intentions.

She looked across the field of political philosophy and rewilded it with what, to her, was most important of all: human experience. When she spoke of freedom, she was not talking about an abstract freedom that could be conjured up out of the minds of men and willed into the world, often at a terrible cost. She meant the freedom that was already latent, waiting among us, and which is realized only when we act together. Her political heroes were those who trusted in other people more than in abstractions: the economist, Marxist, and revolutionary Rosa Luxemburg, the American Founding Fathers, the French Resistance, the Hungarian revolutionaries from 1956, and the students who protested against the Vietnam War and the lies that America told itself in order to wage it in the 1960s and early 1970s.

"As a woman I have no country . . . As a woman, my country is the whole world," Virginia Woolf wrote in her famous anti-fascist essay *Three Guineas,* first published on the eve of war in 1938. In the same year, Hannah Arendt was living in the refugee community in Paris's fifteenth arrondissement, working for Youth Aliyah, a Jewish nongovernmental organization settling young people in Palestine. Like millions of others at that time, she literally had no country; she was stateless, and would remain so until 1950 when she acquired American citizenship.

Arendt was just as much a cosmopolitan thinker as Woolf, although notably less of a feminist. Yet, by the early 1940s she was in no place, and in no mood, to celebrate a borderless world. *We lost our home, which means the familiarity of daily life,* she wrote from New York in a 1943 essay. News that the concentration camps were also *corpse factories* (her phrase) for European Jews had not long filtered through to the refugee community. She was thirty-six, roughly at the midpoint of her life, and that essay, entitled "We Refugees," was one of the most beautiful, lyrical, and devastating pieces of prose she would ever write:

> *We lost our home, which means the familiarity of daily life. We lost our occupation, which means the confidence that we are of some use in this world. We lost our language, which means the naturalness of reactions, the simplicity of gestures, the unaffected expression of feelings. We left our relatives in the Polish ghettos and our best friends have been killed in concentration camps, and that means the rupture of our private lives.* [4]

The loss was total. Worse still, it barely registered in her new country nor, indeed, in much of the Allied world, which had no problem in recognizing Nazi barbarism but some difficulty in accommodating the new guests from no-man's land. *Apparently nobody wants to know that contemporary history has created a new kind of human beings—the kind that are put in concentration camps by their foes and in internment camps by their friends,* she added.

Hannah Arendt's statelessness was not incidental to her political thought; it gave her the perspective she most valued: the viewpoint of those who knew exactly what the reality was beyond the

lies and propaganda, the confected outrage and the false justifica-
tions for cruel and murderous policies. She called this the *priceless
advantage* of the pariah. *One of these days,* she wrote in a letter to her
second husband, Heinrich Blücher, in 1955, *I will be able to describe
the actual domain of political life, because no one is better at marking the
borders of a terrain than the person who walks around it from the outside*
(*WFW* 236).

There is a reason why current authoritarians, as they did in the
mid-twentieth century, deliberately cultivate widespread cynicism
with their indifference to reason and reality: it keeps the political
field clear of challengers. Arendt wanted politics to be more
crowded, busier, livelier, more unpredictable. "Hannah was always
more for the Many than for the One," wrote her friend, the novelist Mary McCarthy: "which may help explain her horrified recognition of totalitarianism as a new phenomenon in the world."[5] The
"many" was not the masses, but the plurality of the human condition which she believed to be the natural enemy of totalitarian
thinking—would that we could see it.

Thinking about what we are doing begins with trusting our
aversions to ready-made political and social narratives. *I hate to be so
difficult, but I am afraid the truth is that I am,* she once wrote, declining
to take part in a public debate which she knew was being staged for
a boo-hiss audience and which she therefore wanted no part of.[6] In
truth, Hannah Arendt dreamed of a world in which the majority
were happy and able to be difficult whenever it was morally or
politically necessary.

*It is as though mankind had divided itself between those who believe in
human omnipotence (who think that everything is possible if one knows how
to organize masses for it) and those for whom powerlessness has become the*

major experience of their lives, she wrote in the 1951 preface to *The Origins of Totalitarianism* (OT xxv). It was then and it is now. But toward the end of her life she also wrote: *We are* free *to change the world and to start something new in it* (CR 5). That freedom begins not with what she once called *reckless optimism,* but with the determination to exist as a fully living and thinking person in a world among others (*OT* xxvi).

Those who knew her confirm what surviving film footage of her interviews and lectures captures so well. She was brilliant in public, and performed her thinking with all the intense virtuosity of the Shakespeare soliloquies she loved. Elegant, long-fingered hands would cup both her chin and her cigarette, and smoke would rise over her face like a mask through which she would sound her thoughts in a deep-throated, careful, accented English. A pause, an outbreath of smoke, an upward look, a smile that got wider with age. *Well I can't help that,* she'd reply to questions she thought particularly obtuse, her eyes slightly widening beneath the lids. But she always held something back. Watching and reading Hannah Arendt, I am often captured by the sense that there exists something she will not give up; something precious, mysterious even to herself, but very strongly present. But isn't that just the point of all of this? she might say now, chin resting in her smoking hand from her place in the bar in the underworld where the lost angels of the last century gather at dusk. That we are unknowable even to ourselves, maybe especially to ourselves and yet capable of collective miracles? Isn't that what you must fight for again now?

Hannah Arendt at the University of Chicago, 1966.

CHAPTER ONE

Where Do We Begin?

It belongs to totalitarian thinking to conceive of a
final conflict at all. There is no finality in history—
the story told by it is a story with many beginnings
but no ends.

—*The Ex-Communists*

On a cold and drizzly March day in 1962, Hannah Arendt lay in a hospital bed in New York, gazing thoughtfully up at the ceiling. The day before a truck had slammed into the taxi she was riding in through Central Park, smashing up her face and teeth and breaking nine of her ribs. She did not know how the truck had come to hit the taxi or how her body had got so broken because, as had become her habit of late, she had been using the ride for some precious reading time. One moment there had been words echoing in her head, the next, darkness.

When she regained consciousness she checked that she could still move and then, with considerably more attention, tested her memory; *very carefully decade by decade, poetry, Greek and German and English, then telephone numbers,* she recalled in a letter to Mary McCarthy. *Everything all right.* In that same moment, she realized she had to make a decision: she could die or choose to stay in the world. She was fifty-five years old. Death did not particularly frighten her, but *I also thought that life was quite beautiful and that I'd rather take it* (*BF* 126–27). As she squinted at the hospital ceiling through her undamaged eye, she recognized a familiar feeling: elation.

It had been a long time since Hannah Arendt had been so still, her hands free of either luggage or books, her mind free to roam. Events had moved so fast over the past year; at moments it had seemed as though her entire life was being replayed before her. Each time she'd caught her breath something else had happened and she had sped on again.

A year earlier, she had gone to Jerusalem to cover the trial of the senior Nazi Adolf Eichmann for *The New Yorker*. Eichmann was responsible for organizing the transportation of Jews from across Europe to their deaths in concentration camps in the east. He had escaped through one of the Nazi ratlines five years after the war ended, having hidden low in the countryside farming chickens. In May 1960, Israel's secret service agency, Mossad, caught up with him in Argentina, drugged and then bundled him onto a commercial flight and brought him back to Israel to face trial. Abduction was a deliberately dramatic gesture—fugitive Nazis and international opinion were supposed to take note—but not an unreasonable option.

Hannah Arendt also wanted to catch up with Adolf Eichmann, which was why she had swiftly written to *The New Yorker*'s editor, William Shawn, offering to cover the trial for the magazine. By this point, she was a well-known intellectual in the United States. Delighted, Shawn gave her as many words as she needed and an open deadline. The five articles that would eventually be published as the book *Eichmann in Jerusalem: A Report on the Banality of Evil,* appeared a year after her accident in the spring of 1963.

The journey to Jerusalem was personal. Adolf Eichmann's lifetime was also Hannah Arendt's lifetime. The career Nazi and the Jewish political theorist were born barely seven months apart. Their lives were already twisted around one another's before her famous book bound their names together forever. He had spent his life in the service of a monstrous regime that had murdered millions and decimated Europe's politics and morality. She had spent hers working to defy, escape, and destroy that same regime using the only weapon she knew she could rely on: her mind. Hannah Arendt did not just want to see Adolf Eichmann in the flesh; she was searching for a missing piece of her own history. *I would never be able to forgive myself if I didn't go and look at this walking disaster face to face, without the mediation of the printed word,* she wrote to Karl Jaspers in December 1960. *Don't forget how early I left Germany and how little of all this I really experienced directly (AKJ 409–10).*

She had fled Germany in 1933 after the Reichstag decrees made life there impossible for Jews and those who had the resources to do so began to leave for good. Sixteen years later, in her new home, New York, she completed the longest and most meticulously researched book she would publish in her lifetime, *The Origins of Totalitarianism.* Nazism was undoubtedly tyrannical, and self-evidently fascist in its gray-black glamour, racist mythology, and disregard for the rule of law. However, Arendt argued that modern dictatorship had an important new feature. Its power reached everywhere: not a person, an institution, a mind, or a private dream was left untouched. It squeezed people together, crushing out spaces for thought, spontaneity, creativity—defiance. Totalitarianism was not just a new system of oppression, it seemed to have altered the texture of human experience itself.

Toward the end of her book, Arendt looked further east to Stalin's Soviet Union and began to spot a pattern. Totalitarian regimes did not simply command obedience from the top, as had most tyrannies over history, but rather were organized like an onion. There was a dark heart at the center, but the system's inhumanity soaked through every layer. Its odor dominated everything, even as there were those who claimed they could smell nothing at all. Clearly there were architects of evil at the regime's core, men who set out to dominate, conquer, lie and manipulate, murder and terrorize, and there were obviously sadists, willing torturers and executioners, delighted to help them to do so. But this was not enough of an explanation for evil on this scale.

Totalitarianism had normalized mass oppression and murder at the heart of Europe. How did that happen? It was too easy to say that people were brainwashed. Nor would it do to plead, as many had after the war, that they had no choice, that they had feared for their lives. Others did not comply. They disobeyed. And while it was true that many had paid with their lives for their defiance, others survived to tell their stories because it turned out that you *could* disobey in certain circumstances. There was an entire universe of perplexities in the space between collusion and resistance. Brush past these too quickly because they are too difficult or obscure, Hannah Arendt feared, and the risk was not only that we would fail to understand the nature of modern evil, but also how to defy it.

She had been gathering material on anti-semitism, imperialism, and totalitarianism since she had left Berlin aged twenty-seven (although up until the late 1940s relatively few, including Arendt, used the word totalitarianism, which was first coined by the Italian "philosopher of fascism," Giovanni Gentile, in the 1920s). The end of the war, the Nuremberg trials, and the Nazi mania for self-archiving had created a superabundance of evidence and documents with which she could complete her book in 1949. But back then her formidable scholarship was not enough to capture the deep human sense of the questions she knew were key to understanding the nature of totalitarianism. How—*how*—had men become so inhuman? And, as importantly, had they really stopped being so? These were the questions that she hoped going to Jerusalem might help her answer.

Eichmann's was a new kind of crime: a crime against humanity itself. With others, he had murdered Jews, the Roma, disabled and queer people simply because of who they were. His crime was both against large groups of people and against the very idea of human plurality—that, to Arendt's mind, was what made it a crime against humanity. Eichmann could not tolerate the existence of different kinds of people in his world, so he exterminated them. It followed that his was also a new kind of trial. The Nuremberg trials had put crimes against humanity on the international books for the first time, but the genocide of the Jewish people had been deliberately muted and few Jewish witnesses were heard on the stand. Now, in Jerusalem sixteen years later, survivors stepped forward to speak for the first time of what they had witnessed and endured. To say it was a historical trial was an understatement.

But the prosecution saw an ancient crime in modern garb, and portrayed Eichmann as the latest monster in the long history of anti-semitism who had simply used novel methods to take hatred for Jews to a new level. Hannah Arendt looked at the scrawny man wearing an ill-fitting suit and sniffing loudly in his bullet-proof box and thought she saw someone more familiar. Here was a small, vain person blathering away self-importantly, seemingly unaware of what he was actually saying, who he was saying it to, or where he even was—in Jerusalem, the Jewish state, explaining away his role in the genocide of the Jewish people to Jewish people, many of whom already knew his reputation for horror intimately.

Whether he was trying to persuade the court that he was a mere cog in a machine obeying orders (fooling nobody, including Arendt), talking up his brilliant career in the SS, or pleading his exquisite humanity (it was he, he boasted, who had insisted on limiting the number of persons per cattle truck, the conditions were so inhumane), Eichmann's lack of moral, social, historical, of *human* awareness had dumbfounded her. Eichmann was that man, known certainly by every woman and by quite a few men too, who you wish had not sat beside you. Words pour from his mouth but he speaks in secondhand sentences, clichés, and stereotypes. He imagines he is profound, clever, sympathetic even, but you know that for him you are not really there at all: your existence, let alone your perspective, is simply not significant. He cannot see you any more than he can hear what it is he is actually saying. He appears animated but feels detached. He is not stupid, but neither is he as exceptional as he believes.

This was undoubtedly evil, but it was shallow, not profound. Eichmann was a genocidaire, obviously, but his demeanor at least (we'll come to the truth of Eichmann's performance in chapter nine) suggested that you didn't have to be full of brilliant satanic cunning to be so oblivious to the existence of other people as to make their elimination, and their suffering, seem an entirely plausible part of a day's work.

Arendt had written about how ordinary people were capable of unspeakable cruelties in *The Origins of Totalitarianism*. Much of this began, she said, with Western imperialism, with racism, conquest, and greed, and with an organized brutality that then leaked back to a Europe wrecked by war, unemployment, and poverty. But she had not understood then just how far-reaching, and how deeply permanent, the legacy of this ordinariness was. Devils you can fight. It is comforting to imagine that Nazis and totalitarians can be put back in a box simply by vigorously reasserting moral and traditional norms. But as we know, they do not tend to stay in those boxes. An evil that has seeped into human experience like this (like a virus, Albert Camus had suggested in his 1947 novel *The Plague*) needed new ethical, political, and legal instruments to counter it. But here was Eichmann, sitting in his glass box in 1961, with his outrageously grotesque banality, behaving as though he and his crimes had not altered the fabric of moral experience forever. Far from giving her answers, Jerusalem left Arendt with more questions.

The trial had adjourned in August 1961; the final judgment would not be delivered until December. Back in New York, she looked both askance and eagerly at the mountain of new documentary material growing on her desk, including the translations of the court's proceedings handed out to journalists each morning, Eichmann's original police interviews, and the transcript of tapes of an earlier interview he had given to a Dutch journalist and Nazi named Willem Sassen in Argentina. Those tapes (only made available in full after the trial and the publication of Arendt's book) revealed Eichmann openly boasting of his role in the genocide of the Jews with the same vapid enthusiasm with which he had attempted to debate the moral and philosophical difficulties of his situation with the judges in Jerusalem.

Yet, before she could even get to this material, she had another book to deliver to her publisher, a sprawling comparative study of modern revolutions she had been working on for the past three years, and a class on Machiavelli to teach at Wesleyan University, a private liberal arts college in Connecticut. The quiet autumn hum of academic life was short lived. In October, her husband, Heinrich Blücher, like her a refugee and inveterate smoker, suffered an aneurysm.

Blücher was the dapper, slightly older man from Berlin who, one spring evening in Paris, in 1936, had chosen to sit beside her in the Café Le Soufflot on the hill leading up to the Sorbonne. Since then, he had never left her side and she had never stopped being pleased about it. Their rich intellectual and personal intimacy was her ballast against totalitarianism. Hannah Arendt knew she could take on Adolf Eichmann because she had Heinrich Blücher. She was devastated at the thought of his loss. Mary McCarthy, a specialist on the Italian Renaissance, stepped in to take over her class (we might pause here for a moment of envy for those students taught to read Machiavelli that autumn by Hannah Arendt and Mary McCarthy) and Arendt rushed back to New York to supervise his recovery. The rest of the autumn semester was a blur of anxiety, trains back and forth from New York to Wesleyan, books half-read, proofs half-edited, letters answered late. All the while, she felt the unwelcome presence of Eichmann in his cell in Israel awaiting his fate, still no doubt performing his platitudes to anyone unfortunate enough to be in there with him, and the huge task that awaited her of working out how to write about what exactly it was she had experienced in Jerusalem.

The verdict came in on December 15. Eichmann was found guilty on all charges. She was pleased, but now there was the work of reading and interpreting the judgments too. Had the law risen to the challenge presented by this new kind of criminal or had another opportunity to square up to the moral ruin of Nazi totalitarianism been missed? She did not yet have time to find out. Uncomfortable with institutional life of any kind, she had chosen to be an itinerant academic. She now had to prepare for classes at the University of Chicago in January. No sooner had that weekly commute from New York begun, a virus crept into her lungs and would not move. The stubborn capacity for endurance which, next to her mind, had been Hannah Arendt's second most reliable weapon could not shift it. Her doctor prescribed antibiotics which her body, with an allergic spasm resembling her moral revulsion in Jerusalem, violently rejected. By the time she had got into that taxi in March 1962 she was already ill and exhausted.

You don't get much of a sense of a bodily life in Hannah Arendt's writing and biography. There is an adolescent fleshly frisson in her early letters to Martin Heidegger and a much more intimate and mature sensuality in those to Heinrich Blücher. There are illnesses, aches, pains, and the peculiarities of aging recorded in letters to her close friends. She pays quiet and respectful homage to the trials and rhythms of the laboring body in *The Human Condition,* the book she wrote after *The Origins of Totalitarianism,* and to the personal confidentialities of love and pain. But just as it was axiomatic that the intimacies of bodily and private life should not be matters of public concern in her thought, so too in her surviving writing is her body kept properly tucked away from view.

Yet, there is no denying that her body caught up with her in the months following the Eichmann trial. The sheer physicality of the horror of the Holocaust made itself publicly present in the Jerusalem courtroom like never before. She had deliberately, coldly said her critics, kept her distance from the cries and sobs, the howls of anguish and the bodies of witnesses, one of whom literally collapsed under the weight of memory. She worried that the trial's theatricality might detract from the complexity of its legal task. But history will make itself felt, and often in defiance of the mind. Nor, in the end, did her body's vulnerability worry her. Frailty, like the human condition itself, was simply another fact of life.

The accident, when it came, was a kind of late rebirth. Instead of being born pure and pristine, she was shot back into the twentieth century bloodied, bruised, and broken as, she might well have remarked to herself, was fitting given that the horrors of her century had left nobody unscathed. Like many survivors of serious accidents, she was elated in her hospital bed because she had lived to love a world whose beauty had just become more vivid. But by this point in her life Hannah Arendt also knew what this rebirth really meant: she could begin again. For now, she had no choice but to stop, let the quiet of the invalid settle about her, wait, and think.

Like many refugees of her generation, Hannah Arendt was an expert in the art of starting over. Forced on the run by Hitler in 1933, she had not so much made a new life each time she moved country, as shifted her perspective to better see what life looked like from a new angle. *Thinking means that each time you are confronted with some difficulty in life you have to make up your mind anew,* she wrote in her final book, *The Life of the Mind* (*LM* 177). It was a lesson learned through experience. But making up your mind again doesn't simply mean adapting to a new reality by learning to fit in or lowering your expectations. For Hannah Arendt, it meant comprehending what was new about that reality so as, when necessary, to resist it.

In this, she was a product of the same totalitarianism that uprooted her, or more accurately perhaps, she was its intellectual nemesis. Everything about Hannah Arendt's life—how she thought, loved, lived, worked, wrote, and taught—was anti-totalitarian either by default or intent. Her capacity to always see the world anew and be accordingly perplexed, surprised, and appalled was her most adaptable weapon in this struggle. To grasp at reality as though it mattered because it *does matter* was her first response to the moral lifelessness of her age.

When people talk of a particular view as being "Arendtian," they're often referring to this stubborn insistence on the messy reality of history. The same stubbornness also means that it is difficult to derive a political or philosophical orthodoxy from her work. She believed that reality required responsiveness, not dogma. There are coordinates—thinking, love, the importance of moral responsibility, and political visibility are constant mantras throughout her thought. But as the contemporary political philosopher Martin Jay once remarked, Arendt's writing is more of a "force field" than a coherent political theory.[1] Across the fifty years of her writing life, throughout her major works and many essays, ideas appear and reappear, bumping against one another, new topics and new circumstances, to make different intellectual shapes and patterns that illuminate then fall back into the shadows only to shine brightly again later. When Hannah Arendt spoke of the life of the mind, she emphatically did not mean the sort of mind that develops steadily as it ages, mastering complex problems and setting the absolute terms for its disciples to follow. She meant a mind that is indifferent to chronological time, that hops about a large canvas of thought and experience, looking again and beginning again, whenever required.

Like many women thinkers, she was frequently admonished to "stay in her lane" or, more aggressively, to stay out of whichever lane she was seen to be encroaching on. Several historians denounced *The Origins of Totalitarianism* and *On Revolution*. Neither book conformed to conventional historical methods and nor did she pay what many saw as due reverence to the established norms of academic discourse. Her refusal to be guided by existing norms and orthodoxies was quite deliberate. *Comprehension . . . does not mean denying the outrageous, deducing the unprecedented from precedents, or explaining phenomena by such analogies and generalities that the impact of reality and the shock of experience are no longer felt,* she wrote in *The Origins of Totalitarianism. Comprehension . . . means the unpremeditated, attentive facing up to, and resisting of reality—whatever it may be or might have been* (OT 7).

The realities she faced up to were not always ones that other people were ready to think about. Probably few intellectuals of her generation were more known about than actually read. Fewer still, perhaps, read and then misunderstood. The margins of interpretation often taken as a sign of profound complexity in the writing of male European intellectuals were in her case more often deemed obscurities in need of correction. In the 1960s, everyone had strong opinions about *Eichmann in Jerusalem* whether they had read it or, as remains the case today, merely read about it. Prissy mutterings about an "Arendt cult" first emerged in the 1950s from a committed Left that objected to her anti-communism (had Arendt had more sympathy with psychoanalysis, she might reasonably have called this "projection"). The "cult" charge was repeated in the wake of the publication of her reports on the Eichmann trial which saw her accused, among other things, of downgrading Eichmann's role in the Holocaust. It lingers today, and while perhaps the striking iconicity of her image hasn't always helped, it is not hard to detect a whiff of misogyny in the evident pleasure taken in proving Hannah Arendt wrong (and, usually, "arrogantly" wrong).

She *was* sometimes wrong, principally about the politics and history of race in America, and her tone was sometimes arrogant. But she was never stupid, which cannot be said of other twentieth-century intellectual giants, including, most notably, her teacher and lover Martin Heidegger, whose Nazi past is overlooked as regularly as "what Hannah Arendt got wrong" is debated. The most wounding charge in the scandal following the publication of *Eichmann in Jerusalem*—that a Jewish woman who lost her home, language, living, entire way of life, members of her family, friends, and at key points almost her own life to the Nazi genocide was somehow insensitive or indifferent to its tragedy—has always stood as its own kind of indictment.

She was fearless in her thinking because she felt, although without grandeur, that that was what her age demanded. *What*

*Hamlet said is always true: "The time is out of joint; O cursed spite / That
ever I was born to set it right,"* she remarked more than once (*PP* 202).
Shakespeare set Hamlet the puzzle of proving that his father had
been murdered and that a terrible crime had happened right at the
heart of the state. His curse, perhaps the most modern of curses,
was to try and establish whether the lines of authority could be
fixed after political power had been so totally and outrageously
abused. They could not, and the endeavor drove him mad. Totalitarianism had left the modern world in the same position. Hannah
Arendt took a very different path from Hamlet's tragically self-
destructive vengeance. It was *because* the world was out of joint
that things could be different, that things might, indeed they must,
begin again, she insisted instead.

This puts the moral and political onus squarely on each new
generation. There is all the difference in the world between having
to exist—why was I ever born?—and having the capacity for a
truly human existence among others, as Hamlet knew to his cost.
This was twentieth-century existentialism's common starting
point, and Hannah Arendt's too. There is no authority, no ready-
made meaning, that can be passed down through the generations.
We skate on thin ice. But unlike some of her philosophical contemporaries, she did not think this groundlessness made existence
itself absurd. Nor did she believe it possible to transcend the con-
straints of existence through sheer will. Believing that thought
alone could shape the world had already proved to be philosophers'
most lethal illusion. The tragedy of turning ideas, even good ideas,
into reality by violence, be it bloody or administrative, was there
for everyone to see by the middle of the twentieth century.

Except that not everyone did see it. One of the reasons the

Hannah Arendt, 1944.

world is such a mess is that in the rush to make it better even the most sharp-eyed among us consistently fail to see what is right under our noses. The confident theories and the lofty ideas had kept on coming, apparently regardless of recent history. This was in part the lesson she finally took from Eichmann's trial. The moral obscenity of the Holocaust had to be recognized, put on trial, grieved, and addressed. But it could not be made right with existing methods and ideologies. The banality with which the crime was executed needed to be reckoned with precisely *because* of the persistence of moral thoughtlessness—and its murderous consequences—in modern culture. You cannot simply will this evil off the face of the earth with a few good ideas, let alone with the old ones that allowed it to flourish in the first place. You have to start anew.

The really shocking thing for Hannah Arendt was that the world was not shocked enough. She feared that her contemporaries had not registered just how profoundly Western culture *was* completely wrecked by the mid-twentieth century. She shared Hamlet's incredulity that nobody else could see the ghosts and were carrying on as though nothing had happened. Even after the Holocaust, after the gulags, even after Hiroshima and Nagasaki, and after the late colonial and imperial wars that ran steadily and lethally through the rest of the twentieth century from Algeria to Vietnam, it was as though somehow, tragically, the point kept on getting lost.

The error which she claimed many of her existentialist contemporaries made was to assume that the modern catastrophe was now a personal problem and that the dilemma about how to survive can now only belong to individuals. She was not so much concerned about "bad faith," Jean-Paul Sartre's famous description of how we habitually deny that we are, in fact, free to make choices about our inauthentic lives. Instead, she worried that an obsessive preoccupation with living an authentically free life meant that people had lost the capacity to see that what had gone wrong was not individual existence but *our plural existence*—our politics, in other words (*PP* 202). It's not you, it really is us.

The *danger lies in becoming a true inhabitant of the desert and feeling at home in it,* she wrote in her notes as she prepared to teach a class at Berkeley in 1955. She had her eye on the easy enchantment of her students by the existential glamour boys of both American and European post-war culture, many of whom appeared to be rebels with no evident cause save to rebel some more (*PP* 201). Totalitarianism thrived in desert conditions, she warned them. There is nothing like a political and existential void for making an atrocious idea welcome. If nothing makes sense, then anything is possible. As populists and propagandists know, whipping up fake storms in the wastelands gives the appearance of action, meaning, purpose, salvation. This is pseudo-action only (as today's social media storms again illustrate), yet with each passing tempest people become less, not more, sensitive to suffering, and less able to judge. Life, politics, and suffering itself become tedious. Then the big men with the big "impossible" ideas move in and suddenly the world is at war with itself again.

Hannah Arendt was born Johanna Cohn Arendt on October 14, 1906, in Linden-Limmer, now a southern suburb of Hannover, but then a fast-growing town buoyed by the industrial revolution. Her father, Paul Arendt, was an electrical engineer. Her mother, Martha Cohn, a trained musician. Educated, progressive, secular Jews, the couple leaned Left politically. Arendt was born on the corner of the busy tree-lined Marktplatz, just as the leaves were turning red. From her window, she would have been able to watch people come and go, buying and selling, busy with living. Like those in other European towns and cities at the turn of the century, the people of Linden had a strong image of themselves as confident middle-class citizens. The marketplace had been built to provide the town with a civic center as recently as 1894. The new town hall stood opposite the Arendts' house. Underneath the trees, there was an ornate fountain on top of which stood the figure of a night watchman, keeping the inhabitants of the Marktplatz safe as they slept, ready for a new day of industry, progress, and civic life.

Hannah Arendt was an expected event in the lives of her parents, insofar as any child that arrives new in the world is ever quite what their parents expected. Certainly, she was much loved and cherished. Her mother kept a detailed diary of her development, "Our Child" (*Unser Kind*), with the obsessive diligence of many a new parent whose bookishness hadn't quite prepared them for the wonder of their own child: "The temperament is quiet but alert. We thought we detected sound perceptions, aside from general reactions to light, in the seventh week. We saw the first smile in the sixth week, and observed a general inner awakening. The first sound began during the seventh week."[2] If we want a provisional biographical answer to the question as to why Hannah Arendt came to think in the way she did, it is because she was first lovingly thought about.

The obsessive attention of new parents is a universal phenomenon, but excitedly recording a "general inner awakening" belonged to the Arendt family's class, time, intellectual and cultural milieu. Grandchildren of the Enlightenment, like many of their generation they were committed to free thinking. That is what Martha Arendt was searching for in her newborn: the first sign of a light going on in her mind, "baby's first thought." One of Arendt's favorite eighteenth-century philosophers, Gotthold Ephraim Lessing, called this *Selbestdenken,* which translates literally as "self-thinking," but which is more commonly translated as "thinking for oneself."

The image that Arendt used to describe Lessing's thought later could equally apply to her own: *instead of fixing his identity in history with a perfectly consistent system, he scattered into the world, as he himself knew "nothing but <u>fermenta cognitionis</u>."*[3] For Lessing, as for Arendt, thought ferments because it *responds*—to the environment, to events, to circumstances, to other people, to change, and to the unexpected.

Hannah Arendt's parents believed in the progressive power of free thinking. They imagined, by and large, that because people were learning to think for themselves, their world would improve. They could not have imagined that their daughter would spend a lifetime defending free thought against a mindset that believed that the very existence of Jewish-Germans like themselves was superfluous.

Germany's industrialization had brought her engineer father to Linden and had provided the impetus to build the Marktplatz. In Solingen, approximately two hundred miles to the south, Adolf Eichmann's similarly placed but notably un-bookish father worked as an accountant for a transport company. Yet, the pretty German towns with their fountains and tree-lined marketplaces disguised a dangerous rootlessness that had been spreading across the world for quite some time. Rapid economic expansion and greed had gobbled up lives in colonial Africa, South America, and Asia. Closer to home, European workers had begun to notice that what they got in return for their labor came at an exorbitantly high human cost. The pace of progress was already depriving communities of a place in the world. Resentment against the democratic elites brewed and the sharp-eyed began to spot political opportunities.

A *subterranean stream of European history* which *hidden from the light of the public and the attention of enlightened men* was able *to gather an entirely unexpected virulence,* Arendt later wrote about the period of her childhood (*OT* 8). Mainstream media and enlightened commentators either ignored or trivialized anti-semitic extremists and right-wing *crackpots* (her word) because they seemed too self-evidently extreme and broken to bother with (an error repeated in the early twenty-first century). Prussia had emancipated its Jews in 1812 but Hannover had only done so as recently as 1842. Emancipation turned out to be a cleft stick, as Arendt would later argue in a biographical study of the eighteenth-century German-Jewish salonnière Rahel Varnhagen. Legal inclusion also fueled the social politics of exclusion. After Jews were granted equal citizenship, religious and cultural differences were interpreted with a new vigor. The first explicitly anti-semitic parties in Germany and Austria appeared in the late nineteenth century. In France, where the tradition of anti-semitism was never quite extreme or murderous enough for the Nazis (for a while Eichmann and his officers struggled to persuade the occupied French to surrender their fellow Jewish citizens to the gas chambers), the affair of the falsely accused Jewish officer Alfred Dreyfus in 1894 was an early demonstration of how easy it was to whip up a racist mob by capitalizing on the widespread dislike of social elites.

Hannover was not free of anti-semitism in the 1900s, but the streets through which the infant Hannah Arendt was pushed in her perambulator could at least boast a tolerant architecture. The New Synagogue, opened in 1870, was built on the left bank of the Leine and rested under the shadow of the imposing Protestant Lutheran Church of Saint Johannis. Down the road swelled the roof of the

Basilica of Saint Clemens which stood just opposite the city's main Catholic church. The buildings were a mix of European, gothic, and Romanesque styles. A visitor would have had to have got pretty close before realizing which was *schul* and which was a Christian church. In 1938, not even seventy years later, no time at all in the life of most religious buildings, the synagogue was razed during the Nazi-incited *Kristallnacht* pogrom against the Jews. Today, a small monument marks the gap where it once stood, just in front of a post-war apartment block. The bell towers of the other churches still stand in the sky. The *subterranean stream of Western history* had *finally come to the surface* (*OT* xxvii). It had all happened so quickly.

The first time I visited the city in 1986, Hannover was all about dancing to Simple Minds in basement discos and rumors of sex in the Eilenriede Forest. One of the main routes into the GDR began in Hannover and friends would talk about their trips to see grandparents in the east in their families' new VW Golfs (by then Volkswagen had established itself as the city's major company). There were few car trips that began from the other direction. By 1989, barely three years later, the wall had come down and the Cold War had ended. Distant cousins suddenly arrived in their Trabants, sometimes with the grandparents in the back. Soon, trains and buses brought others, suitcases in one hand, children in the other. Another subterranean current had risen to the surface: freedom and, most precious in those first months, freedom of movement. Many of my friends, and certainly their parents, had dreamed of just such a moment, but few had anticipated that it would actually happen in their lifetimes. It had also all happened so quickly.

We cannot help being born, where we are born, and in what

time. That beginning is not our responsibility. But we can learn to respond to the world we are born into, however fast-moving or bewildering that experience might be. Thinking, Hannah Arendt came to argue, is how you get your second, third, and fourth birth and so on, according to whatever changes you are confronted with. Although she was born in Hannover in 1906, she first began to think almost 600 miles to the east and north, in a city called Königsberg, the intellectual center of Europe's Enlightenment.

CHAPTER TWO

How to Think

> There are no dangerous thoughts, thinking itself is
> dangerous.
>
> —*Thinking and Moral Considerations*

Königsberg, 1783, the bell from the cathedral chimes and a man checks his watch as he crosses the Holz Bridge, as he always does at this hour. The man is the philosopher of reason, Immanuel Kant, and he knows that within two minutes he will cross the fourth bridge to the Kneiphof, the island that floats in the middle of the city, before walking over the fifth bridge onto the Pregel River's other bank, and then back onto the sixth (also the first bridge he began on) which will take him home to start his afternoon's work. Some days he will cross all seven of the city's bridges by walking south to the Holz Bridge, but not today. As everyone who lives in Königsberg knows, if you want to cross all seven bridges you will need to have made at least eight crossings, six bridges needs more than seven, five more than six, and so on. Famously, it was not possible to walk across both banks of the river and visit the two islands in its center without crossing one of the bridges of Königsberg twice. As the mathematician Leonhard Euler had demonstrated in 1735, you didn't actually need to cross the bridges to demonstrate this truth, you could use reason instead. A relatively simple graph, now named Euler's Graph, converted the bridges and banks into vertices and edges and told you all you needed to know: it was mathematically impossible to cross a bridge only once if you wanted your feet to touch both riverbanks and islands, and that was the end of the matter.

Kant probably tried not to think about Euler's Graph on his daily walk. He believed, indeed he lived, for reason and for the truths that could be uncovered with the human mind, but the fact that Euler had produced another theorem to prove the existence of God irritated him. God and bridges were not in the same category. You do not experience a bridge in the same way as you experience God, so you had to think about them differently. There was *Vernunft*, reason, the means by which you worked things out, and *Verstand*, intellect, understanding, and reflection, which we use to search for meaning. Things do not exist just because you rationally conceive of and can control them in your head. You had to *think about* your thinking if you really wanted to know the meaning of things such as God, freedom, faith, morality, and human existence, even if the end result was just to demonstrate that such things were indemonstrable. It was how you perceived the world that mattered: the categories you put things into, how thought was organized for you, and how you organized your thoughts in response. Reflection, *Verstand*, he thought crossly, was precisely why he was free—*free*—to determine whether today would be a six-bridge or a seven-bridge walk *for himself*, theorem or no theorem, graph or no graph.

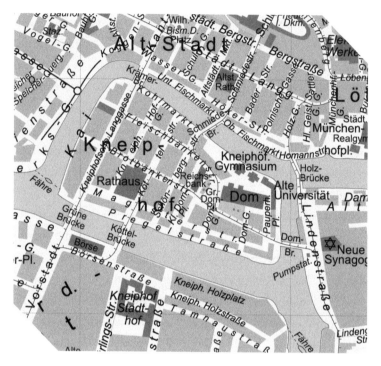

Map of Königsberg, 1905.

Almost a century and a half later, the young Hannah Arendt runs across the same bridge. The same cathedral bell chimes at the same time, but she doesn't quite hear it. Her mind is somewhere else. She knows she is late, after all she is running, but she is not quite sure what she is late for. Something is not quite right. She stops, spins on her heel, temporarily lost. The *Neue Synagogue* is before her; she remembers that she has just visited Rabbi Vogelstein to talk about God and the state of her faith, but also because she liked the sound of his voice and the way he took her seriously. Now she needs to decide whether to backtrack over the Holz Bridge across the island and follow the longer but prettier way home or take the Dom Bridge, the shorter route that will take her past Kant's old house. She opts, as she usually does, for the latter.

Where had she been just now? Lost in thought. But where *do* I go when I think (she thinks because she cannot stop and the fact of this incessant thinking also interests her)? Sometimes I am, and sometimes I think, but can I think and be at the same time? Because it feels like when I'm thinking, I also vanish from the world. I don't of course—more's the pity. She glimpses a group of young men walking slowly toward her; students from the Albertina University; *Stuko* members perhaps, a couple of badges catch the sunlight. They certainly see her. Whisper it (but make sure that she can hear): *Jüdin,* Jewess! Their gaze hits something tender, like a bruise. Ernst Grumach's gaze, on the other hand, she remembers as though from nowhere, touches the same spot with an altogether more pleasurable effect. She decides to turn her confused footspin into an ironic little dance of defiance. *Quatsch!* she shouts silently, returning their gaze over her shoulder with a smile, whipping her plaits through the air. Then she runs toward the bridge.

In the way I think and form judgments, I'm still from Königsberg, Hannah Arendt told the German historian Joachim Fest in a 1964 interview: *Sometimes I hide that from myself, but it's true.*[1] It was in Königsberg that Kant discovered that it was because we could think that human freedom and dignity were possible. No sooner had the thought taken hold that we alone could reason humanity into existence, give each other human rights, dignity—the freedom to walk across any bridge we wanted—than the possibility of doing the exact opposite emerged. Kant's famous moral maxim is that we

Hannah Arendt as a child, sitting on a balcony. Date unknown.

must not use other people as a means to our own ends. But we could, couldn't we? others replied, and then they did. *It is as if Man had never before risen so high and fallen so low,* Arendt later wrote; *it requires heroism to live in the world as Kant left it.*[2]

A busy port and the major administrative and intellectual center of Prussian life, Kant's Königsberg was thriving and diverse. The so-called "Venice of the North," thanks to the seven bridges, had been settled by Mennonites, Huguenots, English traders, and Jews, among others. The famous cosmopolite who never traveled did not need to go too far to hone his arguments for a "universal state of human beings." Kant's life might have looked dull, the daily walks measured by the cathedral clock bell are legendary, but his philosophy was expansive, worldly, and, in theory at least, liberating. Our existence depends on how we think for ourselves and so for and with one another, he reasoned. All the grand theories, theorems, and graphs, the mind-blowingly complex, beautiful, occasionally tedious, philosophical reasoning that followed in his name really begins with one simple idea: that we think and that how we think has moral consequences.

Arendt grasped the radical simplicity of Kant's central insight early on and never lost sight of it. She would go on to challenge his cool rationality, but she never gave up on the importance of his central moral promise: because we have reason and moral agency we can, indeed we *must,* act to make the world a good place, whatever the cost. *Nobody has the right to obey!* she insisted in the aftermath of Eichmann's trial. She was quoting Kant back at Eichmann, who at one point had attempted to defend himself by citing Kant's argument that we are morally obliged to obey the law of our rulers. This argument totally falls apart if the rulers are lawless, Arendt countered; Eichmann had conveniently forgotten, if he had ever really grasped, Kant's much harder lesson about the categorical imperative: *Kant's whole ethics amounts to the idea that every person, in every action, must reflect on whether the maxim of his action can become a general law. In other words . . . it really is the complete opposite of obedience! Every person is a lawgiver. In Kant, nobody has the right to obey.*[3]

The imminent prospect of unreason—madness—had driven the Arendt family from Hannover to Königsberg, the home city of both parents and their extended families; exiles from the anti-semitism of mid-nineteenth-century Lithuania and Russia. Her father, Paul Arendt, had contracted syphilis as a young man. This was not unusual in Europe, and early twentieth-century literature may well have cast the quiet despair of the era differently had it been less so. The reality of the disease, however, was cruel and punishing. Paul Arendt's symptoms had subsided by the time he married and the young family had hoped for the best. Hannah was barely three years old when the first signs of dementia appeared. The couple knew that Paul Arendt would soon retreat into madness before leaving both the world altogether, and Martha and their child alone. They returned to Königsberg and Hannah Arendt left her birth home to find her true intellectual home.

She was barely sixteen when she first read Kant's *Critique of Pure Reason* (1781). Around the same time, she began organizing a Greek reading group for her friends outside school hours, partly because she objected to getting up early to attend the Greek class at school. It's no surprise that Hannah Arendt was precociously clever, but to fixate on her exceptional mind is to miss something that is important about her lessons in thinking: thinking is ordinary, she teaches; that is its secret power.

Everybody thinks, sometimes well, sometimes badly; not all the time, of course, otherwise you would never get anything done. Most of the time, our everyday thinking stays invisible, which is as it should be, but what worried Arendt was the assumption that other people, clever, learned, and powerful people, therefore did all the important thinking for us. Others reason, we follow. Instead, she took from Socrates the idea that the "two-in-one" dialogue we have going on in our heads all the time is the origin of both thinking and morality. *Talking-to-yourself is basically thinking—a kind of thinking that isn't technical, and of which anybody is capable.*[4] This was why Socrates would say that it was better to be at odds with the whole world than to fall out with oneself. Better to quarrel with others than to censor yourself for shame.

The soundless voice with whom you would converse on your daily walk to school—this was always thinking as much as being the proud possessor of powerful reasoning for Hannah Arendt. The stories you tell yourself, the poems you juggle out of words as you slip in and out of the high visibility of early adulthood; all these are apprenticeships in thought. Of course, it is quite possible to have stupid conversations with yourself, and many poems are no sooner written than regretted at any age (*I dance and dance / In ironical glory,* she wrote in an early poem). But the thinking self is where morality began for Arendt.

She had the good luck to be born into a cultural milieu where thinking for the sake of thinking was taken seriously. In this matter, Arendt was as much a child of the *Haskalah,* the Jewish Enlightenment, as she was of Kant and Lessing. One of her closest friends, Anne Mendelssohn, was a descendant of Kant's own good friend, Moses Mendelssohn (Arendt's first boyfriend, Ernest Grumach, had been Anne's before, and the two women would remain friends for life). Mendelssohn had paved the way for the *Haskalah* by demonstrating that it was possible to live by the principles of both the Enlightenment and Judaism. Later German-Jewish thinkers argued that reason required the abandonment of Judaism altogether and urged complete assimilation. But they had not reckoned on the rise of anti-semitism in the twentieth century. Arendt's was not a religious family, but their Jewishness was not a matter of indifference either. It could not have been even if they had wished it so. The subterranean current pushing against the values of tolerance, friendship, and reason was already rising to the surface.

Even as a girl, Arendt knew that to be Jewish meant that she would always be more, or even less, of a thinking person so far as other people were concerned. Whatever she was thinking, wherever she was in her head, someone crossing a bridge from the opposite direction was there to remind her that they had thoughts about her and that those thoughts had consequences for how she lived. Nobody is ever allowed to retreat from the world into their own minds completely, and racism and sexism keep some visible whether they like it or not. Arendt first met the reality of her Jewishness in the streets and in the classroom. Her mother taught her that if her teachers made anti-semitic remarks, she was to tell her and she would deal with it. The anti-semitism of other children, on the other hand, was on her. She learned to be tough.

And she learned to disobey. She would later castigate herself for her fearful inwardness as a teenager—she started to read the existential trailblazer Søren Kierkegaard about the same time as she first pulled Kant down from her family's bookshelves. But she always knew a wrong when she saw it. When a teacher at her school made a blunder—we don't know precisely what was said, but we can guess that it offended Arendt's precocious intellectual and moral sensibility—she organized a protest. The students boycotted the teacher and the school expelled Hannah Arendt. She went to Berlin where she sat in on classes at the university and then she returned to Königsberg and passed her *Abitur* with flying colors.

Paul Arendt died in 1913, the same year as did her beloved

grandfather, Max Arendt. Adolf Eichmann's mother died a year later in 1914. His family had also moved, from Solingen to Linz in Austria. About the time that Arendt was reading Kant and organizing boycotts, Eichmann was struggling at school and hiking through the woods reclaiming German nationalism with the *Österreichischen Wandervogel,* the Austrian "Bird Wanderers," a scouting organization with violently right-wing ambitions. He had not yet shown much aptitude for anything, although he did learn to play the violin.

Because of the importance of the larger-than-life intellectual men in her life, biographers have often dwelled on the early death of Arendt's father. Her best biographer, her former student Elisabeth Young-Bruehl, who later became a psychoanalyst, tells the story of her intellectual development through the men who helped to shape it. It's an enviable list of paternal substitutes: Martin Heidegger, Karl Jaspers, Walter Benjamin, the Zionist-intellectual Kurt Blumenfeld, Heinrich Blücher, and later the Austrian writer Hermann Broch. But this is not a thesis that would have particularly interested Hannah Arendt.

The problem with psychoanalysis, she thought, was that its plots tended to make the lives of the most fascinating people commonplace: if we all have father complexes, then what more is there to say? More fundamentally, she believed that it was an error to confuse biography with the life of the mind. *The thinking ego is sheer activity and therefore ageless, sexless, without qualities and without a life story* (*LM* 43). Hannah Arendt very much liked having a life story, an age, a sex, and plenty of interesting personal qualities, but she liked having a thinking ego at least as much.

For Arendt, this "thinking ego" is not always the same as the "self" of consciousness, and so to an extent she shared with psy-choanalysis the idea of a divided self. As she came to argue, there's a kind of hidden thinking that runs alongside us, keeping check on us and the world. We do not always know quite who we are, in other words, which may not be a bad thing, especially when po-litical and social conformity are being demanded of us. From the perspective of other people, of course we appear as one person, one identity—she, he, they, Black, brown, white, other; this is the given plurality of the world. But as soon as I try to confirm an identity to myself and say, proudly or defensively, or maybe tenta-tively and curiously, "I am I," I've also revealed my own inner difference from myself. *I am inevitably* two-in-one—*which incidentally is the reason why the fashionable search for identity is futile and our modern identity crisis could be resolved only by losing consciousness*, she wrote in 1971, setting her face against what we would now describe as iden-tity politics.[5]

Arendt valued perplexity over identity; thinking for oneself, and quite often against oneself, was her touchstone. By thinking, she did not mean the cool reason of enlightenment thinking, but the constant work of reflection, questioning, and perplexity— Kant's *Verstand. I do not believe that there is any thought process possible without personal experience. Every thought is an afterthought, that is, a reflection on some matter or event. Isn't that so?* she once remarked.[6] Reason will only get us so far, and blindly obedient reason, as Eichmann had shown, can be catastrophic. The epigraph to her final book, *The Life of the Mind,* was from Plato's *The Statesman:* "Every one of us is like a man who sees things in a dream and thinks he knows them perfectly and then wakes up to find he knows no-thing."

Embracing perplexity was Arendt's first line of resistance against the absolutism that so often drives terror and violence. Yet thinking alone could not hold the political and moral line, as she would discover in 1933, not nine years after she left Königsberg in 1924 to study philosophy and theology in Marburg. Many academics and intellectuals showed themselves willing to align themselves with National Socialism, some of them former colleagues and friends. She would never forget how supposedly clever people made bad moral and political decisions in the 1930s and then pretended that they hadn't. *Never again! I shall never again get involved in any kind of intellectual business!* she firmly instructed herself after she left Germany.[7] Philosophy might teach you to think for yourself, but politics and history meant that smart Jewish girls would eventually have to find their own way across the bridges.

Hannah Arendt's student house in Marburg is on a winding back lane leading up to the Landgrave Castle, which has quietly dominated the town's skyline since the thirteenth century. Outside, next to the fence, there is (what else could there be?) a cigarette-vending machine—the perfect shrine to Hannah Arendt—and a temptation, even for those who have not smoked for years, to sit on the steps and feel the smoke move out from your lungs and up over your face in contemplative homage. Sleet whipped up the lane when I visited so alas, no smoking. I was, unsurprisingly, the only visitor to the castle's museum.

Like hundreds of museums in provincial towns across Europe, the Landgrave Museum of Cultural History tells a story that begins with suits of armor and ends with the drawing-room furniture, cutlery, and tableware of the continent's bourgeoisie. The objects are beautiful, the industry behind them admirable, but few of us who were born in the twentieth century can walk through these museums without reflecting on the history that these objects imply but rarely make explicit.

A quiet, hardworking, predominantly Protestant, bourgeois university town, just four months before Arendt arrived, the Nazi *Völkisch* gained three times more votes than the national average in Marburg in the Reichstag elections of May 1924. It was a protest vote and it would take some time for local Nazis to make good on this gain, but the town of tradespeople and soft-spoken academics, where many prided themselves on their indifference to national or party politics, had shown itself willing to at least begin to blame the Jews and leftists.[8]

In one of the museum's display cases, two headless women modeled the fashion of 1920s Marburg. The liberating loose folds of one of the dresses resembled those worn by Arendt in photographs of her student days. It was a soft brown earth color, just as she liked to wear (green was another favorite color). Between the two mannequins was a black-and-white photograph of male students posing outside one of the bars in Marburg's Marktplatz, smiling and smoking, their arms draped across one another's shoulders. Student dueling and other militaristic societies encouraging male bonding were popular in Marburg. These were the young men every woman, and every Jewish student, would study alongside.

In early 1920, more than eight hundred university students heeded the national call to join the *Studentenkorps*—the so-called *Stuko*—for "peacekeeping" duties following the November Revolution in 1919. Amidst post-war political chaos, the Social Democratic Party had aligned with the Right and the army, including the violent *Freikorps,* to squash the more ambitious revolutionary Left led by Rosa Luxemburg and Karl Liebknecht's Sparticists. On March 25, one group of Marburg's *Stuko* left for Thuringia to escort suspected Sparticists from Mechterstädt. By dawn, fifteen of the prisoners were dead, shot in the back, in the face, at close range, their corpses left dumped on the road, shrouded by the early morning fog. In the investigations that followed the massacre, the students were acquitted—twice. There is now a plaque on the university's walls commemorating the event with deep regret.

A week after my visit to Marburg, on February 19, 2020, Tobias Rathjen, a right-wing terrorist, murdered nine people in Hanau, just sixty-five miles to the south. He had targeted customers smoking in two Turkish *shisha* bars in the town. Rathjen was forty-seven years old, trained as a bank clerk, and had a degree in business management. In the twenty-four-page document posted online explaining his "philosophy" that is now obligatory for small-time genocidaires, Rathjen had written about the voices in his head that controlled his thoughts and actions. He claimed that they were part of a worldwide central intelligence agency that could be defeated only through the "annihilation" of Germany's ethnic minorities, a project he declared he had happily signed up to. He could hear the voices in his head, but clearly Rathjen could not hear his own voice as he wrote. He had decided not to have a conversation with himself. According to the *Guardian* newspaper, a "few days before the attack Rathjen uploaded an English-language video to YouTube in which he warned Americans that they were controlled by devil-worshipping 'secret societies.'"[9]

This might merely have been the sad, mad, final gesture of a very ill man were it not for the fact that millions of Americans already believed the same.

Hannah Arendt had planned to go to the Philipps University in Marburg, then famous for its distinguished neo-Kantian faculty, to learn to think a bit more like Kant. Hermann Cohen, the Jewish philosopher celebrated for his rigorous and insightful commentaries on the philosopher, had taught at Marburg until his death in 1919. Arendt imagined she would be treading in some formidable intellectual footsteps, but then she walked into Martin Heidegger's classroom (number eleven in the Old University Building), and soon she would learn that thinking wasn't simply something you did with your mind. Thinking was existence itself. Thinking was passion—and passionate.

For some, Hannah Arendt's relationship with her philosophy professor is the love story of two brilliant minds, tragically marred by some poor decision-making in unfortunate historical circumstances. For others, the Heidegger affair is enough to put them off Arendt entirely. How can we trust the judgment of a woman who not only forgave her onetime Nazi lover (Heidegger joined the National Socialist Party in 1933), but then went on to promote his books and supervised collections and translations, rehabilitating his reputation?

However the story is told, Hannah Arendt is frequently represented, as a colleague once put it to me, and to use a British expression, as a "numpty." We had been watching Margarethe von Trotta's 2012 biopic, *Hannah Arendt,* which shows the young

Arendt falling to her knees at his feet in a shadowy attic bedroom. Everyone is allowed to be a numpty at eighteen (or indeed at any age): but was it Arendt or Heidegger who was the fool? A cursory glance at their letters shows just how much Heidegger needed Arendt: her thought, her person, early on her body, always the reflection of his brilliance in her mind, to the point at which very often, he refused to see who she really was at all. Hannah Arendt did not just fall in and out of love with her professor; throughout their relationship she was facing up to, and resisting, the complex reality that was Martin Heidegger. The affair, like much else in her life, taught her to think both with and against her own experience.

We don't have many of the letters that Arendt sent to Heidegger. He destroyed most of them as, marriage and reputation at stake, he thought they had agreed. Luckily, Arendt, the wiser of the two and already as much of a historian as a philosopher, kept many of his. Professor Dr. Martin Heidegger (aged thirty-six) to his student, "Miss Arendt" (aged eighteen), February 10, 1925: "Be happy!—that is now my wish for you," he begins promisingly, but quickly there is a caveat: "Only when you are happy will you become a woman who can give happiness, and around whom all is happiness, security, repose, reverence, and gratitude to life." Only by giving her happiness (to whom?) will she really be able to take advantage of what university life can offer. Too many of her sex, Heidegger then cautions, force "academic activity" which can leave them "helpless and untrue to themselves." Preserving her "innermost womanly essence" he concludes, will be decisive when "individual intellectual work begins" (*AMH* 4).

Sitting in her student room in the second semester of her degree, reading her new lover's letter, Arendt may have hoped she had found her dream: a love of both mind and body. Then she reads the letter again. This is a bit patronizing, a quietly defiant inner voice possibly whispers in the back of her mind, why can't I just think and be happy? And what *is* "innermost womanly essence"? It was never a question that would seriously preoccupy her. Far more interesting than Heidegger being patronizing, sexist, and self-important was what he said about "being" itself.

Cozily cocooned with his students in the sturdy flint-gray fortress-like walls of Marburg's Old University Building in the autumn of 1924, Heidegger looked intently at the young men and women before him and told them that being was profoundly hazardous. We are born—thrown—into the world, with nothing save the frail fact of our existence to see us through our allotted time on earth, he said. This is the Wile E. Coyote moment of existentialism: the point at which we run off the cliff but keep running even as we look down and see there is no longer any ground beneath our feet. What enables us to keep running—at this point in classroom eleven, Hannah Arendt lifted her head and fixed her professor with an intense gaze—is thinking. The good news is that despite, in fact thanks to, the nothingness, because we think, we can grasp the reality we find ourselves in. There is no moral groundwork, as Kant had once hoped there might be; in fact, the ground itself is always trembling. But this same absence of concepts and frameworks allows us to see the reality of the world as it is. There is an existential void. The world is meaningless and yet this is exactly what makes life so vibrant and real. Yes, we are running on thin air but from that position, suspended between the cliff edge and death, our back paws pedaling furiously, we also get to feel the wind on our faces, note the sharp blue of the sky above and the snowy tops of the fir trees below.

It is thinking, Heidegger said, passionate, serious, never-ending thinking, that gives existence meaning. In Marburg, the girl once lost in her own thoughts in Königsberg now learned that in fact, she had been making and unmaking her existence all along. She was making sense, she was making herself real, whatever the boys from the *Stuko* thought—or her lovestruck professor for that matter.

Arendt later described her cohort of students at Marburg as *resolute starvelings,* desperate for something more than a conventional philosophy course that would prepare them for knowing repartee over bourgeois dinner tables; *what they did want,* however, she added, *they didn't know*.[10] Heidegger's genius was to make "not knowing" the starting point for his teaching. Heidegger did not think *about* things, he simply, and intoxicatingly, *did* thinking. You listened to his lectures as you might walk in the woods, seemingly without purpose, but burrowing deeper into thickets of thought. Students flocked to his classes to experience thinking in realtime with a man who seemed to share their resolute restlessness. It helped that he was a charismatic and eloquent teacher and that words fell from his lips like icicles thawing on a waterfall.

Words mattered for Heidegger. Everything we could possibly know about existence, he argued, we know only because we are speaking beings. The key text for his classes in that autumn semester of 1924 was Plato's *Sophist*. The sophists were skeptical about the existence of gods and other big metaphysical claims, but very good on rhetoric. Only man is the measure of man, they taught, and at its root, that measure is made up of language. The fact that we are wordy creatures is one of the essential romantic tragedies of Heidegger's philosophy. We can never say it all; there is always something that remains unsayable, uncommunicable; an unspoken part of us that is always alone. The only certain thing we can know about ourselves is that we will die, but only time will tell us that and what we were. As we live, we keep our words, like our thoughts, moving.

The combination of Heidegger's narcissism with his Nazism eventually drove the lovers apart. When they finally met again after the war, in Freiberg in February 1950, they celebrated their reunion with a long conversation about language as they walked through the woods up to the *Schlossberg* that sits on the high hill overlooking the town. Arendt had written him a note to say that she was back, as though she had never been away from Germany, never been exiled, and as though she had not just finished writing *The Origins of Totalitarianism,* in which she had very precisely attempted to put the horrors of the past twenty years into words. The next morning, he arrived at her hotel. Arendt stood up from her breakfast, smoothed down her dress and calmly walked toward him. Both knew that to speak together was to confirm their own way of being together, but they also understood that their talk about language acknowledged that something could not be spoken between them. So much of their relationship had always existed in the nuance of a poetic image, at least for Heidegger, who often found that the world appeared better when refracted through an image or a metaphor, especially when reality proved difficult or unyielding. "When, at our first reunion, you walked toward me in your most beautiful dress . . . you stepped through the past five years," he wrote to her afterward: "Hannah—have you seen the brown of a freshly plowed field in the light of dusk? Having endured everything, ready for everything. May your *brown dress* [emphasis original] remain the sign of that moment of reunion for me.

May this sign become ever more revealing to us" (*AMH* 76). But by then, a lot of blood had flowed under a lot of bridges.

Four years before that meeting, Arendt published an essay, "What Is *Existenz* Philosophy?" in *Partisan Review,* one of New York's most influential literary and political magazines. A brilliant account of the emergence of existentialism in the early twentieth century, the essay was also an intellectual autobiography of how the philosophy she had absorbed in her student years had weathered the storms of exile, total war, and genocide. Her answer was: not well.

By 1946 everything had unraveled. In April 1933, Heidegger had taken over the presidency of Freiberg University. In his now infamous Rector's Address, he vowed to take the university into a new era of National Socialism. In the hall of the college building where he spoke, you can still see Hans Adolf Bühler's massive 1911 fresco of an unrepentant-looking Prometheus, surrounded by admirers, catching a few beams of dusty light from the hall's high windows. The neo-fascist artwork (Bühler was a member of the Militant League of German Culture) would have been the perfect backdrop to Heidegger's declaration of a new dawn for German universities. The following month he joined the Nazi Party. Soon, he would be signing his name to a memorandum ordering that Jewish members of the faculty could no longer teach at the university, including his former mentor, the pioneering phenomenologist Edmund Husserl. The winter before, he had responded indignantly to a letter from Arendt, by then living in Berlin, asking him whether the rumors about his anti-semitism were true. He had petulantly replied that he had been on sabbatical, away from academic affairs and was therefore not responsible. "I am now as much an anti-Semite" as I ever was, he concluded, unreassuringly, before pleading stupidly, "above all it cannot touch my relationship to you" (*AMH* 52–53). By July 1933, Arendt had fled Germany. She would not return for another sixteen years.

Her essay in *Partisan Review* was one of three lead pieces in the 1946 winter issue. The other two were an essay by the British writer Stephen Spender called "German Impressions and Conversations," documenting a visit to post-war Germany, and an extract from a chapter of Jean-Paul Sartre's first novel, *Nausea,* "The Root of the Chestnut Tree." Only Arendt's name was misspelled on the contributors' page: "Hanna Arendt is a frequent contributor and was a student of Karl Jaspers in pre-Hitler Germany." Sartre (born a year before her) was "one of the foremost" writers of his generation and Spender (three years her junior) "the well-known writer and critic"; apparently neither were ever anybody's student. In his piece, Spender described the obliteration of a country and continent. In his, Sartre described the repugnance of contemporary existence. It was left to Arendt to explain how the recent catastrophe of war and existentialism might be connected.

Existentialism, she argued, had shown how it was possible to let go of the metaphysical super-plots that had held philosophy back, and had opened up new paths to explore how we might be human together. With existentialism, Kant's grand project for a universal humanity based on moral reason had been replaced by a more *modest humanism,* she said. This humanism lay at the heart of the phenomenologist Edmund Husserl's philosophy, without which Heidegger could not have made his break with metaphysics.

Arendt had moved to Freiberg to attend Husserl's classes in 1925. It was Heidegger who had pushed for the move. Although it was common for German students to switch universities, there was little reason for Arendt to do so. She was doing well, had made good friends, such as Hans Jonas, another friend for life, liked the town, and was in love. Heidegger persuaded her that she wasn't fitting in in Marburg, by which he no doubt meant that she wasn't fitting in with his life there. *I left Marburg exclusively because of you,* she wrote to him the day after they had met again in 1950, *as a matter of love for you—not to make things more difficult than it must be* (*AMH* 60).

In Freiberg, she lived on the leafy and affluent Schwimmbadstrasse just around the corner from Husserl's bright white and shimmering art-deco apartment block on Lorettostrasse. Nearly ten years later in the winter of 1932–1933, Sartre, along with Simone de Beauvoir, first heard about Husserl's phenomenology from Raymond Aron, who had been studying philosophy in Berlin (and who would later write a critical review of *The Origins of Totalitarianism*). All four young thinkers realized that Husserl's phenomenology had quietly shaken the grounds of philosophy for good. What was up for debate was how philosophy might respond.

The magic of how we experience the world is at the heart of Husserl's thinking. We live, he said, in a constant dance between the acts of consciousness through which we reach out into the world, and the phenomena we reach for. As Arendt put it in her 1946 essay: *The seen tree, the tree as an object of my consciousness, need not be the "real" tree, it is in any case the real object of my consciousness.*[11] It doesn't matter that the tree I see in my mind's eye is not the actual tree: what matters, what is special, is how I wrap my mind around the tree with my thoughts.

There is no master plot in Husserl's thinking, no grand reckoning with either God or nothingness, but simply the promise of a modest new home for humanity in the *small things,* as Arendt described them; in the emerging catkins, for example, that she may have noted on her walk down the Schwimmbadstrasse to the university, or heading up the street in the opposite direction, in the black of a winter tree against the white wall of Husserl's apartment block on the corner of the Lorettostrasse.

There was also a Husserlian tree in the extract from Sartre's *Nausea.* Antoine Roquentin, a disgruntled, middle-aged academic living in a tired, gray, damp French port, discovers the meaning of existence in the roots of a chestnut tree: "and there it was: all of a sudden, existence was there . . . that root was made out of the very stuff of existence," Sartre writes. Roquentin is as repelled by his own existence as he is by that of the roots: "soft, bare disorderly masses, monstrous and obscene in their frightful nudity."[12] The dyspeptic existential anti-hero of the latter half of the twentieth century had struck his first fictional pose.

By contrast, in her essay, Hannah Arendt argued that if the world looked hideous in 1946, if existence made you gag, this probably had less to do with the frightful nudity of tree roots reflecting the absurdity of your own existence than with recent systematic attempts to eliminate humanity. Sartre's eventual solution to living in a morally obscene world was to seize one's own existence and commit to revolutionary change. In a later essay, Arendt worried that as radically political as his humanism was, Sartre's utopian image of man re-creating the world in order to make it less absurd was still prey to the delusion that *Man is his own God*—and that the world and the people in it could be made into an idea of

Man's image, with all of the Promethean dangers evident to any-one who had experienced them as directly as Hannah Arendt had.[13]

Existentialism had crashed into a history it hadn't seen coming and the result had been catastrophic. Arendt concluded that Husserl's thinking was genuinely liberating but that its apparent modesty masked a lingering and, as it had turned out, fatal arrogance about our place in the world and the limits of our existence. Existence was not all there was. There was also history. Just months before his death in 1938, at the age of seventy-nine, Edmund Husserl was evicted from the white-walled apartment block in Freiberg that he loved so much after a campaign orchestrated by his anti-semitic Nazi neighbors.

I never had any professional or personal attachment to old Husserl, Arendt wrote to Karl Jaspers in July 1946, as she completed her essay. Yet, she had read the 1933 memorandum forbidding Jewish faculty to teach and knew that it, and especially Heidegger's signature at the bottom, had *almost killed* the old man. Heidegger was not just Husserl's boss, he was his former student and a friend. *Truly irreparable things often—and deceptively—happen almost by accident, sometimes from an insignificant line that we step across easily, feeling certain that it is of no consequence anymore, that wall rises up and truly divides people* (*AJK* 47–48), she wrote to Jaspers. She was talking about Husserl; and she was talking about herself.

After their reconciliation, she would attempt to defend Heidegger for the memorandum which, as Jaspers had pointed out, was a circular anti-semitic directive and issued across Germany's universities.[14] But in 1946, Hannah Arendt was clear that Heidegger had crossed a line. This wasn't simply a personal or political, or even just philosophical, line. Heidegger had failed to connect his thinking to the reality of the world he lived in, and that was unforgivable. Halfway through her essay, Arendt delivered the most uncompromising condemnation of Heidegger that she would ever publish.

Having thrown Being off a cliff, the Heidegger of the 1930s did not really know what to do with moral responsibility. Kant taught that *every individual represents humanity,* that's why we have moral obligations to one another. I find my humanity reflected in you, you find yours in me: that's the basis of our shared morality and our collective ethical groundwork, however shaky that might turn out to be. Heidegger's self, by contrast, lived *in absolute isolation,* under self-imposed lockdown, and represented *no one but himself.*[15] Heidegger did not mean to be an anti-social nihilist, she noted (indeed, he would change his position on the significance of others later in his writing), but it was hard to see where you might go once you had lost the idea of universal human rights—Arendt would battle with the same question in *The Origins of Totalitarianism,* as we will see in the next chapter. A lapsed Catholic, Heidegger was good on how existential guilt kept us tethered to other people, but Arendt was unconvinced that a fretful guilty self alone was enough to weather the political storms of the 1930s. In 1946, she knew why she was right to worry. Heidegger had sought redemption in the myths of National Socialism.

Left alone with the splendor of Being, Heidegger had attempted *to bring in by way of an afterthought, such mythologizing confusions as Folk and Earth as a social foundation,* she wrote. This was not philosophy, she complained, but a politically dangerous *naturalistic superstition.* The meaningless nature of social existence could not be solved by people *willing themselves into an Over-self*.[16] That was to turn existentialism into an apology for fascism.

Later, in 1953, in her *Denktagebuch,* the "thinking book" in which she would first experiment with her ideas, Arendt would describe Heidegger as a fox who had become ensnared in his own philosophical den.[17] In 1946, her contempt for his carelessness was much more direct. It was muddled logic that led Heidegger to stick his paws into the jaws of a trap that was well signposted for all but the most quixotic of forest animals in the 1930s, she argued.

Arendt, too, started with the assumption that man was not at the center of things but eventually came to a very different conclusion. The great Kantian project of humanity had failed, certainly; it was no longer possible to recognize ourselves in unifying concepts of Man and his dignity, but what was now left was human plurality. It was the human condition that existentialism truly asked us to reckon with.

If there is a man who can be described as Hannah Arendt's true paternal substitute, it was Karl Jaspers, with whom she studied in Heidelberg. The town was the final destination in her university education in Germany's south, and in many respects was the place where she became her own thinker. A practicing psychologist who became a philosopher, Jaspers had a grounded, curious care for his world and the people in it, and Arendt loved him for it. *Lieber Verehrtester* she would begin her letters, my dear venerated one. "Dear Hannah!" he would reply or sometimes "Dear Hannah Arendt!"; always excited to be in communication with her. Their letters range from their first meeting up until his death in 1969.

They discussed everything. In a letter prior to her fiftieth birthday he wrote to reassure her about the menopause: "Women become more beautiful with age." Arendt replied that she was more worried about the requirement to become dignified *and with the best will in the world, I don't know how I'll assume that. And one does not exactly want the alternative of being ridiculous either* (*AKJ* 301–302).

It was a shared relish for life's pleasures and realities that united Arendt and Jaspers. He had studied the extremes of the human mind closely during his time as a hospital doctor. His wife, Gertrud, was Jewish, as were many of his friends and the students closest to him. Jaspers stayed in Germany, survived the terror, and mourned the country and culture he still loved until his dying breath, even after he moved to Switzerland in the last decades of his life. Once friends, his relationship with Heidegger would never recover after what he saw as his betrayal of both the people they had in common and philosophy itself.

It was Jaspers who cleared Arendt's path back to existentialism's initial promise of a richer and riskier new humanism. He was one of Europe's first world comparativists, along with figures such as the philosopher and philologist Ernst Cassirer (with whom Anne Mendelssohn studied for her PhD) and the art historian Aby Warburg. Jaspers argued that the world's philosophical systems were in fact mythological structures that sheltered us from the hard facts of our existence. They were *Weltanschauungen* or views of the world which tell people compelling and meaningful stories about themselves and work pretty well until, that is, they don't—when wars, fascisms, totalitarianisms, and genocides arrive, when an economic crash or a virus knocks not only life but philosophical narratives off course. It is these "extreme situations" that show us how precarious existence really is.

With Jaspers, Arendt argued in the conclusion to her *Partisan Review* essay, existentialism was able to leave its fateful egoism behind. Starting with the extreme situations themselves, he advocated a new kind of philosophy, one which would teach nothing specific but would instead be a *perpetual shaking up, a perpetual appeal* [the emphasis is Arendt's] *to the powers of life in oneself and others*.[18] Like his contemporaries, Jaspers used philosophy against itself, dissolving its concepts, deconstructing its false mastery. But where others left ruin in their wake, Jaspers left the human character of philosophy improved, like Heidelberg's ruined castle tower which, as Mark Twain once quipped, looked much better in decay than it ever did intact. This perpetual overhaul of philosophy is itself an appeal to life, one's own and also to those of other people. For Heidegger, other people, although structurally necessary, are threats to authentic existence—because we spend too much time under their gaze. But for Jaspers, existence *can develop only in the togetherness of men in the common given world*.[19] We are running on air but we run together—if only we can find ways of communicating between ourselves. There is always hope.

After 1933, Hannah Arendt was not so sure about hope, but she would always keep her political faith in the possibilities of human communication. We think, talk, and narrate alongside others as friends, but also as citizens of different cultures, traditions, and countries. Communication is always difficult, sometimes impossible, but it is also what keeps humanity in prospect even in the most extreme situations, *especially* in the extreme situations when communicating might be the only option we have left.

Arendt had gone to Heidelberg to work with Jaspers on her doctoral thesis on Saint Augustine and his writings on love, neighborliness, and community. Later, especially in *The Human Condi-*

tion, she would spend a great deal of time puzzling over how and whether it might be possible to create a politics that could build on the mysteries of human community. Which bits of our moral and ethical lives had to stay hidden and private if they were not to be contaminated or co-opted by totalitarian fictions of collective life? How might we build a secure politics that can respond to extreme situations without falling into death-dealing myths of together-ness? How can we keep our politics alive and human enough to let what Arendt came to call the *miracle* of human freedom, first dis-closed to her by Kant in Königsberg, open as a possibility?

By the time she was living in Heidelberg, the affair with Hei-degger was more or less over. Their letters became more sporadic, although no less controlling on Heidegger's side. Not long after he found out that she was dating the clever, young, and very stylish Benno von Wiese in 1928, he sent her a small flurry of flirty letters—while forbidding her to write back to him unless he ex-pressly asked her to. She deliberately hadn't given him her Heidel-berg address, but he had tracked it down.[20] Unsurprisingly in these circumstances, the relationship with von Wiese didn't last, and in September 1929, she married Günther Stern, the son of the child psychology pioneers Clara and William Stern and a cousin of Wal-ter Benjamin. She had first met Stern in Marburg where he was a post-doctoral student working with Heidegger. In the 1930s Stern wittily de-Judaized his name to Anders—Other—to protect his journalism career. Funny, smart, and deeply thoughtful, although the marriage did not survive, Stern-Anders would be a friend for life, helping Arendt escape Europe and providing financial support during her first years in New York. In the same year that Arendt published her *Partisan Review* essay, Anders published his own reckoning with Heidegger, *Nihilism and Existence,* in which he, too, berated post-war philosophy for focusing too much on the nihilism within the self and not nearly enough on the moral, political, and material nihilism of totalitarianism.[21]

In September 1930, Arendt and Anders met Heidegger in Heidelberg where he had been visiting Jaspers. Anders later caught the train back to Frankfurt with his old teacher. As the two men met on the platform, Arendt held back. At one point, Heidegger looked straight through her. *I had already stood before you for a few seconds, you had actually already seen me—you had briefly looked up. And you did not recognize me,* she wrote to him the same day. It reminded her, she said, of a cruel game her mother had once played where she pretended not to know her child. *And then when the train was about to leave. And it was just as I had imagined moments before . . . you two up there and me alone, completely powerless. As always, nothing was left for me but to let it happen, and wait, wait, wait (AMH* 52). She had vanished from the world again.

Except, of course, she had been invisible only to Martin Heidegger. In reality, Hannah Arendt was already mastering the art of disappearing into her own thinking, only to reappear in the world on her own terms.

The walls of the Old University in Marburg are hung with photographs and biographies of its esteemed women alumni and professors. Hannah Arendt is there, of course, on the ground floor in the corridor facing the courtyard. The day I visited, the low winter sunlight from the stained-glass windows gave her a halo and wings. I sent a copy of the image to the noted Hannah Arendt scholar, and her former student, Jerome Kohn. We had been due to meet in New York but the beginning of the coronavirus pandemic had stopped us. "I photographed this image of Arendt in the Old Building of Philipps-Universtät, Marburg, last month," I wrote in an email: "The light from the window gave her a sweet angel of history look." The reference was to Walter Benjamin's famous interpretation of Paul Klee's tiny painting of a large-headed, startled angel being blown backward as the catastrophe of history builds at his feet. Benjamin owned the painting and had written about it in his *Theses on the Philosophy of History* which he had entrusted to Arendt just as the two of them were making plans to flee Europe in 1940. When she returned to the University of Freiberg in July 1967, passing through its great hall under the giant mural of Prometheus, it would be to lecture on Walter Benjamin and his angel. Martin Heidegger was in the audience. "Yes," Jerome Kohn replied to me: "The Angel of History, but not Klee's Angel staring in utter bewilderment as he's blown backward into the future, and ruins pile up and up before him. HA, on the contrary, seems to be thinking of how to put it all together *anew.*"

CHAPTER THREE

How to Think Like a Refugee

> The world found nothing sacred in the abstract
> nakedness of being human.
>
> —*The Origins of Totalitarianism*

Hidden behind a gray concrete wall on the Damascus Road in Beirut is a rarely visited Jewish cemetery. The poet Yousif M. Qasmiyeh had been promising to take me there for months, but when we finally visited in spring 2018, the gate was locked and it was difficult to see anything unless you walked backward into the road, which nobody in their right mind would ever do in Beirut. So, we tiptoed and jumped in the April sunshine and finally caught a glimpse of the odd Star of David between the old and naked branches of the lilac trees.

Yousif had recently been writing a series of poems about the cemetery in his birthplace, Baddawi, a Palestinian refugee camp, 50 miles to the north of Beirut.[1] Baddawi Camp was established in 1955, seven years after more than 700,000 Palestinians had been forced from their homes during the war that created the new State of Israel in 1948. Since the civil war in Syria began in 2010, the camp had been hosting another generation of refugees and the cemetery had become crowded. History is not always buried with people: sometimes the graveyards make it more visible. "Born in Haifa in 1945 . . . died in Baddawi in July 2016 . . . Palestinian from Syria" read the words on one of the new tombs, compressing a lifetime of refugee history onto one stone.[2] Haifa was a key port for crude oil under the British mandate. During the Second World War, boats carrying Jewish refugees attempted to dock there only to be towed out to sea or sent back to Europe by the British. At the beginning of 1948, roughly equal numbers of Arabs and Jews lived in the city. By May, less than a quarter of the original Arab-Palestinian population were left.

The borders we have today on the maps of Europe, the Middle East, and Asia were made by generations of population move-ments, of people being shoved into and out of new nation states, sometimes through war, sometimes through treaties and policies, and nearly always with violence. The maps show nothing of the human cost of the experiment, begun in the late nineteenth and early twentieth centuries, in making new nations out of people who were all supposedly ethnically alike: but the cemeteries can be more revealing. By winter of the next year, severe flooding washed away the wall we had hopped up and down in front of on the Da-mascus Road. The Jewish graveyard was suddenly exposed to the city where hardly any Jewish people now live. The cemetery dates back to the 1820s, but the tombs that were newly revealed by the moved earth belonged to those who had been buried there in the 1940s.

The Jews are dying in Europe and are being buried like dogs, Hannah

Arendt concluded in a letter she wrote to the philosopher and historian Gershom Scholem in October of 1940. She was writing to
tell him about the death of their mutual friend, the so brilliant, so
hopeless, Walter Benjamin ("Benji"), who had just taken his own
life in Portbou on the Spanish border, having been told that the
papers he had obtained in Marseilles may have been the right ones
when he left, but the visa rules had now changed, and he was going
nowhere except back over the mountains. Benjamin had been talking of suicide for some time. Interned in Colombes Stadium, just
outside Paris, in 1939, he'd *entered into a kind of asceticism. He stopped
smoking, gave away all his chocolate, refused to wash himself or shave, and
more or less refused to move a limb* (*AGS* 6). Like many refugees, he was
trying to make himself vanish before others got the chance to do it
for him. He seemed to have recovered when he and Arendt met up
again in Lourdes after the fall of France where they spent their days
playing chess and reading the newspapers. But when news reached
them that other Jewish refugees had started to kill themselves, he
began to talk about suicide again. When Hannah Arendt made her
own journey out of France by train, four months after Benjamin
died, she stopped off in Portbou to find his grave. *The cemetery looks
off a small bay, directly onto the Mediterranean. It is carved in stone in ter-
races; the coffins are shoved into these stone walls. It is by far one of the most
fantastically beautiful spots I have ever seen in my life.* But Benjamin was
not there. He had, it seemed, indeed been buried like a dog. *His
name was nowhere* (*AGS* 9).

Today, Israeli artist Dani Karavan's memorial sculpture, *Passages, Homage to Walter Benjamin,* stands next to that cemetery on
the cliff in Portbou. Designed to look like a small refuge or shelter,
(you might miss it if you weren't looking for it), once you peer

inside, a stairway tunnel takes your eye down onto the blue of the Mediterranean and to the same fantastic beauty that arrested Arendt as she left Europe. A quotation from Benjamin's *Theses on the Philosophy of History* is written on the base: "It is more arduous to honor the memory of anonymous beings than that of the renowned. The construction of history is consecrated to the memory of the nameless," it reads. Benjamin had written the *Theses* in Paris in January 1940 and had given Arendt a copy to look after in Marseilles while they were both waiting for exit papers. She was quite probably carrying the manuscript in her suitcase when she stopped off at Portbou.

Benjamin's words have aged unfortunately well. Karavan's memorial was completed in 1994, just one year before Europe's Schengen Agreement went into effect. Created to allow free movement within the European Union, thanks to Schengen, the platforms that once bustled with travelers and customs officials under the huge glass and iron roof of Portbou station are now empty, save for a few locals, hikers, and the sunbeams that catch the dust in the summer. A big new border has taken the place of the small borders that used to form a spiderweb across the continent. Part sea, part old-style barbed wire, part digital, part legal, part criminal, this border is solid only in its purpose to keep people coming from the south and east out. Between 2014 and April 2022, nearly 24,000 migrants were recorded as missing in the Mediterranean.[3]

Hannah Arendt was not one of Benjamin's "anonymous beings," but one of the few fortunate "exception refugees" to escape Europe. Between August and December 1940, the Emergency Rescue Committee operating out of Marseilles under the direction of the legendary people rescuer, the American journalist Varian

Fry, submitted over 1,137 visa claims to the United States Department of State. Only 238 were granted.[4] Arendt, who, with hundreds of others, had made regular and dangerous trips to the southern port to hustle, fill in forms, and petition, was just about well-connected enough to be one of them. Her mother, now widowed once again after a second marriage, was not and Arendt had to leave her behind. Martha would later join her daughter in New York, but was miserable there and died in 1948 on a boat headed for London, where many of the Cohn-Arendt family had fled.

Today a sepia haze has settled over Arendt's generation of refugee writers and intellectuals. They were fleeing European fascism's most obscene moment, yet their exile is often treated as though it were another chapter in the story of the writers and cosmopolitans who made the world seem edgy and glamorous in the twentieth century. It's also typically assumed that this is a story solely about Europe and the United States; as though brilliant minds shifted across the Atlantic only, shining together in sparkly new intellectual constellations, while down on the earth the masses were dully terrified out of their homes and across borders that many of them did not even know existed until one day they were told to pack their bags at the point of a rifle. Arendt certainly mixed in circles in which the privileged super-mobility of the cosmopolitan was often mistaken for the tragic genius of the exile, but she herself never shirked away from the realities of statelessness and migration.

Instead, she understood from experience that to become a refugee was not simply an accident of war or natural tragedy, but structural to the way the modern world was organized. In *The Origins of Totalitarianism,* which she began researching during her refugee years, she would show how the long history that made mass displacement an everyday reality began with racism, imperialism, and the seemingly insatiable expansion of global capitalism. As with today's, the anti-immigrant politics of her time were driven by populist and nationalist movements in the northern and western metropoles and a willingness on the part of political opportunists to override the law and international norms. Nor did she have much faith in post-war humanitarian and human rights solutions. It is not just that refugees are vulnerable people requiring hospitality. We do not simply need to care more. Hannah Arendt argued for a harder truth: the anonymity and vulnerability of placeless people is also, potentially at least, everybody's problem because it exposes the weak spot at the heart of a system that relies solely on the reliability of nation states and human goodwill.

Exiles used to be the glamour boys, and less frequently girls, of myth and history: the banished and the brilliant, the sad and the interesting. By contrast, Arendt's generation discovered that all it took to become a refugee was to be born into the wrong race, religion, class, place, or time. *Everywhere the word "exile" which once had an undertone of almost sacred awe, now provokes the idea of something simultaneously suspicious and unfortunate,* she wrote in an article entitled "Guests from No-Man's Land" in 1944.[5] The *chances of the famous refugee are improved, only just as a dog with a name has a better chance to survive than a stray dog who is just a dog in general,* she later added in *The Origins of Totalitarianism* (OT 365).

Thinking about how Europe had got to a point where burying refugees like dogs was an unremarked commonplace, Arendt used the phrase the *boomerang effect* to describe how imperialism's unique brand of administrative and racist dehumanization had spun back home to Europe in the 1930s and 1940s (OT 4). She was one of the first, in fact one of the few, European intellectuals to grasp that the organized barbarity of modern totalitarianism was not an aberration belonging only to Nazi Germany or Soviet Bolshevism, but was of a piece with a longer imperial and colonial history of dog kicking and dog burying. The *corpse factories* of the Holocaust were like nothing else that had ever happened on the European continent, the impossible had been made possible and a line had been crossed forever. But the conditions that created industrial-scale genocide in Europe were familiar from elsewhere. Anti-colonial thinkers in the later mid-twentieth century, such as Frantz Fanon, Aimé Césaire, and the late Albert Memmi, also pointed out that from where they were standing the tearing of people from their land and homes, pushing them into camps and slave labor, turning lives into commodities and wars into a means of ethnic cleansing, appeared neither novel in their coolly administered execution nor unprecedented in their cruelty.

What few in the twentieth century could anticipate was that the age of the refugee would turn out to outlast the age of total war and genocide. The boomerangs have kept on spinning; their flight paths making new shapes for misery, loneliness, and anonymity as they twist across the earth. The problems that Hannah Arendt identified about human rights, national sovereignty, and the weakness of humanitarian solutions remain. And the nakedly racist cruelty which many had hoped the post-war human rights regime might at least temper is back.

In *The Origins of Totalitarianism,* Arendt writes about *holes of oblivion*. These were the concentration camps and ghettos, the detention centers, as well as the unmarked graves, whose aim was to make those who dwelled in them invisible. Like George Orwell's "memory holes" in *Nineteen Eighty-Four* in which all books, documents, and archival material that contradicted the party line were incinerated, holes of oblivion were designed to expunge whole slices of reality, history, and humanity from human consciousness altogether. These were not metaphors. Orwell and Arendt wanted the world to understand that something new and outrageous had happened. Men had always attempted to bend reality to their wills. Now they were attempting to eradicate it altogether. The aim was to render people's experience of the world itself superfluous.

The ultimate holes of oblivion were the Nazi death camps, which were intended to consign the Jewish people to oblivion forever. The existential, moral, and historical horror of that fact lies behind everything that Hannah Arendt wrote after the war. Yet she also recognized that there were other ways of getting people to disappear besides killing them. Labor and detention camps, *once popular even in nontotalitarian countries,* she pointed out, were also useful *for getting undesirable elements of all sorts—refugees, stateless persons, the asocial, and the unemployed—out of the way* (OT 574).

The Nazis' holes of oblivion project had one crucial and precious flaw: the holes were dug by human beings. *Nothing human is that perfect. One man will always be left to tell the story,* she later wrote in *Eichmann in Jerusalem.* She had been listening to the testimony of Zindel Grynszpan, who, along with 12,000 others, was beaten over the border into Poland in October 1938 in the first stages of the mass deportations that the Nazis euphemistically described as Jewish "migration" (Eichmann had been promoted to First Lieutenant and appointed to the Central Agency for Jewish Emigration in Vienna three months earlier). "*Juden raus* to Palestine!," the mob screamed as the Jews were marched through Hannover, her birth-place, to a waiting train. "Run, Father, run, or you'll die!" Zindel's eldest son cried as they were ordered across the border, German guns trained on their backs (*EJ* 228–29). The simplest way to pry open the holes of oblivion, Arendt realized in Jerusalem, is to speak of them.

She did not quite know it then, but in the early 1930s Arendt was already working on the first of what would be many missions to salvage Jewish history from oblivion. She and Günther Stern-Anders had returned from the south to settle in Berlin in 1931. Finally shaking Heidegger from her feet, she made up her mind to turn away from philosophy, immersed herself in reading German Romanticism, and began work on her second major study for her *Habilitationsschrift* (the first was her thesis on Saint Augustine), a critical biography of eighteenth- and early-nineteenth-century Jewish *salonnière* Rahel Varnhagen. This early study, only pub-lished as a book in the 1950s, would be one of the most intensely personal of all her writings.

Rahel Varnhagen is best known today as the clever and devoted fan who created the cult around the Romantic novelist Johann Wolfgang von Goethe. In novels such as the tragedy of youthful introspection *The Sorrows of Young Werther* (1774) and the more prescriptive primer in bourgeois life *Wilhelm Meister's Apprentice* (1795), Goethe invented characters with lives real and rich enough to suggest that there was a social world full of generalizable hu-manness to which everybody might belong—at least in fiction. Goethe showed *the infamous prosiness of our whole little lives,* Arendt wrote, the fictions by which we might live and love (*RV* 115). The daughter of a Jewish merchant, smart and complicated, Varnhagen wanted Goethe's prosy existence badly. She organized her life around love affairs and intense friendships which she recorded in hundreds and hundreds of letters. She ran a salon and filled her tiny Berlin apartment on Jägerstrasse with writers, politicians, nobles, and the celebrities of German Romantic culture. More than anything, Varnhagen wanted to live life to the fullest within a society of equals, such as Goethe's novels tantalizingly portrayed. She wanted to belong.

But there was a problem: in the end that enlightened society of so-called equality and rights did not want her. She was unable to become one human being among others *because of the ban, imposed from the outside, against a Jew's [sic] becoming a normal human being* (*RV* 216). Varnhagen worked hard to circumvent the Jew ban: she changed her name, married a gentile, and was baptized. But she was never just a parvenu, which was why the young Hannah Arendt was so fascinated by her. Varnhagen's courage, her stubborn will to exist as an individual equal in the world, her original cleverness; all of these came about not despite but *because* she was an outsider, a pariah, and a Jew.

Rahel Varnhagen could not help being who she was, and in the end, this gave her an uncommon but precious advantage. She understood how the world was and exactly where she was in it because she had no choice but to do so. Because she *had no home in the world to which she could retreat from her fate there remained nothing for her but to "tell the truth"* (*RV* 54). Truth-telling is what you do when you have nothing else. *To be sure, no one understood the rain better,* Arendt observed, *no one showed so clearly what rain was like, than the person who happened to have no umbrella and therefore became soaking wet* (*RV* 94). Rahel had followed the eighteenth-century call for universal human rights and placed her hope in a better and more equal society. In her quest, undertaken earnestly and entirely in good faith, she had exposed the fault lines of Europe's grandest humanist political project. The reality was that she remained a pariah. The advantage was that she could now see European culture for what it was.

Arendt found the same pariah's viewpoint in the writing of Franz Kafka, whose work she was introduced to in Berlin by Walter Benjamin, Gunter Stern-Anders's cousin, who was one of the very first to recognize Kafka's genius. In the mid-1940s, newly arrived in New York, one of her first jobs was working for the publisher Schocken Books, where she edited Kafka's diaries. She wrote two essays on his fiction in this period (partly in homage to Benjamin), each demonstrating how what other readers might regard as surreal was in fact a description of Jewish reality in twentieth-century Europe. In Kafka's *The Castle,* she writes, the character K turns up to a village mistakenly thinking he has been asked there to work. His ensuing nightmare adventures in the castle's labyrinthine and meaningless bureaucracy, and his frustrations with gullible and superstitious villagers, reveal the lot not only of Jews, but of migrants, refugees, and strangers everywhere. "You're not from the Castle, you're not from the village, you are nothing," the pub landlady yells at K at one point. "You are one thing though, a stranger (*Sie sind nicht as dem Schloß, Sie sind nicht aus dem Dorfe, Sie sind doch etwas, ein Fremder*), one who is superfluous and gets in the way everywhere, one who is a constant source of trouble."

But the really significant thing about K, Arendt says, is that he is not a hero or a pioneer, but an ordinary man of goodwill who arrives at a new place merely asking that his human rights be respected. By beginning his novel with that quiet request for human dignity Kafka shows how empty human rights are. The point for Hannah Arendt was to never stop asking for human rights, even as evidence of their applicability to oneself is glaringly absent. The simple ask, she observed, is itself the privilege—maybe the only privilege—of the strangers and pariahs for whom human dignity is regularly denied.

Thinking alongside other writers for Arendt was at once an exercise of imagination, an act of solidarity or friendship, and a springboard for criticism, understanding, and, when necessary, dissent. She had a rare talent for literary biography and would later regularly write character portraits of her contemporaries and friends, as well as historical figures. Many of these she would finally collect in the 1968 volume *Men in Dark Times*. Her range was wide. She wrote about Bertolt Brecht, Walter Benjamin, Rosa Luxemburg, Karl Jaspers, Herman Broch, and the Danish writer Isak Dinesen (Karen Blixen), but also Pope John XXIII; in *The Origins of Totalitarianism,* with wit and insight, about the nineteenth-century British prime minister and novelist Benjamin Disraeli; and the English colonial adventurer Lawrence of Arabia.

Being able to think from another's point of view was a life-long ethical, intellectual, and political commitment. Yet this early biographical experiment was different. She wanted to think exactly *like* Rahel Varnhagen, to shadow her thought and experience as closely as she could so that she might better understand her own emotional, intellectual, and at the time often perplexing life. Much of the final book is made up of direct chunks of quotations from Varnhagen's own writing, as if Arendt already knew that the documents she was citing were about to disappear too as, indeed, many

soon did in the Nazi pillaging of Jewish archives (many of Varnhagen's papers were lost forever).

She drafted most of the manuscript in Berlin. The last two
chapters, and the most directly polemical, she finished in exile in
Paris, by which point it had become clear just how wet the Jews of
Europe were getting. She called the last chapter of her book "One
Does Not Escape Jewishness." Reading the book now, it is often
difficult to tell where Varnhagen's voice ends and Arendt's begins.
When she wrote about Rahel in the 1800s she was also writing
about herself in the 1930s.

It was because she was passionate, committed, and curious that
Varnhagen finally embraced the reality of living as a Jewish woman
in the early nineteenth century. Writing about her life helped
Hannah Arendt to do the same in the mid-twentieth century. One
passionate love affair, a rebound marriage to a friend, much intense
reading, fretful dreaming, and earnest questioning had all thrown
Arendt back upon herself in Berlin in her twenties. This turned
out to be exactly the position she needed to be in to comprehend,
and survive, what followed. The reality was that a Jew could not
stop being a Jew, not in an anti-semitic society governed by an increasingly violent racist ideology. "*Jüdin,* Jewess!" the boys had
cried on the bridges of Königsberg. *Hier bin ich!* she replied, the
ghost of Rahel Varnhagen beside her, fifteen years later.

The manuscript on Rahel Varnhagen would not be published
until 1958. When it was published in Germany a year later, the
editors at Piper Verlag shortened the subtitle from *The Life History
of a German Jewess from the Romantic Period* to *A Life History.* Arendt
protested furiously.[6] Rahel Varnhagen's Jewishness was never
going down a memory or oblivion hole again.

Rahel Levin Varnhagen. Drawing by Wilhelm Hensel (1822).

After the election of Adolf Hitler in 1933, the rain started to pour hard in Berlin. Günther Stern-Anders's Jewishness, his red politics and even redder friends, such as the playwright Bertolt Brecht, drove him out of the city in February following the Reichstag Fire decrees. Arbitrary arrests and detention, the banning of political organizations, and censorship swiftly followed, as overnight the German nation state became a police state. *What happened,* Arendt remembered of the first days of the terror that followed, *was monstrous . . . an immediate shock for me and from that moment on, I felt responsible. That is, I was no longer of the opinion that one can simply be a bystander.*[7] The existential groundlessness she had learned about from Heidegger in Marburg became a grotesque historical reality. Now there really was nothing below her and her friends other than an abyss. It wasn't only existential, but political courage which was required.

She stayed in the city just a few more months, working to help others leave. At the turn of the eighteenth century, Rahel Varnhagen's small apartment had been heaving with people desperate to be seen in society. In the spring of 1933, Hannah Arendt's small apartment on Opitzstrasse was a safe house for Jews, leftists, and

Hannah Arendt. Passport photo (1933).

anti-fascists desperate not to be seen. Throughout those days she reminded herself of the lesson she had learned from Varnhagen: *I realized what I then expressed time and again in the sentence: If one is attacked as a Jew, one must defend oneself as a Jew. Not as a German, not as a world citizen, not as an upholder of the Rights of Man, or whatever,* she later said. *But what can I specifically do as a Jew?*[8] The scholar and thinker turned activist.

Given her later commitment to the importance of political visibility, there's a neat irony in the fact that Hannah Arendt's first activism was undercover. Kurt Blumenfeld, the leader of the Zionist Federation of Germany, enlisted her help in compiling a dossier of anti-semitic statements made, not by the obvious Nazi ideologues, but insidiously by professional and government organizations, clubs, journals, and charities, etc. The goal was to present this evidence to the Eighteenth Zionist Congress in Prague that summer. The state archives revealed what the newspapers were not reporting: that anti-semitism, long the curse of Europe, was hardening into a widespread and focused political movement. Blumenfeld had been a friend of her family's back in Königsberg. They met again when she and Hans Jonas invited him to speak to students about Zionism in Heidelberg in 1926. She was never convinced by his arguments for Zionism, but she always loved Blumenfeld, who was handsome, erudite, and with whom she enjoyed hilarious impromptu poetry and singing contests late at night. As with the other men who stayed close to Hannah Arendt over the years, he took her seriously from the first time he met her. Their bond was broken shortly before his death during the controversy that followed the publication of *Eichmann in Jerusalem*. He had heard that her book misrepresented the work of the Jewish councils in the Holocaust. She was devastated, furious at the idea that the man who first taught her how misinformation worked had been misinformed on his deathbed.

Blumenfeld wanted someone who was good at archival work; he also needed a clean skin: if caught, the federation would be accused of concocting fake news. Arendt's relationship to Zionism was complex and critical, but she wholly approved of telling political home truths to the Jews of Europe in 1933 and had been public in her qualified support for the Zionist cause which, she believed, unlike other political movements at the time, was at least seeing Hitler straight. She got to work in the Prussian State Library archives and spent several weeks carefully curating *a beautiful collection of materials*.[9] After only a few days' work, she was arrested crossing Alexanderplatz on her way to lunch with her mother, who was also taken into custody. A search of her apartment turned up academic notes and a few pages of Greek which took the police several hours to decode—as Greek. The questioning of Martha Beerwald (as she now was, after her second marriage) yielded nothing because she knew nothing. Arendt's interrogation, which she claimed took place over eight days, delivered a series of well-calibrated, utterly persuasive, and charming lies.

When I first read about this incident in Elisabeth Young-Bruehl's biography as a student thirty years ago, I puzzled over why it was necessary to search the archives to find hard evidence of a programmatic anti-semitism which I wrongly assumed must have been self-evident to most Jewish people in Europe by the 1930s. I was yet to experience the vertigo of living in a political era when facts became so difficult. In 1933, many people, including Jewish people, were having trouble appreciating the dangers that

Arendt and others saw clearly. Later, the Third Reich took care to disguise its most naked savagery, except when it served to terrorize its victims. In 1943, Eichmann dressed up Theresienstadt (Terezin) in northern Czechoslovakia as a "model ghetto" for a Red Cross inspection. In New York, the German-Jewish weekly *Aufbau* speculated that the "model ghetto" would later be used as an alibi. Hannah Arendt wrote a letter to the magazine to point out that even this interpretation of Nazi lies missed what was actually going on. Theresienstadt was not a model, but a deliberate and distracting fake. The fact was that the Jews were being massacred. This may have been the first time she'd read about Eichmann and she was already in no doubt about his capacities for murderous deception.[10] More than many, Arendt was always prepared to believe the worst.

There was another puzzling issue about the rise of Nazi ideology in this period that would preoccupy her in the years to come. How did political lies get to work so well? At what point did the manufacturing of images start to impinge on reality? The Nazis were not only adept at spinning out hateful fictions. They also turned their lies into facts. In *The Origins of Totalitarianism* she called this the *propaganda effect of infallibility:* the trick of appearing omnipotent by prophesying a future that you then make happen. Hitler wanted the world to believe that the Jewish people were a global threat. So, in the first stages of what became the Final Solution, he shoved them over his borders to become a "refugee problem" and a "migrant crisis" for others "too." This would not be the last time that cynical political operators would use refugees as propaganda effects in this manner, even if the intent, so far, has never again been so monstrous.

Arendt had the good fortune to be arrested by a rookie Gestapo officer as yet unpracticed in the art of finding conspiracies whenever you encounter a Jewish person. He bought her cigarettes and good coffee. She softly blew her smoke just close enough to his face for him to feel a connection between them, while he pondered what to do. I got you in here. I shall get you out again, he told her, which somehow he did. She left Germany with her mother following the increasingly busy Green Front route through the forest of the Ore Mountains. Their last night in Berlin was spent drinking the contents of a wine cellar that had been abandoned by another fleeing Jewish refugee. It was, Anne Mendelssohn later recalled, "the most drunken night of our lives." So far, Hannah Arendt might have added, who never lost her appetite for getting very drunk with close friends.[11] At the German border, they slipped into the front door of a safe house for lunch. They left that evening through the back door, which was in Czechoslovakia. Franz Kafka could not have plotted the story of Hannah Arendt's final escape from Germany any better.

In January 1961, just as she was preparing for her visit to Eichmann's trial in Jerusalem, her close friend, the American poet Robert Lowell, sent Arendt a new poem, "Pigeons (for Hannah Arendt)." It was one of a series of loose translations of the poems of Rainer Maria Rilke, a poet who she had first begun to read and study in Berlin in the 1930s. "I hope you'll let me dedicate it to you out of gratitude," he wrote. "I wonder if it isn't (quietly) one of my finest poems?"[12]

> *The same old flights, the same old homecomings,*
> *dozens of each per day,*
> *but at least the pigeon gets clear of the pigeon-house . . .*
> *What is home, but a feeling of homesickness*
> *for the flight's lost moment of fluttering terror?*

Pigeons fly and pigeons home. But in Lowell's poem, it is the instant of flight itself that reveals the meanings of both home and

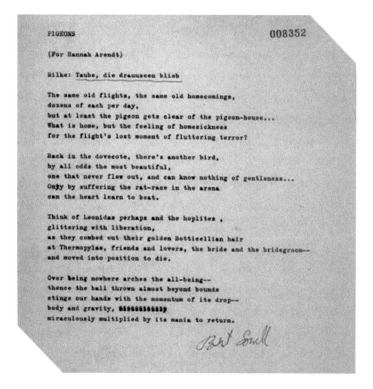

PIGEONS   008352

(For Hannah Arendt)

Rilke: Taube, die drauusseen blieb

The same old flights, the same old homecomings,
dozens of each per day,
but at least the pigeon gets clear of the pigeon-house...
What is home, but the feeling of homesickness
for the flight's lost moment of fluttering terror?

Back in the dovecote, there's another bird,
by all odds the most beautiful,
one that never flew out, and can know nothing of gentleness...
Only by suffering the rat-race in the arena
can the heart learn to beat.

Think of Leonidas perhaps and the hoplites ,
glittering with liberation,
as they combed out their golden Botticellian hair
at Thermopylae, friends and lovers, the bride and the bridegroom--
and moved into position to die.

Over being nowhere arches the all-being--
thence the ball thrown almost beyond bounds
stings our hands with the momentum of its drop--
body and gravity, █████████████
miraculously multiplied by its mania to return.

Excerpt and facsimile of "Pigeons (For Hannah Arendt)" by
Robert Lowell, from Collected Poems *by Robert Lowell.*

freedom. Getting clear of the pigeon house is its own "moment" to be grasped—and lost.

Arendt loved Rilke for the way he expressed the essential homelessness of modern times.[13] A moment on a mountain, another with a rose, talking with an angel, the instant a pigeon takes flight; the images in his poems are points of resistance and solace in a world that moves too fast and too ruthlessly. Like Friedrich Nietzsche, Rilke rejected the idea that history was an inevitable story of progress and development, and so too (suitcase permanently to hand from 1933 to 1941) did Hannah Arendt.

Instead, Homer was her model historian, the first, she later said, to look at events from a variety of perspectives. History began when Homer, in the *Iliad, decided to sing the deeds of the Trojans no less than those of the Achaeans, and to praise the glory of Hector no less than the greatness of Achilles*.[14] Lifting himself free of the warring sides, the poet told the story of the Trojan Wars as though from above—like a bird. As the French philosopher and mystic Simone Weil, also an exiled thinker, pointed out in the 1940s, Homer may have inherited this viewpoint from the generations of refugees uprooted by the wars.[15]

By the twentieth century, historians had lost Homer's commitment to impartiality. Men began to plot history, seeking to control the future by interpreting the past according to philosophy and theology, and later, and disastrously in Arendt's opinion, nineteenth-century ideologies based on economics, technology, race, and nationalism. History became *a man-made process, the only all-comprehending process which owed its existence exclusively to the human race*.[16] The thicker the plots, the looser the connections with reality became.

By contrast, to grasp the "moment of flight," like Lowell's pigeon, is to live with the uncertainty of the present, between past and future. It is a different way of being in time, with a pigeon's-eye view of world history. Hannah Arendt's own moment of "fluttering terror" forced her to look at the pigeon-house differently. Statelessness made (and makes) history look different. From 1933 onward, the history she told was always in a sense refugee history. What if, she asked, the idea of a political home was not necessarily to be found in European ideas of nations, nationalism, and sovereignty? What if refugees have something new to say about how to organize our politics?

In 1938, following the Nuremberg Laws, Arendt was formally stripped of her citizenship. Her official expulsion was listed in the Reich's mouthpiece, the *Deutscher Reichsanzeiger,* in Berlin on April 27, 1938. With the stroke of a pen she, along with millions of others, was stateless. The list's publication in the press was intended to humiliate. At this stage, the aim was to force the Jews to leave ("migrate") voluntarily, even as the financial terms of exit consigned many to penury and the choice was no choice at all. Not long after, Adolf Eichmann would begin actively researching alternative destinations in his role as the Reich's leading "expert" on the "Jewish Question," including Jewish "reservations" in Nisko, Poland, and on the island of Madagascar. In reality, there was no home for Europe's Jews to go to in 1938. *Once they had left their homeland they remained homeless, once they had left their state they became stateless; once they had been deprived of their human rights they were rightless, the scum of the earth,* was how Arendt described the situation in *The Origins of Totalitarianism,* her suitcase only recently unpacked for the final time (*OT* 341).

Statelessness was a new weapon in the modern armory of

twentieth-century human cruelty. For Hannah Arendt, its harsh realities dealt a final death blow to the Enlightenment dream of universal human rights. Without the civic and political rights that come with citizenship, human rights were pretty much meaningless, she argued. Most refugees will ask for a national home before they ask for human rights, and for very good reason. In a homeland you have legal and political rights. Human rights were (and remain) far frailer things. The refugees of the 1930s made this frailty starkly visible. *The conception of human rights, based upon the assumed existence of a human being . . . broke down at the very moment when those who professed to believe in it were for the first time confronted with people who had lost everything except the quality of being human,* she wrote in 1949. *The world found nothing sacred in the abstract nakedness of being human* (OT 380). It still doesn't.

For a long time after the Second World War, states would rarely deprive people of citizenship, not wanting to be seen as using Nazi techniques to police national frontiers. Human rights legislation was drawn up against making people stateless, conventions were signed and protocols agreed to, including the United Nations Declaration of Human Rights (1948), as well as the 1951 Refugee Convention and the 1961 Convention on the Reduction of Statelessness. Protecting citizenship would remain a moral and political baseline for Hannah Arendt throughout her life. She was appalled when plans were proposed to strip Americans of their citizenship during Senator Joseph McCarthy's anti-communist purges in the 1950s. *Deprivation of citizenship* should be *counted among the crimes against humanity,* she urged, and argued hard for a constitutional amendment that would confirm citizenship as an inalienable right.[17]

In the early decades of the twenty-first century, the practice of denaturalization crept back. In April 2022, the UK government passed a bill allowing ministers to deprive people of citizenship without having to give them notice. The reason given for this legislation was national security. Following the rise of the so-called Islamic State, the government did not want to let people back into the country who it knew would be hard, if not impossible, to police. Neither was it certain that it would be possible to get enough firm evidence to ensure convictions, given that many alleged crimes took place in war zones. But the politics behind the law was also nationalist and populist, which would be reason enough for Hannah Arendt to have been alarmed. Nor would she have been persuaded about the security benefits, at least not in the long term. By casting people out you create new generations of stateless and rightless people. It is foolish to think that this makes anybody more secure.

After Berlin, she settled in Paris where she lived in small hotel rooms in the fifth arrondissement to begin with, then the fifteenth, then finally in the sixteenth on the tiny winding rue Servandoni just opposite the Luxembourg Gardens, in the same pension where William Faulkner once lived. Paris was humming with legal and illegal refugees, turning their collars up in the streets and casting furtive looks at one another across smoky bars and at metro stations. Every now and then Action Français would march down the boulevards under the banner *La France aux Français* to remind them that the ultranationalism they had fled was fast catching up with them.

Arendt would regularly meet with other exiles in a café on the rue Soufflot on the hill leading up to the Sorbonne. They included the Austrian writer Stefan Zweig, whose melancholy laments for a lost European literary culture irritated her intensely. Later Zweig, like Benjamin, would kill himself and she would write a scathing review of his final book, *The World of Yesterday* (1942), in which he lovingly recalled living in Vienna in the first decades of the twentieth century. Zweig never really was in that yesterday world of art, love, and books, she bristled: Europe's cosmopolitan culture was always an illusion for the Jews.[18] She attended the Hegel scholar Alexandre Kojève's lectures. At the Institut pour L'Etude du Fascisme, she heard Walter Benjamin give a talk that would become one of his most famous essays, "The Author as Producer," about how to rearrange the way the world looked so as not to succumb to fascist narratives.

Paris for refugees in the 1930s was less the glitter and glamour of contemporary popular imagination than grime and grind. The exiles were more often tolerated than welcomed. The writer and journalist Arthur Koestler complained that he was never invited to dinner by his French acquaintances (although that might just have been specific to Koestler, who was not always the best of guests). For the most part, the refugees lived in parallel intellectual circles to Parisian thinkers and writers. Hannah Arendt certainly became acquainted with rising intellectual stars like Simone de Beauvoir and Jean-Paul Sartre, and with Albert Camus, whom she liked rather more, but she did not spend her time socializing with them in bars and cafés. She had other things to do.

One of those things was falling in love with a Marxist cabaret performer, Heinrich Blücher, who she had first noticed in the Café Le Soufflot. Blücher was thirty-seven when they met, with a history of communist activism and a previous marriage that he kept secret from her for a little too long. In Paris illegally, he would dress up with the studied nonchalance of a regular bourgeois and spend his days strolling through the city's art museums, disguised as a local. She called him *Monsieur*. A political street fighter with a head full of books and a passion for life, and above all for her, there really was nothing not to love about Heinrich Blücher. Martin Heidegger had always been a bothersome third in her marriage to Günther Stern-Anders and when Nazism became a fourth their relationship drifted. The prurience generated by her relationship with Heidegger has overshadowed Hannah Arendt's more singular romantic achievement: to fall permanently in love with a funny, clever, and thoughtful man who loved her back (if not always entirely faithfully—theirs was a twentieth-century European love match). He was her *four walls,* she wrote to him, just days after she had met Heidegger again in Freiberg in 1950, just for the avoidance of doubt. Where "I am, I am not at home" but "where you are with me there is my home," he replied (*WFW* 128, 132–33).

Hannah Arendt was a serious lover, as Heidegger had discovered to his cost. She never doubted that love was a realm of authentic existence, but like many women she feared that in committing to love she might lose her own mind and independence. She never stopped believing her luck that she had managed to get both the *"love of my life" and a oneness with myself* (*WFW* 40). In Blücher, she recognized another intellectual outsider. A working-class autodidact, his reading and understanding took place from outside the hierarchies and snobberies of academic institutions. Everything she and Blücher read and discussed together could be approached anew.

She later told people that it was Blücher who introduced her to politics and history, and her biographers have largely been happy to repeat this line. He was the Marxist materialist who seduced the philosopher-theologian back down to earth. But it's not exactly true. She was already reading Marx, Luxemburg, Lenin, and Trotsky in Berlin, and there were few more direct encounters with contemporary politics in 1933 than that from the inside of a Gestapo cell. What is true is that the pair pooled their reading and sensibilities in an effort to understand the increasingly strange world taking shape around them. *The Origins of Totalitarianism* would undoubtedly have been a different book had Arendt not understood how imperialism produced the conditions for totalitarianism. But that does not mean that she couldn't have written it without Blücher's influence. What it means is that if two people feeling the rain fall directly on their faces set out to comprehend the nature of the rain because it happens that their lives depend on it, one of them might end up producing one of the most significant works of political theory and history of the twentieth century.

Hannah Arendt had not come to Paris to fall in love. She came *to do practical work—exclusively and only Jewish work.*[19] She specialized in youth work. Even before the rise of the Nazis, Jewish migrants had poured into Paris from across Eastern Europe. After 1933 they were joined by families from Poland, Germany, and Hungary. Many sent their children ahead alone. One of these was Herschel Grynszpan, the youngest son of Zindel Grynszpan, whose testimony she would later listen to in Jerusalem. Aged just fifteen, Herschel arrived in Paris illegally to wait until he was old enough to be permitted to travel to Palestine by himself. In the meantime, he was declared stateless and in 1937 was told to leave France. He went underground, cut himself off from support, and slowly spiraled into his own mind. Toward the end of October 1938, he received a letter from his father describing the family's brutal deportation to Poland. On November 7, Herschel walked into the German embassy on the rue de Lille and shot a minor Nazi diplomat, Ernst vom Rath. He had been looking for the Nazi ambassador, Johannes von Welczeck. The "revenge" taken for Herschel's desperate act was *Kristallnacht,* the orgiastic smashing of Jewish businesses, synagogues, and skulls that took place through the night of November 9 across Germany and Austria.

Hannah Arendt was not working with Jewish youth out of humanitarian sentiment. Her motivation was political and existential. The Jewish people had to exist: it was that simple. She had taken Heidegger's lesson about the importance of being in the world and applied it to her own people. Unlike Heidegger, she understood that it was not some *Völkisch* nationalism that might enable a people to exist but a more morally complex politics.

She worked first for Agriculture et Artisanat and then for Youth Aliyah, both of which recruited and trained young people for emigration to Palestine. Many people working for these organizations had an explicit and committed Zionist agenda. Others, such as her friend Chanan Klenbort, from whom she learned some Hebrew, explicitly and committedly did not. Arendt's own focus was on getting the *waifs,* as she called them in a propaganda piece she wrote in 1935, to a place where they stood a chance of existing, not simply as survivors or recipients of charity, but with dignity, as Jewish people.[20] This was the same reasoning that later led her to campaign for a Jewish army during the war. Revisionist Zionists, who wanted a Jewish-only state, campaigned for the same as part of a preemptive claim for Jewish territorial sovereignty. Arendt's argument for a Jewish defense was simpler: if you are attacked because of who you are, you have the political right to defend yourself *as* yourself. Anything else is to concede to the wishes of fascism and to conveniently disappear.

There is a 1935 photograph of Hannah Arendt accompanying some of the children on the boat from Marseilles to Haifa in Palestine. They were headed for Ein Harod Kibbutz, one of the very first kibbutzes established in Palestine in the 1920s and a popular destination for many fleeing Europe in the 1930s and 1940s. Arendt and the children are on a lower deck, shielding from the sun. The children are beautiful: tanned, grinning, very much alive. Shirts are pressed, sleeves are rolled. The boys muck around. Everyone is facing the camera, as though to acknowledge that this is a moment of their lives when they need to be seen. Everyone, that is, except Hannah Arendt, who, although smiling slightly, has her eyes closed against the wind whipping up from the Mediterranean.

From an Israeli, European, or American perspective, the photograph shows Jewish refugees fleeing for their lives, to safety and a homeland. This history will look very different from a Palestinian perspective: the same refugees were also a new generation of colonialists, coming to settle on their land. The point is not to determine which perspective has more claim, as though different refugee histories can be resolved in some kind of ultimate court of appeal. The challenge is to look at both histories at the same time—pigeon vision, as Lowell, after Rilke and Arendt, might have called it.[21]

Setting her face against the wind ten years after that boat trip to

Hannah Arendt and the children of Youth Aliyah on a boat to Palestine, 1935.

Palestine, Arendt would go on to argue that the creation of Israel as a Jewish state was an existential threat not only to the Palestinians but for Jewish people too. Once in New York, she wrote and campaigned on Jewish politics with a determined tirelessness. The fast wit and original intelligence of her prose quickly gained her recognition in the overlapping circles of refugee, Jewish, and literary New York where the question of Palestine was urgent. She wrote regularly for *Aufbau* and worked alongside other activists who were committed to a Jewish homeland but increasingly troubled about the creation of a Jewish-only nation state.

Not long after her arrival, at the Biltmore Conference, held in the famous hotel of the same name, the Zionist movement broke with tradition and formally demanded a Jewish commonwealth in Palestine. Arendt, along with other bi-nationalists, such as Judah Magnes and Henrietta Szold (the activist and director of Youth Aliyah), was horrified. Not only would the new state be surrounded by hostile neighbors, but the problem of statelessness would not have been solved: *On the contrary, like virtually all other events of the twentieth century, the Jewish question merely produced a new category of refugees, the Arabs, thereby increasing the number of stateless and rightless by another 700,000 to 800,000 people (OT 368).*

The "Jewish question" has now been replaced by the "migrant question." Hannah Arendt might point out that the wrong noun remains next to the word "question," and that it is not refugees and migrants who require "solving," but how we do our politics that requires more critical attention. She would never lose faith with the idea that it might be possible to fulfill Kant's injunction to view everyone as an end in themselves, and to do so through po- litical means. We *are* put on the earth to try to make things right for one another; that's how we make a world. But she doubted very much whether the bold humanitarian and human rights ini- tiatives of the post-war period could fix what had been broken, and worried that in some respects the fixing might make things worse, especially as humanitarian agencies became bigger, more internationalized, and more bureaucratized. Holes of oblivion can change their shape.

The problem, as she came to see it, rested not with how we treat people less fortunate than ourselves, but with the more fun- damental question of what kind of political community we wish to live in. *We became aware of the existence of a right to have rights . . . and a right to belong to some kind of organized community, only when millions of people emerged who had lost and could not regain these rights,* she wrote in 1949 (*OT* 376). That meant the right to *live in a framework where one is judged by one's actions and opinions,* the right to speak, to be seen, to appear as a person before others. The *right to have rights* guarantees the only right that perhaps matters: the right to be in the political conversation.

Political theorists have since complained, with justification, that she was frustratingly vague on the type of political community that might best guarantee such a right to have rights. She had some models. She liked the fluid democracy in the soviet councils from the early months of the Russian Revolution and in the worker's councils that flourished during the short-lived Hungarian Revolution of 1956. She admired the revolutionary associations that paved the way for the United States of America. She supported the idea of a post-war federation of European nations (but would have disliked the over-bureaucratized European Union of the 2000s) and for a time mooted the idea of a Palestine within a larger commonwealth of post-colonial states. Insofar as she was sympathetic to modern democracy (like many political thinkers of her generation she was skeptical about the wisdom of majority rule and distrusted the party system), she liked it as direct, lively, and as unpredictable as possible. But to demand a coherent political model from Hannah Arendt is to risk missing her refugee's lesson. Political models look very different to those who are excluded from them. What might happen if we thought about our politics from outside our pigeon-houses?

Paris has a new generation of refugee and migrant youth, the boys, and less commonly girls, from northern and sub-Saharan Africa, Syria, Palestine, and Afghanistan. In the early days of the coronavirus pandemic they were among the first to wear masks in the streets. The rest of Paris was in *confinement,* but in the months before vaccination a mask was better protection than nothing when you had no safe place to stay inside. For similar reasons, the refugees of Baddawi Camp in Lebanon went into self-imposed lockdown long before the United States and many European countries.[22] Migrants and refugees did not need government-appointed behavioral scientists to persuade them about their vulnerability: they knew it.

The masks were also a way of marking the Paris boys out. They wore them over their noses and mouths, but also drooping under their chins as they spoke or hanging from one ear, like an accessory; *gestes barrières* with added cool. The masks were a way of being seen and not seen at the same time. Hardly anyone else was wearing masks in those early months when the streets were also empty of the camouflage of the crowd. When you are constantly under surveillance, at risk of detention, police violence, and deportation, a mask also has extra benefits. The boys were hiding in plain sight, but they were also showing the city, and one another, that they existed.

Perhaps refugees have always worn masks. In 1943, by then safely in New York but reeling from news of the death camps, Arendt wrote what I think was her most blistering and beautiful essay. It was called "We Refugees" and begins with the memorable first line: *In the first place, we don't like to be called refugees.* It is a sentence that masks and unmasks the reality of refugee existence at one and the same time. Arendt is ventriloquizing, as she so often does when she has a serious point to make. In the first place, "we" do not like to be called refugees because we want to assimilate, we do not want to be seen. But being seen *as* a refugee is the reality every displaced person has to confront. Her ironic

put-down of the refugee parvenus who deny that reality is mer-
ciless:

> Some day somebody will write the true story of this Jewish emigra-
> tion from Germany, and he will have to start with a description of
> that Mr. Cohn from Berlin, who had always been a 150 percent
> German, a German superpatriot. In 1933 that Mr. Cohn found
> refuge in Prague and quickly became a convinced Czech patriot. . . .
> Time went on. . . . Our Mr. Cohn then went to Vienna; to adjust
> oneself there a definite Austrian patriotism was required. The Ger-
> man invasion forced Mr. Cohn out of that country. He arrived in
> Paris at a bad moment and he never did receive a regular residence
> permit. Having already acquired a great skill in wishful thinking,
> he refused to take mere administrative measures seriously, convinced
> that he would spend his future life in France.[23]

By 1943, Hannah Arendt knew that behind Mr. Cohn's many
masks were suicides, unmarked graves on the clifftops of the Mediterranean, and horror.

But she had also come to realize that for refugees the best defense is to know the reality of your existence without giving in to
despair. It was possible to wear the mask of the refugee with the
kind of creative and critical defiance that comes from knowing exactly what your place in the world is and what that says about the
condition of that world. The final paragraph of "We Refugees" is
at once a minibiography of her own refugee journey and a call
from her century to those migrants, refugees, and activists in ours
who also understand that it is with their existence, and their rights,
that the truth of our current predicament is revealed most starkly:

Those few refugees who insist upon telling the truth, even to the point of "indecency," get in exchange for their unpopularity one priceless advantage: history is no longer a closed book to them and politics is no longer the privilege of gentiles. They know that the outlawing of the Jewish people in Europe has been followed closely by the outlawing of most European nations. Refugees driven from country to country represent the vanguard of their peoples—if they keep their identity.[24]

From Portbou, Arendt and Blücher traveled to Lisbon. During the still moments of the days of early 1941, waiting for the boat that would take them to New York that May, she would watch the garbage, laundry, and morgue trucks depart from the back gates of the Hospital Santa Marta next door to her room in number 6a on the Rua da Sociedade Farma at the top of the city. Lisbon was disorienting. The city itself is easily navigable: you are either going up or down a hill and everything is pretty. But the estuary of the Rio Tejo is so huge that it looks like the sea, and it can take awhile for the visitor to establish which direction will take them out to the Atlantic, to America in Arendt's case, and which to the Portuguese-Spanish border and back to Europe.

Portugal's leader, António de Oliveira Salazar, was a fascist and an authoritarian but neither an anti-semite nor interested in getting embroiled in the war, so he kept the country neutral and its ports open. When Arendt and Blücher arrived in January 1941, the city was full of refugees, English spies, secret police, people smugglers, and Nazis. They killed time waiting for their boat, walking through the gentle grandiosity bequeathed to the city by the slave trade and drinking port in the cheaper bars, maybe too early in the day, as their room was small and there wasn't really much to do but wait and watch the mist come in as though from nowhere. They had left their books in a trunk with the landlady in their Paris lodgings. Nine years later, Hannah Arendt would return to collect them during her first visit back to Europe.

Today you can take the Chemin Walter Benjamin, clearly signposted from the mayor's office in Banyuls-sur-Mer on the border in southern France, through the vineyards, up into the Pyrenees, beyond the treeline, and then down through the cacti into Portbou and Spain. It is a stunningly beautiful but not a particularly easy climb. It would have been no journey for a skinny middle-aged man who had been preparing for his final disappearance from the world for several months. Once you reach the summit of the mountain, there are only rocks and complete silence. There is not a bird in the sky to see you.

CHAPTER FOUR

How to Love

> Men get together as persons because they need each
> other (love).
>
> —*Denktagebuch/Daily Thinking Book*

O n May 15, 1940, on the orders of Paris's Gouverneur Générale, Hannah Arendt reported to the Velodrome d'Hiver,
an indoor sports center near the Eiffel Tower, with a blanket and
a small suitcase containing some clothes, her papers, and a couple
of paperback novels by the popular Belgian crime fiction writer
Georges Simenon. It was, she reckoned, a good time to learn
how the police operated. Two years later, the stadium would be
crammed with Jewish people rounded up on Nazi orders to be sent
to Auschwitz in the infamous Rafle du Vel' d'Hiv, following the
decision made at the Wannsee Conference in January that year to
"free" all Europe of Jews and implement the Final Solution. The
SS Councillor for Jewish Affairs (Service IV-J), Theodor Dan-
necker, gave the orders to French police after having agreed on his
quotas for the number of victims to be delivered, including over
four thousand children, with his boss, Adolf Eichmann.

Arendt was lucky to have been interned before the Nazi occupation, and not as a Jew but as an "enemy alien." Along with other German and Austrian women, Jews, refugees, dissidents, and a few genuine Nazis, from Paris she was sent to the Gurs internment camp in the southwest of France, on the plains beneath the Pyrenees. As those who live on the plains know, if you can see the mountains, it means the weather is about to change. Most of the time, they are shrouded in their own weather system and the horizon appears flat. When the wind blows hot in the long summers it can sometimes feel as though nothing will ever change again.

Arendt stayed at Gurs for a mercifully brief six weeks. When France fell in June 1940, she was one of a small group of women who took their fates into their own hands and escaped. Arthur Koestler recalled seeing the women, the *Gursiennes,* walking through the country lanes, their uncut, undyed hair swept up into the turbans *à la mode* of European women in wartime.[1] She went first to Lourdes, where she knew Walter Benjamin had fled, and then to the town of Montauban, about 90 miles to the east. There, she was reunited with Heinrich Blücher when they found one another in the street. This fact is often recounted with wonder in biographies, but in the early days of the war, as is often the case now, refugee and survivor networks were tight and people knew where to go to find one another. Montauban was well known as a town of refuge and had welcomed Spanish, German, and Jewish exiles since 1933. In the summer of 1940 it was packed, especially the library, where people took refuge from the heat to read, think, or simply to sit alongside one another in the cool.

Still, I remarked to my husband, as we walked through Montauban's narrow lanes, it must have felt like a miracle to catch a glimpse of a familiar gait walking ahead of her before she realized that it really was Heinrich Blücher, still wearing his bourgeois Parisian disguise but now looking distinctly out of place. We were visiting the town in the brief summer interlude of Europe's first Covid year. The newspapers were reporting that people needed human contact; we must socialize, the authorities urged us, carefully. The hot air was thick with the vivid intensity of forgotten everyday street life. I had known about the library and that Arendt and Blücher had lived above a photographer's shop. My husband had done some sleuthing and presented me with a vacation gift: the address of their apartment—3 Côte de Bonnetièrs—which turned out to be exactly opposite the old Bibliothèque municipale. I carefully counted the sixty steps across the square that it would have taken Arendt to get from her stuffy room to the cool companionship of the library. The next day we drove to Gurs.

In the library Arendt read Carl von Clausewitz's classic political study of international relations, *On War* (1793), and Marcel Proust's *Remembrance of Things Past*. She kept herself close in these days, alert, her inner bows drawn. One of her friends from Gurs camp, Lisa Fittko, who later guided Walter Benjamin over the Pyrenees, recalled running into her as she walked alone in a meadow just outside Montauban. "Do you want to come to Lourdes with us?" Fittko asked. *I feel safer alone,* was the reply.[2]

The majority of women had remained in Gurs, imagining that they might be found by family or friends. That autumn, they were joined by six thousand Jewish people from Baden and Saarplatz. Adolf Eichmann had personally overseen their (illegal) deportation south with the help of the Vichy regime. Those who did not die of dysentery, typhus, hunger, madness, or grief would finally be bullied into cattle cars in the 1942 and 1943 round-ups and murdered in Auschwitz. In the summer of 1945, the Maquis liberated what was left of the camp. For a short time, it housed collaborators and stray German soldiers. By winter that year, the flat rows of the wooden prison had all been burnt to the ground for firewood. Later, a forest was planted in their place.

Today, high trees offer the shade denied to the inmates of the camp, and birdsong accompanies the soft crunch of the gravel paths built to guide the few visitors between the spaces where the barracks once stood. In 1994, the same year he completed his Walter Benjamin memorial in Portbou, Dani Karavan built a reconstruction of one of the huts, adding a railway line stretching eastward from its door, running incongruously between the gar-

View of Gurs Transit Camp with the Pyrenees, 1940–1941.

dens of the houses built around the camp in the immediate post-war years before remembering had properly begun and when forgetting meant that you could buy land cheaply.

When the Gouverneur Générale issued his proclamation ordering all enemy aliens between the ages of seventeen and fifty-five to report for detention in May 1940, he had also gathered together some of Paris's most blazing and energetic refugees: writers, scientists, dancers, musicians, artists, engineers, workers, teachers, doctors, builders, and intellectuals who, on arrival in camps across the south of France, set about recording what was happening around them, making something of it, for one another and for the future. The prisoners of Gurs labored hard to keep clean, flush the sewage, fetch water from the wells that were inconveniently situated at the far end of the camp, to cook, pray, find solitude, sleep, and keep sane. As they struggled some also sketched, drew, wrote, talked, and composed songs. "Ich kann Sie nicht mehr seh'n die Pyrénéen" ("I Can No Longer See the Pyrenees") was one camp song. Others taught their neighbors what they had learned of philosophy, literature, art, politics, and the world. Arendt ran a minicourse on political theory in the women's barracks.

The artists Jacob Barosin, Eva Liebhold, and Karl Schwesig were interned in Gurs. So too, with her grandfather, was the painter and genius Charlotte Salomon. In her masterpiece *Life? or Theater?* Salomon recalled her grandfather's constant invitations to share his bed and confessed to poisoning him after they had escaped to Nice. She was gassed, with her unborn child, in Auschwitz in 1943. One of the most prolific artists in the camp was Lili Andrieux, who captured camp life in more than one hundred delicate pencil line drawings. Andrieux would draw every day, moving through the camp with her sketchbook; watching, capturing a pose, a shared task, a conversation, a tired body. Among those she sketched several times is a woman reading. I've often imagined she might be Hannah Arendt reading Georges Simenon.

Lili Andrieux, Woman Reading on Sack (II), *Gurs Camp.*

The site of a former concentration camp is a strange place to begin to think about love. But as Hannah Arendt discovered in Gurs, sometimes love can be not so much all you need as all you've got.

Love is a paradox in Arendt's thinking. As a philosopher, existentialist, and theologian, she argued that love is at the very heart of the human existence; she originally wanted to call her 1958 book, *The Human Condition, Amor Mundi—The Love of the World*. Love is what makes us human, plural, alive to one another and to the human condition itself. Love may be all you have when you're thrown into a place like Gurs. Yet, as a historian and political theorist, she could also see that precisely because love has such earthly power it can be more than human, possibly inhuman, monstrous, deathly—unearthly—and so, politically speaking, very dangerous indeed.

This doubleness—love's duplicity—is not just a dry theoretical matter. Love matters to our politics because it matters to us at the most intimate level of our lives. As we do now, Arendt lived in a world where there was far too much passionate intensity of the worst kind, and not nearly enough neighborly love. Today, howls of injured outrage fill our timelines, while policy advisers keep daily watch on the barometers of the inchoate rage that they believe, correctly, is the cheapest source of political power. Worn down by the politics of extreme emotion, but denied access to meaningful political action, many campaigners and activists urge solidarity, empathy, and community. "Love more!" people cry, and not without reason, but how? And would it make any difference if we did? Might loving not, as Arendt feared, sometimes make things even worse?

Hannah Arendt loved expertly and authentically. She married well to a clever man, an intellectual companion, and a lover, devoted to her mind and success. She made and kept friends for life. She excelled at intimacy, loyalty, support, flirtation, intensity, and above all, honesty. Hannah Arendt, as we might say now, worked at love because she understood that it is only through relationships with other people that it is sometimes possible to exist at all. It was, again, a refugee's insight. *Such letters are like minutely thin, strong threads,* she wrote to Gershom Scholem just after she had finally arrived in New York in the spring of 1941: *We'd like to convince ourselves that these threads are able to hold together what remains of our world* (*AGS* 12).

In her new city, she determinedly gathered old and new friends about her. The Arendt-Blüchers' crowded rooms on West 95th Street and their later cozy apartment on Morningside Drive on the Upper West Side, front door bolted firmly with two locks and a pole, welcomed fellow refugees, such as her Marburg friend, the philosopher Hans Jonas, the existentialist theologian Paul Tillich, and later, his girlfriend Hilde Fränkel, with whom she became very close (an *erotic genius,* Arendt thought), the journalist (and brilliant hairdresser) Charlotte Beradt, and Blücher's old friend from Berlin the songwriter Robert Gilbert. There were also the rising literary and intellectual stars of New York, such as Alfred Kazin, Dwight Macdonald, Philip Rahv, Randall Jarrell, Lionel Trilling, Robert Lowell, his wife, Elizabeth Hardwick (whose 1979 novel *Sleepless Nights* she later recommended to the Rockefeller Foundation for a grant), the painter and scientist Alcopley (Alfred Copley), and the woman who was to become her closest friend for the second half of her life, Mary McCarthy. The refugee friends were new to America. The New York friends were young, often first-generation intellectuals, also trying to figure out the world anew.

By the time the couple moved to their larger apartment on

Riverside Drive in 1959, the legendary "tribe" was firmly in place. Over the years Arendt's parties gained a reputation. "I set my drink down, hard," John Berryman wrote in his 1968 poem about one of them, "New Year's Eve."[3] Everybody did. She had distinct ideas about what was required of hospitality and would press her guests to eat from little dishes of nuts, candied ginger, cake, crackers, cheese, "almost all at once, regardless of conventional sequence or, often, of the time of day."[4] Her penultimate New Year's party was noted in *The New York Times* in 1974, where it was also reported, in tartly smart racist code, that the Upper West Side had become a magnet for "European" (read "Jewish") intellectuals ever since the white middle classes had moved out and the Puerto Ricans and African Americans moved in, meaning that the rents were cheap.[5]

As shabby-chic glamorous as this may seem, the Jack Daniel's and ice served on the same tray as the Slivovitz and chocolate, W. H. Auden the only one wearing a (threadbare) suit, and even that with a crusty leather jacket on top, the truth was that Arendt was quietly working hard to keep the threads between people, and so her world, connected. "Her presence on the West Side was like Lear's on the heath," Alfred Kazin recalled. "The kingdom had been rent . . . she seemed to cry out a wildly urgent need for constancy in life, every instance of life. She was a passionate and anxious friend."[6] This is a little overdone. Hannah Arendt witnessed the tragedy of her age and time at close proximity but never surrendered to it. But it is true that the way she loved, and the way she came to think about love, was possibly her most intense and consistent response to totalitarianism.

In 1946, five years after she escaped from Gurs, she found herself in another hot summer and in another Hannover, Hanover,

Connecticut, enjoying the cool, beginning to read the great theorist of American democracy, Alexis de Tocqueville, and catching up with her Shakespeare. She always liked the peace of summer. The first years in New York had been frantic. Alongside her journalism and activism, she was the family's main breadwinner. Heinrich Blücher struggled both with learning English and with culture shock. Her mother, finally delivered safely from Europe, was miserable. It was only after the war that she found time to begin pulling together *The Origins of Totalitarianism*. That summer she was working on the book's middle section, "Imperialism." The long days helped, but she was struggling, she wrote to Blücher back in New York, to make her arguments about human rights *come out right* (*WFW* 80). The point about being superfluous, she was arguing, imprisoned in a camp, on the run, on the margins, is that you're no longer really in the world—you just exist, a dim figure in the dark background against which everyone else carries on with the rest of their lives; a shadow person among the shadows. She was in the middle of explaining how this made politics all the more important. The dark places of the world cannot be magically illuminated nor can human rights simply be conjured out of good will. Rights need to be made, bolted down with the consent and dissent that comes with politics, with law, with tradition, she wrote. Then she pauses: the shadow life is nothing, is desperate, is utter deprivation, and yet, there is something—love:

> *This mere existence, that is, all that which is mysteriously given us by birth and which includes the shape of our bodies and the talents of our minds, can be adequately dealt with only by the unpredictable hazards of friendship and sympathy, or by "the great incalculable*

grace of love, which says with Augustine, " 'Volo ut sis' " [I want
you to be] without being able to give any particular reason for such
supreme and unsurpassable affirmation. (OT 382)

I want you to be, *volo ut sis*. I think of the boozy smoky Upper
West Side parties, but also of Lili Andrieux crouching in the door-
way of the women's barracks in Gurs with her stubby pencil to
catch the arc of her neighbor's naked arm as she washes at a communal sink and of the quiet breath of intent readers in the companionable cool of Montauban's library.

The "great incalculable grace of love, which says with Augustine,
'*Volo ut sis*.'" It is a beautiful sentence, as graceful and simple as
the love it recommends and one that Arendt would repeat often
throughout her life. But Saint Augustine never said it. It was Heidegger who in one of his early letters to his student girlfriend
sagely, seductively, explained that "to be *in* one's love = to be forced
into one's innermost existence. Amo means volo ut sis, Augustine
once said: I love you—I want you to be what you are" (*AMH* 20).
So now she knew. Except that it turned out that Heidegger was ex-
trapolating overenthusiastically, and Augustine did *not* once say exactly that, according to specialists at least, who report that while he
had a great deal to say about love, the Saint of Hippo never wrote
volo ut sis. (In his eighth sermon on the first letter of John he did
write: *non enim amas in illo quod est; sed quod vis ut sis* (you do not love
what is in him, but what you want it to be). He meant, however,
not that you should love someone for who they are, but for what
God might turn them into, which is significantly different.)[7]

Heidegger knew a good romantic line when he had penned it—who would not want to be loved merely for their existence? Four years later, he used the same phrase in a letter to another lover, Elisabeth Blochmann, also a brilliant Jewish thinker (his wife Elfride Heidegger's friend since childhood), and an educationalist who studied at Marburg where she later returned to teach after the war.[8] Blochmann left Germany for England in 1933, just after Heidegger had given his Rector's Address.

Hannah Arendt's intellectual interest in love began when she very sensibly transformed her doomed love affair with Heidegger into a PhD dissertation on love in the work of Saint Augustine, thereby smartly turning the agony of being in love into the question of Being in Love. Heidegger argued that it was because Being was directed toward the one absolute fact of our death that we are able to grasp our existence in its full and profound authenticity. "This primal forceful *negative* is what is decisive," he wrote to Elisabeth Blochmann in 1929: "to place *nothing* in the path of the depths of Dasein."[9] At precisely the same moment, sitting alone at her desk in Heidelberg writing her dissertation under the supervision of Karl Jaspers, the twenty-two-year-old Arendt was putting the finishing touches to a thesis that argued the exact opposite: no, not only death, Martin, she responded, the nothing that we come from is born of love; it is love that makes our existence, and crucially, the existence of others, meaningful. There is only one mention of love in Heidegger's magnum opus, *Being in Time* (1927), which was one of the reasons Jaspers thought that the whole book was unlovable.

Heidegger had taught her that traditional philosophy was dead, its metaphysical concepts meaningless; what was left was an archive of words and thoughts for the taking. In her dissertation, Arendt plunged into Saint Augustine's archive with all the grace and fearlessness of a young woman who had understood that this also meant that the great texts of world history and philosophy were hers now too: all she had to do was read and interpret them as carefully and honestly as she could. The puzzle she first examined in her dissertation on Augustine would stay with her for life: what is the relevance of other people in our lives? Why do they matter? Why *should* they matter? Or, to paraphrase a common complaint from our public spheres today, why should I care?

Initially, Augustine is not entirely promising with his answers to these questions. He is, as one might suspect of the great author of Christian doctrine, somewhat doctrinaire when it comes to love. You must love your neighbor as you love yourself because that is how God loves you, he teaches. Worldly love, craving others, obsessive wants, apples in another's orchard, erectile overfunction, the "wrong" kinds of love that got the young Augustine into serious trouble on more than one occasion, are as nothing to God's love which drives our very being and awaits us in eternity. Not *cupiditas,* the love that makes wanton idiots of us all, fun as it is, but *caritas,* the love of others for the love of God: that is the true love. When we love with God, we are *sublimely indifferent* to who our neighbor is, just as we should be indifferent to our own desires: we must love as equals before God; that's the whole point of the commandment (*LA* 43). It is wise not to mess with the love of Christian doctrine. It has a moral and unearthly power. It's a tough, often brave, admirable kind of love. It is the love of those who believe it is their duty to love others as they believe God loves them, whatever the cost to themselves.

But, as the young Arendt discovered as she shadowed Augustine's arguments, in the end it's difficult to see exactly where other people as they actually exist (different, difficult, perhaps unlovable) fit into this love affair with God, especially as Augustine also says it is fine to be mean to people for their own good precisely because you love them as God loves you. What if love in the name of God actually damaged our capacity to relate to one another?

Augustine was modern history's first semiotician. He saw the world as a concatenation of signs, all mysteriously connected, buzzing with wonder and grace. To be a good Christian was to interpret the signs correctly as evidence of God's love. In this sense, other people too are signs of God's love, which is why it is acceptable to use others and to love them in worldly ways, because in the end, whoever they are, they signify the one love that really matters. The love story, so to speak, is already written.

And here, for Arendt, was where the problem with love partly began. With a master narrative like this, the margins of interpretation can start to shrink alarmingly quickly. Once you start to do things to people in the name of love, using them to loving ends, the risk is that you might obliterate the singularity of those you claim to love, flattening out their differences, and so human plurality itself, in the name of their rights, their humanity, their sins, their immortality, their race, their vulnerability, their poverty, or whatever else drives your public passion. Millions more people have been loved to death by ideologies, religions, and revolutions than by their lovers (and millions of women by lovers according to patriarchal ideologies). A lot of damage gets done in the name of love. Love, but be careful who you love, Augustine famously instructed. Love, but be careful how you love, Hannah Arendt added: you don't want to be loving people to death.

Augustine says many different things about love at different periods of his life, as Arendt, who read and reread him, often creatively, throughout her life knew. In the end, it wasn't the saintly and austere Augustine who she was really interested in. The thinker the young Arendt fell for, and who she was to keep close to her for the rest of her life, was the less certain mortal, the man who always remained, as he brilliantly put it, "a question to himself"; the existentialist *avant la lettre,* who first loved fecklessly, lost his best friend, fell into nothingness, found himself through God, and then wrote about all of it endlessly, patiently, lovingly, and honestly. This Augustine, Hannah Arendt believed, had some more promising things to say about love.

In Augustine's work, love is also the meaning of being, that for Hannah Arendt was his most important message. Heidegger was right about that. When we are in love, we crave what is absent. Love, in this sense, forces us to exist in time, for to be satisfied in love is only ever something we can imagine for the future. You don't desire what you already have, so being at one in God's love for all eternity at some unspecified, but definite, time is a good bet, for the Christian believer at least. Yet because Augustine is a modern as well as an ancient thinker, he knows that it is not enough to be told we will be loved eventually: as thinking beings we require proof. The proof lies only in the past. We never know for certain where we are heading, that is why we have faith, but we do know for certain that we once came into the world from absolutely nothing. First we weren't here and then we were. All humans share this weird history. It is a fact. For Augustine, this *ex-nihilo* creation means that we can work out that we are creatures of God's love— how else would we be here? For Hannah Arendt, it meant that love, not nothing, existed in the depths of *Dasein.*

Later, in a note to herself, she wrote that it is *only in an unthinkably ironic way—auf eine nicht auszudenkende ironische Weise*—that when we fall in love, we actually become human as such.[10] I like this remark nearly as much as I love "*Volo ut sis.*" In fact, both phrases are saying the same thing. Love is singular, that is both its curse and its sweetest of sweet spots. Love is the infinitely precious apprehension of and pleasure in human otherness. For the lover, there are no more fish in the sea because I want you—this fish in all your magnificent fishiness. But, precisely because of this singularity, to love is also to affirm the plurality of the world; our differences from one another and our ability to love those differences. Because love is unique, because nobody has ever loved as we two, we join the many.

Love, then, is the private passion that makes us both individuals and, whether we like it or not, part of a bigger collective human story. When we love we also bring something new into the world: a couple, maybe a child, maybe not, maybe something else, a home, a project, a lifelong conversation, a garden, a repertoire of silly names and petty arguments, whatever, but something undeniably *new*. "Natality," Arendt would call it in *The Human Condition*: love as the beginning of the world.

These are comforting thoughts to those of us who have only ever found it possible to be in love ironically, never quite able to take the whole thing seriously, no matter that we haven't slept for weeks and can't keep our hands off our phones. Maybe we're not just damaged, cynical, or repressed: maybe to fall in love is indeed to catch yourself in the oldest cliché there is or the Arendtian version of that cliché: *Love is living without a world. As such, it proves to be world-creating; it creates, engenders a new world.*[11] It doesn't matter if you feel ridiculous: you're in love and therefore part of the world, which is, in fact, exactly why you feel ridiculous. This is also not to be messed with, this everyday and sometimes miraculous love. As the prisoners of Gurs knew as well as the New York friends, without a world in which there are others, where there are stories in which a life might be recognized, narratives with beginnings and ends, there is nothing, as she would later put it in *The Human Condition, but eternal recurrence, the deathless everlastingness of the human as of other animal species* (*HC* 97).

In her dissertation, Hannah Arendt scooped out the existential humanist from Augustine and turned him into a thoroughly modern lover for an age of extremes. She also took Heidegger's amorous one-liner and quietly turned it against him. It is not enough just to clear your path of those anxiety-provoking people in the world as you and your *Dasein* stride purposefully and boldly toward death. The world *is* other people, your neighbors, and both they and you exist—if the circumstances allow—because of love. *Volo ut sis* is no blind love born of desperate faith in a loveless world. I want, Arendt tells us—no, not just want—I *will* you to exist (as she would argue at greater length in the unfinished *Life of the Mind*). For Arendt, we do not love out of faith alone, there is a restless moral reason at work too, which begins with the recognition of just how meaninglessness our existence can be, not only for ourselves but for everyone. We are *all* strangers in need of welcome, which is why *I want you to be* remains one of the most powerful statements in her thought.

Aged just twenty-two, Arendt took the words of two men, one who could sometimes be a censorious saint, the other the thinker who had destroyed the metaphysical grounds of modern

philosophy, both uncommonly self-absorbed and more than a little sexist, and turned those words into a modern creation story
about the human condition itself.

As she worried away at *The Origins of Totalitarianism* in Connecticut
in the summer of 1946, Heinrich Blücher was anxious to reassure
her. Their friend Robert Gilbert, he wrote, had described her version of "I want you to be" as "the greatest and most beautiful love
poem in the world" (*WFW* 87). Yet, as Arendt also came to see,
poetry was another part of the problem with love. Poetry is not
politics. "We must love one another or die," her dear friend in the
tatty suit, Auden, had written in his famous poem "September 1,
1939," just eight months before Arendt reported to the Vel' d'Hiv'.
Auden later hated himself for writing those lines. "That's a damned
lie," he said and rewrote them: "We must love one another *and*
die." But even this was too cute for the times he lived in, and he
disowned the entire poem. The critic Ian Samson has described
"September 1" as "the world's greatest Zombie poem." It won't
die because people will always want to believe that love can save us
from killing one another. Putting pretty ideas in one perfect line
was Auden's gift and his curse.[12] As Arendt noted of his poetry
in her beautiful elegy for the poet in 1973, *this kind of perfection is
very rare.*[13]

    I want you to be also refused to die in Arendt's thinking. On the
one hand, she wouldn't let it. Without love there could be no
human condition; without natality there could be no future for
the world. Love is the *pre-political* condition of us being in the
world together in the first place. On the other hand, Arendt

guarded love with a determined vigilance. Love is best when it is both there and not there. She liked to quote another poet, William Blake, on this point:

> *Never seek to tell thy love*
> *Love that never told can be*
> *For the gentle wind does move*
> *Silently invisibly.* (*HC* 51–52)

Love is worldless, and preferably publicly wordless too. But this doesn't make it worthless in historical terms. The Christian political principle which holds that charity can bond us together as a community was designed (partly by Augustine) for a reason: when we're persecuted, outlawed, and despised, loving one another keeps us human, alive, present to one another.

But this is where Arendt's second problem with love begins. She fundamentally distrusted the love that leaked out into the world as charity. *Of course, I am prejudiced,* she wrote in a letter to Auden on Valentine's Day 1960 discussing the nature of forgiveness, *namely against charity.*[14] The two had become close friends after he had written an enthusiastic review of *The Human Condition,* a book, he claimed, that had given him "the impression of having been written especially for" him.[15] Later, after Blücher's death in 1970, as Auden was entering his miserable final years, he proposed to her. She refused promptly and unambiguously. She would never forgive herself for leaving Auden alone, but neither would she have permitted herself to love out of charity.

That was all private; intellectually, Arendt simply didn't believe that charity should be a political principle. Far better to fix things so that people did not end up in death and detention camps, exiled and vulnerable, in the first place. Charity, as she would later argue, is also the case with violence, is a failure of politics.

This later insight gave her even more reason to be wary of the sublime indifference of love as *caritas* that had first troubled her as a student reading Augustine. Writing her book on the histories of revolutions in the late 1950s and early 1960s finally clarified why political love might, in the end, be neither loving nor political. Uprisings in Algeria, Kenya, Cuba, Hungary, and the American civil rights movement suggested that a new age of revolutions was underway. Arendt was excited: revolutions, she thought, could be the best kinds of new political beginnings. But she was also wary. History had taught her that there were good revolutions and bad revolutions and the bad ones suffered precisely because people had followed the injunction to love more. "*Par pité, par amour pour l'humanité, soyez inhumains!*" cried Maximilien Robespierre, architect of the Terror that washed over France in the wake of its revolution: for the love of humanity, be inhuman. This is the problem with zombie love: let it out in the streets and before you know it, they're lined with corpses.

In her early days in New York, Hannah Arendt liked to walk in the parks. She liked Riverside and Hudson Parks by the river best, where she and Heinrich would stroll in companionable silence, and she would compose elegies to the friends she had lost in Europe. The *voices of the dead,* the messengers who *lead us to sleep* reads a poem dedicated to Walter Benjamin. *We, too, have grown tired of streets, cities, of the rapid / Changes of solitude*, she wrote in another.

One of the poems concludes with the title she first wanted for *The Origins of Totalitarianism,* the burden of our time—*A loving couple passes by / Bearing the burden of time.*[16] Ghost companions from Europe, lost neighbors and friends, came out of the mist from the Hudson to be loved again in words.

At some point, the walking stopped. I'm pretty sure she never walked in the park beneath the cliff edge along which runs Morningside Drive where she lived in the 1950s, the craggy rectangled Morningside Park which bisects the territory between Morningside Heights and Harlem to the east. I wonder how long it took her to identify the racialized codes of entry and exit that are written in invisible ink under the reasoned sublimity of New York's street plans and which make the matter of neighborly love far more complicated than the twenty-two-year-old in Heidelberg could have ever imagined. Not long, I imagine. In 1955, the same year that she moved to Morningside Drive, the city approved a plan for Columbia University to build and develop in the park. A fifteen-year-long struggle against landgrabs and gentrification followed, culminating in a campaign of civil and student disobedience in 1968 (which Arendt supported) and, for a time, victory for the idea that the park belonged to the people of Harlem, and not only to those on the Heights.

In November 1962, James Baldwin published "A Letter from a Region in my Mind," the second part of *The Fire Next Time,* a landmark text in modern humanism and a pivotal document in the twentieth-century archive of Black American struggle.[17] Baldwin knew everything there was to know about the reality of New York street plans and mapped their reality with a prose so lucid that to read him you really can believe that in the beginning human love was created with words, that all we now need to do is find them again, and that is what Baldwin had done. His 1953 semi-autobiographical novel, *Go Tell It on the Mountain,* tracks John Grimes through the streets of Harlem over the course of a day, each step part of a greater historical and existential journey as Baldwin tunnels down to the stories of his parents, the South, and the long misery. Toward the beginning of the book, Grimes cuts down from Harlem and looks across Central Park: "He stood for a moment on the melting snow, distracted, and then began to run down the hill, feeling himself fly as the descent became more rapid, and thinking: 'I can climb back up. If it's wrong, I can always climb back up.'"[18]

Just over a week after having first read Baldwin's essay, Arendt wrote to her editor, William Shawn, at *The New Yorker,* who had published it: *Dear Mr. Shawn, When we talked yesterday, I forgot to tell you how deeply impressed I am by the piece of James Baldwin in the magazine. I have hardly been able to think of anything else since.*[19] It's almost as though she had fallen in love. But what touched Arendt was not just the lyricism of his essay: it was Baldwin's argument that sped straight to her heart. *The Fire Next Time* is an indictment of whiteness's claim to be the human condition. It is also, at key moments, an exhortation to love.

"It is the responsibility of free men to trust and to celebrate what is constant," Baldwin writes, "birth, struggle, and death are constant, and so is love, though we may not always think so—and to apprehend the nature of change, to be able and willing to change." It was a passage Arendt might have written herself. The section of the essay that she would have recognized, though, was a passage toward the end, where Baldwin writes of love as "a state of grace":

All of us know, whether or not we are able to admit it, that mirrors can only lie, that death by drowning is all that awaits one there. It is for this reason that love is so desperately sought and so cunningly avoided. Love takes off the masks that we fear we cannot live without and know we cannot live within. I use the word "love" here not merely in the personal sense but as a state of being, or a state of grace—not in the infantile American sense of being made happy but in the tough and universal sense of quest and daring and growth. And I submit, then, that the racial tensions that menace Americans today have little to do with real antipathy—on the contrary, indeed—and are involved only symbolically with color. These tensions are rooted in the very same depths as those from which love springs, or murder. The white man's unadmitted—and apparently, to him, unspeakable—private fears and longings are projected onto the Negro.

Love tears off the masks. Love as a state of being, of grace, tough, universal, daring, brave; love as wanting others to be. Love as what just might—if "the relatively conscious whites and the relatively conscious blacks" do not falter in their duty—make America human. If we are even to think about making that happen, Baldwin concludes, white people must stop firing their darkness into the bodies of Black men and women. They must drop the masks of whiteness. Love a bit, dared Baldwin:

> The only way [the white man] can be released from the
> Negro's tyrannical power over him is to consent, in effect,

to become black himself, to become a part of that suffering and dancing country that he now watches wistfully from the heights of his lonely power and, armed with spiritual traveler's checks, visits surreptitiously after dark.[20]

As she read Baldwin's essay, Arendt had the final proofs of her book *On Revolution* in front of her. She too had been writing about love again and about the quiet grace of compassion at the heart of the human condition. But what love cannot do is brush aside *the drawn-out wearisome process of politics,* she had written (*OR* 77). It's simply too dangerous. That's still right, she thinks, we cannot, *must* not, do politics in the name of love. But Baldwin's words are still in her ears. She puts down her pen, lights a cigarette, pulls her typewriter across the large desk toward her and begins to type.

Dear Mr. Baldwin, she writes. Your essay is a hugely significant political event. You have made me understand what is at stake in American race politics differently. But I am troubled, in fact, *frightened* by some of your words. *In politics love is a stranger, and when it intrudes upon it nothing is being achieved except hypocrisy . . .*

All the characteristics you stress in the Negro people: their beauty, their capacity for joy, their warmth, and their humanity, are the well-known characteristics of all oppressed people. They grow out of suffering and they are the proudest possession of all pariahs. Unfortunately, they have never survived the hour of liberation by even five minutes. Hatred and love belong together, and they are both destructive; you can afford them only in private and, as a people, only so long as you are not free.

It is not exactly a love letter. Perhaps she didn't pull her typewriter toward her. Perhaps she dictated the letter to an assistant (she wrote her letter to Shawn the same day), impatient to put the matter that had been bothering her to rest, to get Baldwin's love off her desk. As we will see, there are enough instances in her writing on violence, civil rights, the late 1960s student uprisings, and revolution to suggest that it was not just love in politics that troubled (*frightened*—her word) Arendt, but Black love and Black power, in politics, on the streets, in the universities and out in Morningside Park. *In sincere admiration, cordially (that is in case you remember that we know one another slightly), yours, Hannah Arendt.*[21]

Baldwin did not reply, at least not directly. But later, in 1969, in response to an interviewer suggesting that as an African American it "was easier" for him to "know who he was" because of his suffering, he called on Arendt's letter to put a check on the dubious idea that the oppression of Black Americans could be redeemed. "Hannah Arendt told me that the virtues I described in the *New Yorker* piece . . . are typical of all oppressed people. And they don't, unluckily, she said—and I think she's entirely right—survive even five minutes the end of their oppression."[22] Maybe Hannah Arendt and James Baldwin were walking in the same park after all, albeit on different paths, probably in different directions and without necessarily making direct eye contact.

It matters, I think, that probably the most historically significant conversation Hannah Arendt had about love was not with Heidegger, or even with Augustine, but with Baldwin, a queer Black American writer, born just a few blocks away from her home in exile. Both Baldwin and Arendt (and Auden to an extent) understood what it meant to find love against the dark backgrounds of racism, fascism, and homophobia in the twentieth century and treasured it, in different ways, for precisely that reason.

In 1965, Arendt translated her dissertation on Augustine into English. *It's a kind of traumatic experience,* she wrote to Mary McCarthy: *I am re-writing the whole darned business, trying not to do anything new, but only to explain in English (and not in Latin) what I thought when I was twenty . . . I am strangely fascinated in this rencontre* (*BF* 190). Maybe it was not only the meeting between the middle-aged woman and her younger self that was traumatic. Maybe it was because what the woman in her twenties could never have possibly dreamed was just how necessary the unpredictable hazards of friendship and of love would be, not just to her life but to her survival and her thought. The translation into English was also a translation of what loving had come to mean to Hannah Arendt over the years, which is why in her rewriting she doubled down on the moral reasoning behind *volo ut sis:* we must will one another to be; it won't stop us dying, it won't transform our politics, but it might keep us human.

The older woman looked back at the younger woman and told her that she did not know how right she was when she argued that love was being and that being was with other people. Hannah Arendt's turn to politics in the 1930s did not make her doubt the importance of love, it had made her more committed to the idea that love is a guarantee of plurality. The love of human difference, the love that makes us all of the world, is a condition of designing a better politics, but it cannot be a political aim itself without wrecking that very premise. Questions of power and difference, of who is deserving of love or not, or of who is lovable or not, are not and never should be questions of politics for the simple reason that the answers to those questions can only be kinds of tyranny. For Arendt, if you don't want people to die in camps or suffer in poverty, exile, and indignity, instead of loving them you would do better to engage directly with *the drawn-out wearisome processes of persuasion, negotiation, and compromise, which are the processes of law and politics*: to act, in other words, and take political moral responsibility in a crooked world (*OR* 77).

CHAPTER FIVE

How to Think—and How Not to Think—About Race

> Race is, politically speaking, not the beginning of
> humanity but its end, not the origin of peoples but
> their decay, not the natural birth of man but his
> unnatural death.
>
> —*Origins of Totalitarianism*

Hannah Arendt wrote to James Baldwin out of a strong political identification. Love is the privilege of pariah peoples as long as they are not free, she told him. She knew this herself from Berlin, from Paris, from Gurs, and from Montauban. Three years earlier, in 1959, she had published an essay called "Reflections on Little Rock." There she criticized the campaign against the segregation of schools in the Jim Crow South. It was wrong and cruel, she argued, to put children in the front line of the struggle against racism. She did not say so explicitly, but she also assumed she knew this herself from her own childhood, and from her work with Jewish children in Paris. But Hannah Arendt did not know the children of Little Rock, Arkansas, nor did she comprehend the history of their fight. Written in a lofty and chiding tone, her essay caused a scandal because in it she had forgotten one of her own lessons: you can't co-create rights and freedom with people who you cannot see.

To think about race alongside Hannah Arendt often also means thinking against her. On the one hand, she is an original and powerful historian of modern racism. By the time she arrived in New York in 1941, her pariah perspective was pretty much fully formed. Over the next thirty years she would find new ways of putting this perspective into writing. *The Origins of Totalitarianism* came first in 1951, followed by *The Human Condition,* her love song to the world, seven years later. She picked up the historical threads of terror and freedom in *On Revolution,* published in 1963, the same year that her most audacious reckoning with totalitarian thinking, *Eichmann in Jerusalem,* catapulted her into public consciousness. In each of these books she pitched plurality against terror and tyranny and the human condition against racist and inhuman ideologies. But her "Little Rock" essay would not be the only occasion on which she would fail to comprehend American racism and Black resistance to it. Commentators have noted that her enthusiasm for America's democracy blinded her to its white mythologies. This is certainly true, but that blindness means that something else sometimes bubbles up when she writes about race. Hannah Arendt was a principled anti-racist thinker, but this did not mean that she always thought well about race.

Arendt spent her first years in the United States still in her thirties, writing, teaching, learning English—her third language (and fourth after Greek)—and finding her feet again. She had been rewarded for her journalism in *Aufbau* with her own column—*This*

Means You! Since 1944 she had worked with the New York–based Jewish Cultural Reconstruction organization, which had been established to track down looted and stolen Jewish religious and cultural artifacts, books, manuscripts, and art. The team worked with refugees and institutions to map a hidden archive of surviving treasures. After the war, Arendt would lead a six-month-long mission back to Germany to retrieve what had been stolen.

Her first mature book, *The Origins of Totalitarianism,* was her biggest historical salvage operation yet. Still young enough to feel new and abroad, New York gave her the independence and distance she needed to look back at Europe, its crumbling nation-state system, ruined political culture, and broken philosophical heart. In his 1995 book, *Archive Fever,* the French philosopher Jacques Derrida described how the passion to preserve the past is also a symptom of the drive to destroy what has made us. Hannah Arendt was archiving a history, the history of totalitarianism, in order to destroy the habits of the mind, the structures of feeling, and the histories of oppression, that had made it possible.

The Origins of Totalitarianism is an unwieldy book and a feverish one too. Never again would she gird her scholarship with so much historical evidence. The footnotes alone are massive. She buttressed her arguments with quotations, amplification, statistics, evidence, and more evidence. She was making good on the time denied to her by the Gestapo in the Prussian State Archives in 1933. Some of her sources were barely off the press before she cited them; others, such as the long history of European racism, trailed back to the eighteenth and nineteenth centuries. Above all, she wanted to denude totalitarianism of its mythic power. History was her weapon.

Derrida also noted that the act of archiving confirms our commitment to survival and the future. Hannah Arendt knew this too.
She feared that the story she was uncovering might disappear at
any moment, as had most of Europe's Jews, as she very nearly had
herself. Famous as one of the first and certainly most original studies of a new political phenomenon, *The Origins of Totalitarianism* is
also a survivor narrative told by a refugee determined to document
the historical conditions of her uprooting. No wonder it was passionate and unwieldy. How do you tell the history of your own
near disappearance? This huge and sprawling text was Hannah
Arendt's most ambitious affirmation yet of her own life. I sometimes think of it as an act of love disguised as scholarship.

Upon publication, she was both praised and criticized for her
passion. *The Times Literary Supplement* condemned her "tortured
and self-torturing sincerity."[1] Others accused her of sentimental-
ity and of lacking sufficient academic disinterestedness. She re-
torted that her subject called for a stylistic approach that was as
quietly outraged as totalitarianism was itself outrageous. Anything
else would be a denial of what had really happened.[2]

The book's status as a classic of Cold War thought has also obscured the extent to which it is, among other things, a study of
modern racism. In fact, the bulk of the book is concerned with this
history. She had started the research for the first section, "Anti-
semitism," in Berlin and Paris. Religious discrimination against
Jewish people had evolved into an ideology of race hatred over the
course of the nineteenth and early twentieth centuries (I was there
to see the end of this, she might have added). In the second section,
"Imperialism," she traced how French and British imperialism had
ransacked Africa and India using ideologies of racial supremacy as

both a pretext and a justification. When Germany, Austria, and Russia then turned imperial racism on Europe itself, the elements that would eventually crystallize into totalitarianism moved into place. *The elementary structure of totalitarianism is the hidden structure of the book, while its more apparent unity is provided by certain fundamental concepts which run like red threads through the whole,* she explained.[3]

One of those red threads, perhaps *the* red thread, was racism and race-thinking. That thread also ran through the politics of the country in which she now wrote. Adolf Hitler had approvingly referenced the oppression of Black Americans in the Jim Crow South. Many whites in America had just as approvingly referenced him back in the 1930s and early 1940s. Just because they had now gone quiet did not necessarily mean they had changed their minds.

In its early stages, the now hidden structure of the book, along with Arendt's fevered outrage, was much more explicit. She planned to call it *The Elements of Shame: Anti-Semitism-Imperialism-Racism.* I like "shame" because it captures her belief that such a profound moral line had been crossed that people could barely bring themselves to speak of it. The ashamed are usually silent, as well they might be in this case: Arendt's elements of shame were anti-semitism, imperialism, and racism, none of which had vanished from the face of the earth with the defeat of Nazism. Another, more Dante-esque early title was *The Three Pillars of Hell: Anti-Semitism-Imperialism-Racism.* Right up until the proof stages the working title was *The Burden of Our Time: Anti-Semitism-Imperialism-Totalitarianism* (this was also the title of the first UK edition). Arendt had now grasped how anti-semitism and imperialism were the elementary structures from which totalitarianism would eventually emerge. *The Burden of Our Time,* taken from her poem about walking alongside the Hudson with Blücher, is a reminder of how deeply personal this book about inhuman and profoundly impersonal political structures was.

The word "totalitarianism" didn't find its way into the main title until just before the book went to press in the autumn of 1950. It was her US publisher that suggested *The Origins of Totalitarianism*. It is a great title and it was a shrewd move to keep an explicit mention of racism and anti-semitism off the front cover. In 1951, many Americans would have been reluctant to think about either as one of the key elements of a political system that was supposedly the antithesis of their own democracy. Far better to get those readers into the book first.

But the muting of racism, imperialism, and anti-semitism had consequences for how the book was, and is, read. The final, and now most read, section of the book, "Totalitarianism," is a terrifying and exhilarating account of a political system in which human spontaneity has all but been eliminated. Death and horror stalk these pages as Arendt brilliantly adumbrates how ideology ripped apart people's experience of the world, bearing down on minds and smashing through laws and institutions with a relentless dark energy, culminating in the death camps and gulags. This was the nightmare of "total domination" that had now arrived in the world and which she feared was here to stay, although possibly not in such a dramatic and extreme form. Tired horror, she would go on to say, can be just as, if not more, morally corrupting than the vivid violence of pure terror.

Yet it was implicit in Arendt's argument that the elements that eventually produced totalitarianism are endemic to most modern political systems. It's not just massively outsize propaganda, unspeakable terror, constant surveillance, fear, censorship, black flags, concentration camps, and public executions you need to watch out for. Racism, political and economic greed were all there at the beginning too. They were the roots.

The first modern superfluous people, Arendt argued, were created by the desire for superfluous wealth. If you want to understand the origins of totalitarianism, look to the origins of Empire. "I would annex the planets if I could," the English vicar's son, mining magnate and whiteness ideologue Cecil Rhodes declared at the height of his mission to turn Africa's resources into pure wealth and its people into the pure labor necessary to produce it. He was totally serious. Arendt opened the middle section of her book, "Imperialism," with Rhodes's mad quote. Much of what followed aimed to take him and everything his deranged ambition stood for down. (I think of Rhodes's words whenever I hear the business mogul Elon Musk detail his plans for annexing the planets as a "solution" to the climate catastrophe.)[4]

Another Englishman, George Orwell, so often in lockstep with Arendt, had earlier made the point, well known throughout Asia and Africa, that human rights were not first demolished in Europe in the middle of the twentieth century but at least a hundred years earlier. What was the freedom the West was fighting for? he asked in 1939. Just whose lives were being counted in the name of white democracy?[5] *Lying under anybody's nose were many of the elements which gathered together could create a totalitarian government on the basis of racism,* Arendt wrote of British imperialism. *"Administrative massacres" were proposed by Indian bureaucrats while African officials declared that "no ethical considerations such as the rights of man will be allowed to stand in the way" of white rule* (OT 286).

The vivid novelty of the third section of her book, "Totalitarianism," eventually overshadowed much of the historical material that preceded it and left the impression that the horrors of imperialism in Africa and India were simply building blocks for a greater horror—the "greater" horror being that its murderousness now extended to white people too. The reason why Europeans were so appalled by Hitler, wrote the Martinique poet and politician Aimé Césaire in *Discourse on Colonialism,* first published in Paris a full year before *The Origins of Totalitarianism,* was because he "applied to Europe colonialist procedures which until then had been reserved exclusively" for people in Algeria, Africa, and India.[6]

In Britain and France, imperial and colonial myths of white supremacy had helped to shore up a sense of a coherent national identity in countries that in reality were far from secure in themselves. Elsewhere, in an increasingly impoverished and unstable Europe, new stories about ethnic difference were invented to account for why some white people were superior to others. In the late nineteenth century, the Pan-Slav and Pan-German movements had started to promote race thinking as an alibi for conquest and domination on the continent. When, some years before the rise of the Nazi Party, the teenage Adolf Eichmann pulled on his shorts and went adventuring in the Austrian forests with the *Österreichischen Wandervogel,* he may not have known much, but he absolutely and enthusiastically believed that he was marching for a greater and unified German master race to take its rightful place at the heart of Europe.

Arendt was clear that racism was not only an accessory to the catastrophe that befell the West in the twentieth century: it *was* the catastrophe. *Racism may indeed carry out the doom of the Western world and, for that matter, of the whole of human civilization,* she wrote. *For no matter what learned scientists may say, race is, politically speaking, not the beginning of humanity but its end, not the origin of peoples but their decay, not the natural birth of man but his unnatural death* (OT 209). The entire idea of race was a myth. Race thinking turned that myth into the ideological wing of a politics of unprecedented administrative savagery. Race was the red thread that connected the camps in Africa with those in Europe, the butchery executed in memorandums and recorded on index cards in imperial London and Paris to those later in Nazi Berlin.

The world was not post-imperialist, still less post-racist, when Arendt began to compile her book in 1946. Post-war, the Soviet Union consolidated its dominions across the East under the banner of Bolshevism and had done so along old Slavic lines. (A brief point of comparison: Vladimir Putin's claims on Ukraine were even more imperialist than those of the Bolsheviks. "Russia was robbed," when the 1924 USSR constitution included a provision allowing states to secede, he wrote in a rambling essay in 2021.)[7] In South Africa, where Rhodes had first experimented in raising hell on earth, the political architecture of apartheid was being moved into place even as Arendt worked on her final drafts. In 1948 the National Party came to power. In 1949, the Prohibition of Mixed Marriages Act was passed and South Africa began to resemble the Jim Crow South more explicitly. This was followed in 1950 by the Group Areas Act which licensed the ethnic cleansing of towns and cities; the Population Registration Act, categorizing all South Africans by race; and the Immorality Act, prohibiting interracial sex. As Arendt well knew, near identical laws against intermarriage and miscegenation remained in place in large areas of the United States.

She would never visit the southern states out of principle, any more than she would have dreamed of going to apartheid South Africa. To her mind, both were abhorrent because they aimed at the complete domination of social and private life by racist ideology. Racism's destruction of private life would be the starting point for her "Little Rock" essay too. Why did American liberals not attack miscegenation laws with the same vigor as they supported the desegregation of schools? she asked. *Racial legislation constitutes the perpetuation of the original crime in this country's history.*[8] Just as Jefferson and the Founding Fathers had failed with slavery, so too were this generation of progressives failing to confront the Republic's ongoing history of racial violence.

The protection of privacy, of love and intimacy, was another of Hannah Arendt's anti-totalitarian baselines. She did not believe that laws could or should make us equal, not because she didn't believe in justice but because she had witnessed the violence of social engineering firsthand. Instead, the law must protect our right to love, she argued, and would never stop arguing both in the United States and in Israel, which after 1948 had also established race-based laws about mixed marriages and restricted the civil rights of children from those unions. She was not just concerned about the boots of bigotry marching into the bedroom. For Hannah Arendt, miscegenation laws are a foremost mark of tyranny because they attempt to prevent even the possibility of a politics of plurality. Without love's children, there can be no new beginnings.

In 1946, as she was working on the "Imperialism" section of her book, the historian and ethnographer W. E. B. Du Bois published his major study *The World and Africa: An Inquiry into the Part Which Africa Has Played in World History.* In the opening two chapters,

Du Bois also connected Europe's collapse into totalitarian barbarism with its histories of imperialism and colonialization, but his history went deeper and further than Arendt's. "One of the chief causes which . . . distorted the development of Europe was the African slave trade," Du Bois wrote, "and we have tried to rewrite its history and meaning and to make it occupy a much less important place in the world's history than it deserves."[9] Du Bois's mission was to show how *all* the red threads from the history of racism were tied together. Slavery was not just America's *original crime* as Arendt claimed, it was Europe's too. It bound middle-class whites of both continents together just as surely as their affluence and cultural self-confidence did. In this respect, neither was it true, as she also claimed in her "Little Rock" essay, that imperialism and fascism were two European race crimes that America was not responsible for.

Hannah Arendt did not read *The World and Africa* when it was published in 1946. I wish she had, not least because Du Bois might have prompted her to think harder about how her adopted country was as implicated in the racialized origins of totalitarian thinking as the continent she had fled. She was certainly aware of Du Bois's work and had read his 1935 book on the African American contribution to post-Civil War democracy, *Black Reconstruction,* closely (her annotated edition can be found in her library at Bard College). It was not the case that she did not know about Black history. But she did not think it was her history. Like many twentieth-century European writers and intellectuals, she was determined to pull apart the myths of white superiority. But it was the dark heart of its lethal narcissism that captured her attention and not the historical realities—or the historical humanities—of the Black lives which were lost to keep that heart beating.

In *The Origins of Totalitarianism* Black lives only ever appear, at best, in the rearview mirror of Arendt's thesis. They *appeared to be phantoms, unreal and ghostlike,* she writes of the Khoikhoi people in South Africa, victims of both the Boers and the English. Arendt is ventriloquizing the primitivist perspective of the colonialists here. I don't think she means that the Khoikhoi people were unreal, although there is enough room for doubt on this point. *They were, as it were, "natural" human beings who lacked the specifically human character, the specifically human reality, so that when European men massacred them they somehow were not aware that they had committed murder,* she continues (*OT* 251). The damning ironic idiom of this sentence is pure Hannah Arendt and captures the outraged soul of her entire moral enterprise. What is this *somehow* that, *as it were,* permits men to murder others like this? Indiscriminately, carelessly, methodically, drawing up kill lists in the morning and then going home to play cricket in the evening? How was that obscenity unleashed into the world right under our noses? These were the same questions that would compel her to attend the trial of Adolf Eichmann in Jerusalem fifteen years later, still looking for answers. But in that very same sentence, that *somehow* (somehow) glides over the murdered and massacred themselves. For all their appearing "natural" in quotation marks, and for all her criticism of racist primitivism, the Khoikhoi people have nothing either to see, say, or do in Arendt's account of their dehumanization but rather fade away into the phantom world of imperial racism, unheard and unseen.

Thirty-six years after Hannah Arendt ran through the streets of Königsberg, another smart fifteen-year-old girl, books clasped close to her heart, was trying to find her way home. She, too, was thoughtful and serious. She also sometimes seized the time walking from school to home or from home to the shops or back from church to lose herself in thought and disappear. But because she lived in Little Rock, Arkansas, the moments when Elizabeth Eckford could slip inside herself were few and precious. She was rarely allowed to forget that she was appearing for others; that she was a Black girl walking alone in the Jim Crow South.

On the morning of September 3, 1957, Elizabeth Eckford was not only fighting for her mind, she was fighting for her life. In case she was in any doubt about this, the mob of white youths surrounding her told her so; specifically, they screamed, they would like to lynch her. She knew that the State of Arkansas would not protect her because when she had walked up the steps of Central High School just a few minutes before, it was against her body that the National Guard had raised their bayonets. In the five more minutes it took her to walk back down the steps, through the grounds, and out into the street, she also discovered that if you appeal for help with your eyes, as children do, to the nearest adult woman with a kind face, if that woman is white what you might get in reply is her spittle on your cheek. Understanding all of this, she knew she must keep walking at all costs, which she did, eyes behind her sunglasses, the layers of tulle petticoat under the special dress she had stayed up late making the night before camouflaging the knees trembling beneath them.

Elizabeth Eckford was the most visible member of the Little Rock Nine, the group of Black teenagers who dared to insist that the law mattered, that they mattered, and to take up their places at Central High in Little Rock. In 1954, the United States Supreme Court had ruled that racially segregated schools violated the Equal

Elizabeth Eckford surrounded by journalists, Little Rock, Arkansas,
September 3, 1957, by Bettmann.

Protection Clause of the Fourteenth Amendment and must be de-
segregated in a case that became known as *Brown v. Board of Education*. Little Rock opted for a go slow response to the ruling which,
when challenged by activists and the local school board, turned
into an active debarring policy. As the new school year approached
in 1957, Governor Orval Faubus called in the National Guard "to
keep the peace"—which turned out to mean keeping the nine
newly enrolled Black children out of Central High.

The photographs taken of Elizabeth Eckford's long walk from

the school steps to the bus stop were reproduced across the world. Nobody could fail to see what happened when a young Black woman claimed her rights and walked alone in the South. As the Eckford family had no telephone, she did not get the message saying that the police would escort the children to school on that first day, so she had gone by herself. The cab firm she was led to by the activist Grace Lorch refused to take her home. The journalists who encircled her, tall, suited, grown white men, kept the mob from getting to her but still flashed their cameras in her face, demanding to know her name, what she thought she was doing, and how afraid she really was. One of them, Benjamin Fine, sat next to her on the bench by the bus stop, put his arm around her, and whispered firmly: "Don't let them see you cry!" "This little girl, this tender little thing, walking with this whole mob baying at her like a pack of wolves," he later wrote.[10] Elizabeth Eckford did not let them see her cry. She shut herself up tight and waited for the bus to take her to the school for the deaf where her mother worked.

Everyone was interested in Elizabeth Eckford, but in another sense, hardly anybody was interested in her. For all the demands made on her that day and since, few white observers at least troubled themselves to ask the one question, according to Hannah Arendt in *The Human Condition,* that must be asked of every newcomer—and every changemaker—in a truly plural world: Who are you? What do your actions and speech—your agency— tell us, who share the world with you, about you?

Certainly not Hannah Arendt herself, aged fifty-one, now an established public intellectual in her new home, who watched the events unfolding in the South from New York with unease. *I think no one will find it easy to forget the photograph reproduced by newspapers showing a Negro girl . . . persecuted and followed into bodily proximity by a menacing mob of youngsters,* she wrote in her essay "Little Rock," which was originally intended for the Jewish magazine *Commentary.* Arendt looked at Eckford and saw a little girl, an achingly vulnerable little *Negro girl. Have we now come to the point where it is the children who are being asked to change the world? And do we intend to have our political battles fought out in the school yards?* she despaired.[11] The answer to both those questions, as the Little Rock Nine and countless other civil rights activists would go on to demonstrate in the months and years that followed, was yes.

But that was not the answer Arendt wanted. In prose Ralph Ellison, author of *Invisible Man,* would describe as "Olympian" (which he did not mean as a compliment), she argued that education was the wrong battle to fight segregation with. The photographs of Eckford and the mob of white teens, she admonished, were like the worst caricature of progressive education, where the adults had divested themselves of all responsibility and left Black children to the mercy of the pack and those in the pack to their worst instincts. Elizabeth Eckford had been failed, by her community, by the NAACP (National Association for the Advancement of Colored People), and, she suggested, in a truly scandalous piece of insensitivity, by her parents.

In the days leading up to September 3, Elizabeth Eckford's mother, Birdie Eckford, had talked over the risks of sending her daughter to school with the editor and journalist Daisy Bates, the president of the Arkansas NAACP. Mrs. Eckford recalled walking as a child with her own mother and witnessing a lynch mob dragging their victim through the streets of Little Rock: "We were told to get off the streets. We ran. And by cutting through the side streets and alleys, we managed to make it to the home of a friend. But we were close enough to hear the screams of the mob [. . .] to smell the sickening odor of burning flesh. And, Mrs. Bates, they took the pews from Bethel Church."[12] Both women knew that what they had to fear for their children went far beyond the supposed anarchy of progressive education. Hannah Arendt was not seeing this—or Elizabeth Eckford—right.

Commentary spiked her article. On September 23, President Eisenhower ordered the 101st Airborne Division into Little Rock and on the 24th the Nine finally walked through the doors of Central High. For the rest of the school year, they battled regular physical and psychological abuse. In the summer of 1958, Governor Faubus made one more effort to delay desegregation and succeeded in shutting down the entire school system for a year. The Nine, their advocates, and the local school board dug in for a long fight.

Surprisingly, so too did Hannah Arendt and published her article in another magazine, the left-leaning *Dissent,* a full year after she had first written it. The predictable outrage was immediate. Not only had she gone too far, but many also found it hard to see where she had gone at all. For most people, at least in the North, the case for desegregation was self-evidently just. If anybody was irresponsible it was a nation that permitted some of its children to believe they were less worthy of educating than others. The harm done to the self-esteem of Black children by segregation had been demonstrated in recent and much-publicized studies that had helped to galvanize liberal opinion and steel the resolve of activists. To argue against the desegregation of schools was monstrous.

Arendt based her case on two arguments. The first was a concern about equality, visibility, and social rights. Anticipating worries in the early twenty-first century about how successful progressivism provokes conservative backlashes, Arendt fretted that compulsory school desegregation risked providing white rage with a phony justification. White resistance to Black people becoming visible agents of political power was probably inevitable, she thought, although it didn't have to be that way. The rise of Trumpism in America would not have surprised her. What scared her in 1957, as it scared many between 2016 and 2020, was the anti-political senselessness of that rage. Why risk triggering a mob mentality that threatened the wider project of political equality? she asked. And why do that while leaving fundamental human rights violations—specifically southern state laws that prohibited interracial sex and marriage—intact? If social prejudices are to be prevented from becoming tyrannical, maybe we should allow people to have their differences and discriminations, even if we find them repellent?

Arendt's experience of Nazism made her hyper-alert to the dangers of one-size-fits-all social solutions. Her migrant experience of American mass society made her warier still. Social conformity was one of the first things she noticed about her new home. *The fundamental contradiction of the country is political freedom coupled with social slavery,* she wrote to Karl Jaspers in January 1946 (*AKJ* 30). When she'd first arrived in the United States, Arendt had been taken in as part of a refugee hosting scheme by a couple in Massachusetts. The deal was that she would help with the housekeeping in exchange for English lessons. Hannah Arendt, unsurprisingly, was the worst au pair and the most interesting of houseguests. She did next to no housework or cooking (although she would maintain throughout her life that she was an expert cook, privately her friends differed on this matter). She preferred to stay up late talking politics with her hosts, particularly with the husband; she couldn't work out whether they were Jewish or not, but suspected there was a story. She was deeply impressed by how naturally the couple took responsibility for local and national issues; attending meetings and writing to legislators exactly as though what they did should, and indeed would, make a difference. People did not behave like this in Europe. Was this perhaps political freedom in action?

But what then puzzled her was that such a politically engaged people could also be so socially conservative. The right to have rights was there, in theory, waiting to be grasped, but the mood was low-key and socially stifling. Arendt wasn't simply being an Old World snob. She had the nineteenth-century French political philosopher Alexis de Tocqueville's famous observation about the paradox of American democracy in the back of her mind. Democracy gives people a singular and precious power, but the tyranny of the majority always threatens. In a democratic republic committed to equality, such as the United States, it does not take much for the demand for social equality, even equality in misery and oppression—*social slavery*—to exert its pressure. In other words, democracy is no guarantee of political or personal freedom. As the writer Chimamanda Ngozi Adichie succinctly paraphrased this paradox in 2022: "We fear the mob, but the mob is us."[13]

The tyranny of the mob does not just belong to fascist and totalitarian societies. It is there too in social democracies. Arendt believed deeply that once people become their own secret police, politics really starts going to the bad. Social media, she might have said, is merely the latest example of how what might look like social liberty can also breed a dangerously oppressive conformity. Few nowadays need lessons in how the internet can raise a mob. We can name and shame, follow and unfollow, but we need to remember that as we do, real political and economic power remains in the shadows. One of Arendt's key historical lessons for today is each to their social own—their own clubs, Tinder accounts, parties, and dress codes—and all to fighting very hard for the political right to be different.

This lesson is at the heart of her distinction between the private, social, and political worlds. Her worry was always that both personal and political life might collapse into an over-socialized existence. In this now perhaps familiar dystopia, social conformists would dictate what you might say or not say, how you might say it, what you should have known better about, your looks, your friends, who you should be having sex with and probably how you should be having it. Morality—thinking—would never get the chance to be the topic of a two-in-one conversation enjoyed in solitude, because it would already be decided by courts of public opinion, which is to say it would be no morality at all. ("I would fear the mob less," Adichie said, "if my neighbor would not stay silent were I to be pilloried.") And political power would remain where it always had, with elites who are happy to let people believe they have social agency when what they actually have is merely the right to feel right, righteous, outraged, or at least not to feel despised and lonely. By contrast, freedom for Hannah Arendt meant being clear about the spaces between people, as well as acting together for a common good when it mattered.

But the Little Rock Nine were not demanding entry into a specialist holiday camp, one of Arendt's more niche examples of the kinds of acceptable social segregation we practice all the time, any more than I would demand to be followed by the Conservative Women's Organization on social media. They were demanding that the law be upheld and the right to the same educational privileges as their peers. They did not wish for everybody to be or to think the same as them; they wished to be young political citizens.

Ironically, the gap in Arendt's argument was the very thing she wanted to protect: the political and personal rights of all Americans, including, most urgently, Black Americans. Her second argument in the article, about political power, was also strange in this respect. The American Republic contained the grain of anti-totalitarianism in its federated structure—this is what made it so attractive to her. Enduring political power, as the Founding Fathers recognized, was achieved by neither force nor violence but rested in the power that is created between people and associations. Where other political systems called on higher powers—God, the sovereign, History, Nature, Terror, the state—the republican tradition begins with the recognition that only the common action of people makes power durable. This doesn't mean that people power is necessarily a good thing. Citizens can just as easily authorize their rulers to do awful things—including depriving them of their own freedoms and turning them into social slaves. But the virtue of a federated and constitutional system was that it put a system of checks and balances in place to hold power to account. It made politics human, both frail and strong—alive.

In the case of *Brown v. Board of Education,* she feared that the Supreme Court was putting the Republic at risk through overreach. This was a peculiar interpretation of the constitutional right to check individual states' power to act in unaccountable ways, not to say of the Fourteenth Amendment. Even if you wanted to defend state autonomy, it's difficult to see how you might possibly do this when, as she also pointed out, those same states were suppressing (and continue to suppress) Black votes, often using a lack of educational attainment as a bar to registration. Hannah Arendt knew all this but chose not to see it when she looked at the photographs of Elizabeth Eckford.

My first question was, what would I do if I were a Negro mother? she replied to her critics in *Dissent,* in a last word on the matter which even the most passionate Arendt fan must wish she had left unsaid:

> *The point of departure of my reflections was a picture in the newspapers showing a Negro girl on her way home from a newly integrated school: she was persecuted by a mob of white children, protected by a white friend of her father, and her face bore eloquent witness to the obvious fact that she was not precisely happy, . . . The answer: under no circumstances would I expose my child to conditions which made it appear as though it [sic] wanted to push its [sic] way into a group where it [sic] was not wanted.*[14]

Hannah Arendt was not Elizabeth Eckford's mother. She didn't have to be to imagine what Birdie Eckford may or may not have done. Elsewhere, it is Arendt herself who urges the cultivation, and education, of an *enlarged mentality* so that we can visit other people's experiences and look at the world from perspectives that are not our own. It is also Arendt who teaches us again and again that judgment is a matter of testing reality: of establishing the facts and dealing with them, no matter how difficult; of laying out the world as it really is, as a prelude to resisting it and making it different.

But she did not check the facts. Elizabeth Eckford was not *on her way home from a newly integrated school:* she was being hounded back home because the school was precisely not being integrated. Black parents, activists, and townspeople had been advised to stay away from Central High that day for fear that their presence would incite more violence, so nor was it the case, as Arendt assumed, that *neither white nor black citizens felt it their duty to see the Negro children safely to school.*[15] Elizabeth Eckford was not *protected by a white friend of her father* in the photograph; she was being shielded by white journalists. Benjamin Fine, the education editor for *The New York Times* who sat by Elizabeth Eckford on the bench, was a friend of Daisy Bates (although not of Mr. Eckford). "Daisy, they spat in my face. They called me a 'dirty Jew,'" he later told her: "A dirty New York Jew! Get him!"[16] The National Guard responded by threatening to arrest Fine for incitement to riot; apparently being a Jewish man sitting next to a young Black woman on a public bench and telling her not to cry was reason enough to drive the white citizens of Little Rock to rip up the sidewalk.

Although she would not have been surprised to learn that the social prejudices of Little Rock's racist mob included violent antisemitism, Arendt did not discuss this connection in her essay. Nor did she scrutinize the personal identification that so obviously drew her to the defense, so she thought, of the children of Little Rock. Asking herself what she would have done were she Elizabeth Eckford's mother was a way of both remembering and not remembering what it was like to be a Jewish girl walking alone in 1920s Königsberg, trying, and sometimes failing, to disappear into her own thoughts—of being denied the right to be invisible in her own unique quest to understand her world.

I should like to make it clear that as a Jew I take my sympathy for the cause of the Negroes as for all oppressed or under-privileged people for granted, she wrote in some preliminary remarks to her article.[17] But some forms of sympathy can be barriers to good political judgment. The one thing, perhaps the most important thing, Hannah Arendt's life and writing teaches us is to take *nothing* for granted. Don't assume, don't accept, test your thoughts against reality, question—do the *work*. Think. But she didn't. Hannah Arendt secretly saw herself in Elizabeth Eckford, that much is true, but it remains the case that she did not see Elizabeth Eckford. *"Neither the 'Negro girl' nor her actions appear to Arendt,"* the philosopher and poet Fred Moten has written: "Eckford is unseen because she is neither seen nor heard to see."[18]

"There are no abstract rules," the novelist Ralph Ellison once explained, describing how although all anti-racism struggles serve the same purpose, they are always unique in context. "And although the human goal of a higher humanity is the same for all, each group must play the cards a history deals them." This, he added, "requires understanding." He was talking with fellow southern writer and literary critic Robert Penn Warren, a regular co-contributor alongside Arendt in the pages of *Partisan Review*. Penn Warren had traveled across the United States in 1964, the same year that the Civil Rights Act was passed into American law, collecting interviews from leading figures, including Ellison, and local activists, which were collected in the anthology *Who Speaks for the Negro?*[19]

Ellison had little patience for whitesplaining northern intellectuals. "Why is it so often true that when critics confront the American as *Negro* they suddenly drop their advanced critical armament and revert with an air of confident superiority to quite primitive modes of analysis?" he asked in the same essay in which he had described Arendt's prose as "Olympian": "why is it that so many of those who would tell us the meaning of Negro life never bother to learn how varied it really is?"[20] It was exactly this brash, careless lack of attention, he explained to Penn Warren in their 1964 interview, that caused Arendt "to fly way off into left field" in her "Reflections on Little Rock" essay.

Hannah Arendt had forgotten that nobody knows more about the tyranny of social life than those who have no say in it but are compelled to exist on its terms. The people who she had once described as living without umbrellas in the rain understand more precisely because they are soaking wet. Black Americans, Ellison said, *lived* the truth of racism, and they were drenched.

For Ellison, understanding is "required" of minorities not out of some sense of enlightened liberal generosity toward the people who make their lives miserable, but because if you do not think all the time, if you do not constantly reflect on your place within the madness, you risk becoming the nobody, the superfluous person that racism imagines and wants you to be. Hyper-understanding is a means of survival. "This puts a big strain—yes, it puts a big strain on the individual," Ellison told Penn Warren. "Nevertheless, isn't this what civilization is about? Isn't this what tragedy has always taught us?"

Tragedy teaches us that the sacrifices we make are never just individual but are meaningful precisely because we exist alongside others. When we act we make ourselves real in the world, visible, courageous even (Arendt, after Aristotle, thought that courage was the most important political virtue). When people leave their homes, take the bus, walk up to the gates, when they challenge society, they lose their privacy, expose themselves, risk everything, and they do not do this simply for themselves, because they want to be heroes (although this, too, can be the case), but out of a tacit, sometimes even unconscious, understanding of their position in relation to others. Such, at least, was Hannah Arendt's argument in *The Human Condition,* the book she wrote after *The Origins of Totalitarianism.* If her first major book told the story of how hell was made on earth, her second was a description of the kind of political humanism that might remove it—or at least diminish its scope.

Arendt's political heroes in *The Human Condition* are us: actors in the world whether we like it or not. Sometimes we are unaware of what our actions might trigger; often we're lost in events, not knowing where the story ends. Sometimes, all we know is that we are in the story and that we must act. Although we show the world who we are through our actions, *it is more than likely that the "who" which appears so clearly and unmistakably to others, remains hidden from the person himself.* Action is the kind of self-expression that matters *because* it is understood by others (*HC* 181).

And this, Ellison explained in his interview with Penn Warren, was more or less exactly what Elizabeth Eckford was doing when she walked up to the gates of Central High on September 3, 1957: making a sacrifice in the tragedy that is America; being a "who" appearing for others. In this matter, neither was she as alone as she looked. "This is the thing," Ellison explained: "my mother always said I don't know what is going to happen to us if you young Negroes don't do so-and-so-and-so. The command went out and it still goes out. You're supposed to be somebody, and it's in relation to the group. This is part of the American Negro experience, and this also means that the idea of sacrifice is always right there."

In other words, because she could not see Elizabeth Eckford acting as a Black American living and acting among other Black Americans, Hannah Arendt did not see that Elizabeth Eckford was taking precisely the kind of walk which she herself understood as enacting the promise of politics. Back in New York, in the summer of 1965, Arendt read Ellison's interview with Penn Warren in *Who Speaks for the Negro?* and for the second time in nearly as many years, stubbed out her cigarette, drew her typewriter toward her, and wrote a letter to a major Black American writer that would go unanswered:

Dear Mr. Ellison,

While reading Robert Penn Warren's Who Speaks for the Negro *I came across the very interesting interview with you and also read your remarks on my old reflections on Little Rock. You are entirely right: it is precisely the "ideal of sacrifice" which I didn't understand and since my starting point was a consideration of Negro kids in forcibly integrated schools, this failure to understand caused me indeed to go into an entirely wrong direction. I received, of course, many criticisms about this article from the side of my "liberal" friends or rather non-friends which, I must confess, didn't bother me. But I knew that I was somehow wrong and thought that I hadn't grasped the element of stark violence, of elementary bodily*

fear in the situation. But your remarks seem to me so entirely right,
that I simply didn't understand the complexities in the situation.

With kind regards,

Sincerely yours,
Hannah Arendt[21]

Ten years earlier, in the spring semester of 1955, Hannah Arendt had taught at the University of California, Berkeley. Without Blücher and her New York friends, she was as alone as she had been since she was in that field outside Montauban in 1940. She disliked the circus of university life, the pointless tediousness of its fussy administration, the pretentiousness of her colleagues, and the draining demand to be on show all the time (the publication of *The Origins of Totalitarianism* had turned her into a minor academic celebrity). Her old teacher, Karl Jaspers, tried to find her congenial European company and sent letters to introduce her to the Romanist Leonardo Olschki and his wife, Kate, who used to live in Heidelberg and were now at the university. Their meeting did not go well. Kate Olschki began by exclaiming conspiratorially that they felt as though they were "living in an African village" in Berkeley. Arendt was disgusted (*AKJ* 257). *One has to take a look at these intellectuals from time to time to realize where it is one definitely does not want to go back to* (*WFW* 234). She retreated to her wood-lined rooms in the Faculty Club, tucked under the trees in a small dell in the middle of campus, where the food was good even if there was always a slight smell of mildew in the air.

While teaching an advanced seminar on totalitarianism she met a young man from Kenya named Julius Gikonyo Kiano. Kiano's family were Kikuyu, many of whom were instrumental in the Mau Mau rebellion against British rule. On his return to Kenya, Kiano was active in the airlifts that sent student leaders to universities abroad to prepare them for decolonial rule (Arendt wrote letters of support for this mission). Eventually, he became a minister in Jomo Kenyatta's independent government. He had first impressed her with his paper on Stalin. *It was the best report given in this seminar. The young man understands everything, and has a facility for order and presentation that makes my graduate students look like pipsqueaks,* she reported back to Heinrich Blücher, who was stuck in a still-wintry New York. *What is happening in this world to make this possible! Beautiful world!* (*WFW* 258). She gave Kiano extra tutorials on Kant in the evenings and at the weekends.

Along with the unrecorded scenes from the Berlin prison where she talked with the young Gestapo officer in 1933, I sometimes think about the conversations and interactions that might have taken place between Julius Gikonyo Kiano and Hannah Arendt behind the walls of her Berkeley office. Did he tell her about the torture camps run by the British? About friends and relatives who had gone missing? About how he was homesick? Did she reply that she remembered some of that herself from when she was his age? Did they talk about how best to protect democracy from totalitarianism? As they pored over Kant together, did Kiano ask how Arendt reconciled the philosopher's imperative to treat everyone as an end in themselves with his racism? Did he perhaps politely protest that he was not as clever as she seemed to think and question her implication that there was something exceptional, still less, beautiful, about his academic diligence? Did she snort and reply that she knew all about being treated as an "exception" as a Jew and an "exception" as a woman and that was certainly *not* what she was doing in his case? Did he raise his brow gently? Might he have put up with her patronizing hauteur because he could see that she was lonely and that deep down that loneliness had awoken an old terror and it was one he recognized? Were they friends?

CHAPTER SIX

How Not to Think

> The ideal subject of totalitarian rule is not the
> convinced Nazi or the convinced communist, but
> people for whom the distinction between fact and
> fiction (i.e., the reality of experience) and the
> distinction between true and false (i.e., the standards
> of thought) no longer exist.
>
> —*The Origins of Totalitarianism*

W hen Vladimir Putin moved against the people of Ukraine
in February 2022, maps showing the borders of Eastern
Europe began appearing in newspapers and on screens with a frequency not seen since the months following the end of the Cold
War. To the east there was Russia, red and large, with Estonia,
Latvia, Belarus, and Ukraine huddled on its borders. Then, to the
west, miles away from Russia proper, right on the edge of the Baltic Sea and squashed between Lithuania and Poland, hung another
section of red; rectangular and tank shaped. This is the Russian
exclave of Kaliningrad, previously known as Königsberg. The
city, and its strategically crucial access to the Baltic Sea, were
"given" to the Soviet Union at the Potsdam Conference and, following his death in June 1946, renamed after Mikhail Kalinin, former Chairman of the Supreme Soviet. The Soviet invasion of the

city had begun in 1945 with the operation "Sacred Revenge" and the mass rape of women and girls. This was the second time Russia had occupied the city. The first was between 1758 and 1761 when a largely nonviolent coexistence was maintained. By contrast, the Soviet occupation was total. Mass expulsions swiftly cleared the city of most remaining ethnic Germans, while from the north and the east, trainloads of people arrived to create a new Soviet and Slavic reality on the streets and in the vacant houses. One totalitarian regime had come to squat in the place vacated by the defeat of another.

In 1924, the year Hannah Arendt left Königsberg to study in Marburg, the city built a large neoclassical mausoleum over Kant's grave just next to the cathedral on Kneiphof Island to celebrate the bicentenary of his birth. The cathedral was damaged during RAF bombings in the summer of 1944, along with all seven of the city's bridges, leaving the cenotaph exposed to the gray skies. During the battle for the city, one Soviet soldier had thrown himself across the grave to protect Kant's memory from Nazi fire. Stalin, the rumor was, had ordered that the mausoleum remain untouched; without Kant there would not have been Marx, he reasoned. But a surviving photograph from around 1951, the year *The Origins of Totalitarianism* was published, also shows the monument graffitied by occupying Soviet soldiers. "Did you think that the Russian 'Ivan' would be standing on your grave???" one had written. "Now you understand the world is material," wrote another.[1]

If Königsberg was the place where Hannah Arendt first learned to think like Kant, Kaliningrad was the place where Soviet-style totalitarianism isolated the birthplace of European cosmopolitan thought from the world, achieving one of its most symbolic, as well as strategic, victories. The fact that her home city was occupied not just by one but by two totalitarian regimes is a historical and biographical irony so outsized that not even Hannah Arendt seemed able to write about it directly. In truth, she couldn't. It was hard to find documentary evidence about the city in the 1940s and 1950s. Karl Jaspers sent her a short early study of Königsberg's wartime history, but for most of the later twentieth century the city was obscured by the very historical forces she was determined to understand.

In another sense, Hannah Arendt never stopped writing about Königsberg-Kaliningrad because she never stopped attacking totalitarian thinking. The response to the closing of the mind must be a mind even more open to perplexity, fluidity, and questioning, she insisted. Against the dullness of dogma, she launched her revitalized version of Kant's *Verstand*—the power of thought, reflection, and the restless search for meaning that might dissolve ideological clichés and crush bogus premises. Against enforced disappearances, she pitched the courage to appear. Against the shutting down of freedom of movement and speech, she reasserted Kant's insistence upon the "freedom to use reason publicly in all matters." *Niemad hat has Recht zu gehorchen—Nobody has the right to obey!* She wanted to represent a bolder, more radical Kant so that she could take back their city, if not in reality then at least in her words.

After the Cold War ended, Kaliningrad opened up to the world. Kant's mausoleum was carefully restored in 1996; soft pink pillars now guard his grave again and the cenotaph has been polished clean. Hotels and apartment blocks overlooking the Leninsky Prospekt flyover, which replaced two of the bridges in the

1970s, were refurbished and listed on Tripadvisor. Tourists arrived to see if they could retrace Euler's theorem on the city's remaining bridges. In 2016 the Dutch artist Ram Katzir exhibited a memorial for Hannah Arendt, "Petrification, 2016," in the Friedland Museum. It was a suitcase made up of heavy stones and bound with wire. "Is it possible to carry a place with you?" a caption asked. Yes, it was: Hannah Arendt carried the philosophical ground stones of Königsberg with her for life.

But it turned out that Kaliningrad was not yet ready for the return of Hannah Arendt. Signs that the city was not as close to the end of its totalitarian story as some had hoped were clear before the 2020s. In 2018 a public row erupted over a proposal to rename the airport after Kant. On YouTube, a vice-admiral in the Russian Navy, Igor Mukhametshin, was shown delivering an anti-Kant tirade to his sailors: "He wrote some incomprehensible book that none of those present today have read and won't read." Contemporary Russian nationalism does not share the same moral universe as either Immanuel Kant or Hannah Arendt.[2] When I reread *The Origins of Totalitarianism* in 2022, the passage I found most chilling was one in which Arendt predicts how the legacies of totalitarianism might be experienced long after the fall of totalitarian regimes:

> *The crisis of our century . . . is no mere threat from the outside, no mere result of some aggressive foreign policy of either Germany or Russia, and . . . will no more disappear with the death of Stalin than it disappeared with the fall of Nazi Germany. It may even be that the true predicaments of our time will assume their authentic form—though not necessarily the cruellest—only when totalitarianism has become a thing of the past.* (OT 593)

. . .

It's like a novel, Mary McCarthy observed of the completed edition of *The Origins of Totalitarianism*. Arendt and McCarthy had clashed in 1945 when they first met at a New York party hosted by *Partisan Review*'s Philip Rahv, McCarthy's ex-lover. Another fierce wit who rarely suffered fools gladly, McCarthy, when they were introduced, made a sarcastic quip about Hitler's unpopularity in Paris. Arendt, exhausted from work and war and grieving her dead, exploded with uncharacteristic and dramatic self-importance: *How can you say such a thing in front of me—a victim of Hitler, a person who has been in a concentration camp!*[3] They met again a few years later, realized that they actually rather liked one another, exchanged apologies, and then, soon after, the first of many books. McCarthy sent Arendt her crisp, slim, satirical *roman-à-clef* on self-important American intellectuals, *The Oasis* (1949). Arendt upped the stakes of their early friendship considerably by reciprocating with the neither crisp nor slim *The Origins of Totalitarianism*.

"Dear Hannah," begins the first letter McCarthy wrote in their long, intimate, correspondence, "I've read your book, absorbed, for the past two weeks, in the bathtub, riding in the car, waiting in line in the grocery store. It seems to me a truly extraordinary piece of work . . . and also engrossing and fascinating in the way that a novel is: i.e., that it says something on nearly every page that is novel, that one could not have anticipated from what went before but that one then recognizes as inevitable and foreshadowed by the underlying plot of ideas" (*BF* 1–2).

A book that is engrossing enough to read in the bath has to have a considerable pull and *The Origins of Totalitarianism* is indeed grimly compelling. Arendt depicts a society of lonely, atomized, lifeless people, *one great unorganized, structureless mass of furious individuals,* characterized by hatred, fear, organized terror, mass death, and unspeakable suffering (*OT* 419). This is a world of science-fiction-level horror; utterly alien, incredible and outrageous. Yet as the story of how this hell came to plant itself on earth unfolds, as McCarthy says, you get a growing and uncomfortable sense that there was something inevitable about it all. I think this is partly because while the history described in the book is extreme, Arendt's underlying "plot of ideas" feels familiar. *The Origins of Totalitarianism* reads like a good novel because it reveals to the reader some experience that they already know, but thanks to its pages can now understand. That is also what can make it as terrifying to read in the twenty-first century as it was in the twentieth.

This is the story of how millions of twentieth-century Europeans willingly came to live in a murderous ideological fiction. Get rid of the epic fantasy that the totalitarian masses were driven by some common purpose, a great and unified idealistic commitment to a bold, passionate, but unfortunately evil, idea. Ditch, too, the gothic horror of cunning and mesmerizing leaders and their dull, stupid, and gullible enablers. The history that Arendt chronicles in the final section of her book, "Totalitarianism," is both more prosaic and tawdrier, which is also why it's familiar.

There were several auguries that foreshadowed the development of totalitarianism. There were racism and imperialism, as we have seen. There were mobs and nationalism in France, pre-Nazi Germany, and Austria. Demagogues whipped up emotions across the continent and authoritarians promised to resolve things for ordinary people in Portugal, Hungary, and Poland. There was fascism in Spain and Italy, which was violent and nasty, but not the total attack on politics itself which came with totalitarian regimes. Across the globe, there were totalitarian movements that gathered up the moment's dark discontent by giving the appearance of unstoppable momentum, but which could be stopped where there was sufficient political room for resistance.

The starting point for all these phenomena in Europe was the uprooting of people that had come with capitalism, imperialism, nationalism, and revolution. The end point for totalitarian regimes was to make human superfluousness a permanent condition for absolute rule. The anonymity of modern life discovered its denouement in a political system in which human beings ceased to matter at all.

In Western Europe, social disintegration had undermined the promises of liberal democracies before they really got started. Previously, the sense of belonging to a class or group had disguised the fact that very little genuine representative democratic activity had been occurring, despite the opening up of the franchise and political emancipation across the continent. For a while, people could afford to be disinterested in national politics because they got their sense of social worth from somewhere else. When the promise of social respect and self-determination that had motivated the fathers of Hannah Arendt and Adolf Eichmann began to crumble under economic chaos and war in the first decades of the century, just how vacant contemporary politics really was became visible. Democracy's dirty secret was out, which was that, in Arendt's words, *democratic government had rested as much on the silent approbation and tolerance of the indifferent and inarticulate sections of the people as on the articulate and visible institutions and organizations of the country (OT 415)*. Bluntly put, a small number of people had governed largely for their own self-interest. When it became clear that political parties were not doing what they advertised and representing the interests of particular groups or classes, a vacuum opened up at the center of political power. A different kind of anti-democratic politics began to emerge. At its heart was a *terrifying negative solidarity* of the formerly *indifferent and inarticulate* (*OT* 419). The dull gray masses which popular imagination associates with twentieth-century totalitarian rule were never really unified, Arendt tells us. Mass movements were created out of isolated loners and democracy's losers.

That was what happened in Western Europe. To make totalitarianism possible in the Soviet Union, Stalin had to re-create the social atomization that historical circumstances had gifted the Nazis in Germany. The Russian Revolution had already disposed of one centralized, unaccountable, despotic rule: Stalin had to invent a new one. Vladimir Lenin, the first head of the new government, believed that strengthening social groups and organizations was the best way of protecting the revolution, so he (briefly) encouraged trade unions and promoted the consciousness of cultural and historical differences among the Soviet countries. Stalin, who assumed leadership in 1924, Bolshevized the revolution's communal political structures and replaced them with his infamous centralized party bureaucracy *whose tendencies toward Russification,* Arendt noted, *were not too different from those of the Czarist regime* (*OT* 425). The liquidation of classes, property owners, and the bourgeoisie, then the peasants, swiftly followed. Hannah Arendt would have probably viewed the Russification that began again under Putin in the first decades of the twenty-first century as less of a plot twist than an unimaginative repetition.

In novels, there is often a moment when characters realize they have been living in a dream (or nightmare), when scales fall from their eyes and a new direction is taken. This happens in plots from history too, but it usually takes longer, and the moment of realization is nearly always too late. *Nothing which was being done, no matter how stupid, no matter how many people knew and foretold the consequences, could be undone or prevented,* Arendt wrote of the interwar period. *Every event had the finality of a last judgment . . . that was passed neither by God nor by the devil, but looked rather like the expression of some unredeemably stupid fatality* (OT 341). The First World War, mass unemployment, inflation, civil war, revolution, pogroms, mass deportations, and mass migration; instead of producing a reality check, the more extreme the circumstances became, the more reality spun out of reach. Artists and writers creatively thrilled to the futility of it all. In nightclubs and bars, people sang of hopelessness with a tired joy. And the more estranged people became, the more resentment seeped into everyday life. Nothing, wrote Arendt, *perhaps illustrates the general disintegration of political life better* than a *vague pervasive hatred of everyone and everything* (OT 342).

Directionless hate was a political opportunity. Rabble-rousers and demagogues stepped into the gap left by democratic failure, paving the way for the big men who became such lethal clichés in what followed. The topsy-turvy logic of totalitarian thinking began to take shape. In Europe and America, wealthy elites conspired with ideologues to try and persuade the miserable and disenfranchised that civil society and the institutions of law and democracy were the real enemy. "Truth," they said, was whatever the "hypocritical" liberal and bourgeois political and social classes wanted hidden—the global elites, the bankers, the Jews, the citizens of nowhere.

Conspiracy theories proliferated because they offered a coherence and a consistency that was lacking in the real world. The most famous conspiracy theory of all, the *Protocols of the Elders of Zion,* vividly detailing a Jewish plot for world domination, first emerged in Russia in 1902. After the revolution, anti-communist exiles brought the document with them to the West where it began to circulate. The fact that it was revealed to be fraudulent in 1921 did not stop Hitler and Goebbels from championing it as evidence of a Communist-Jewish threat later. In the United States, Henry Ford published and distributed over 500,000 copies of the *Protocols,* which were also discussed on national radio by Father Coughlin, the anti-semitic leader of the National Union for Social Justice. The current American right-wing movement QAnon developed its own version of the *Protocols* in 2017. America, they claimed, was being run by a cabal of satanic pedophile cannibals, funded by Jewish financiers.

The extreme ridiculousness of these conspiracies is very much the point. They are designed to appeal to people for whom democratic discourse has failed, people who are not only disinterested in conventional politics but often violently opposed to them. Totalitarian propaganda doesn't follow the usual rules of political persuasion and refutation, but makes a show of standing outside of traditional party politics. The ideologues of the 1930s presented political debate as originating *in deep natural, social, or psychological sources*—in race, class, myth, and historical destiny. Their fights, as Arendt put it, were framed as being *beyond the control of the individual and therefore beyond the power of reason*. Twenty-first-century propagandists similarly pitch their battles as epic and existential. Race and historical destiny remain popular themes; so, too, are gender absolutism, sexuality, the family, God, and a vague but passion-ately hawked "greatness." This kind of "politics" is meant to be mad because the madder the theory, the more distant from a com-monly despised reality it is possible to become. *The masses' escape from reality,* Hannah Arendt observed in a sentence that rears up from the twentieth century into the twenty-first, *is a verdict against the world in which they are forced to live and in which they cannot exist* (*OT* 463).

Nazi and Bolshevik propagandists quickly mastered the art of turning coincidences into plots and making the conspiracies seem real. Random events were interpreted as portents and confirma-tions. But while they temporarily gave the illusion of coherence, the storytelling and lies did not end the chaos; enemies and their plots had to be constantly invented. There were never enough of them. It was exhausting (it is exhausting). Far from unifying iso-lated, scared, and angry people into a great nation or redemptive movement, the reality of having to live with multiple lies made the situation more chaotic. More fictions, more hate, and bigger lies were always needed. It became so difficult to distinguish fact from fiction that entire populations gave up trying. *The experience of a trembling, wobbling motion of everything we rely on for our sense of direction and reality,* Arendt wrote in the 1960s, *is among the most common and most vivid experiences of totalitarian rule.*[4]

The same complex reality that made people susceptible to pro-paganda also made them cynical. Amidst the swirl of fictions, plots, fake news, lies, and super lies, people were prepared to be-lieve the incredible—the reliable cunning and malfeasance of class and race enemies—while keeping some shred of human dignity intact by telling themselves that they knew it was just lies and politics all along. The cynics were not the clever people and the masses were not stupid. So far from reality had everyone traveled that none of it really mattered, even as the flags grew bigger and the demands for oaths of allegiance became even more outrageous.

Cynicism turned out to be one of totalitarianism's most fatal characteristics and may yet become one of its most enduring legacies. The men who administered Hitler's and Stalin's policies did not necessarily believe in racism or socialism, Jewish conspiracies or class enemies, any more than many of the GOP believed that Donald Trump won the 2020 election or the Russian high command thought that the Jewish-Ukrainian president, Volodymyr Zelensky, was a Nazi. But they did—and do—all believe in one thing: human omnipotence and, perhaps most especially, although Arendt does not make the connection, male omnipotence. *Their moral cynicism, their belief that everything is permitted, rests on the solid conviction that everything is possible,* she concluded (*OT* 507). And it was.

The gulags and the Nazi death camps were where the brute reality of all this fiction-making was finally played out. The camps served no purpose, Arendt said, other than to demonstrate the truth of totalitarianism's most outrageous claim: that human beings were now superfluous. "For what purpose, may I ask, do the gas chambers exist?," the French survivor David Rousset recalled the question being asked in the death camps. "For what purpose were you born?" was the answer (*OT* 579).

Beyond the capacities of human comprehension, Arendt wrote in a review of an early account of the death camps. In the archives you can see on her typescript how she's returned the carriage of her typewriter back over the words and then struck down hard on the underline key: *Beyond the capacities of human comprehension*. They had all died together; children, men, women, the dying, and the newborn, *like cattle, like matter into the darkest deepest abyss of primal equality, like cattle, like matter, things*.[5] When she *used the image of Hell* in *The Origins of Totalitarianism,* she later insisted, she *did not mean this allegorically but literally*.[6]

Mary McCarthy had one criticism of her new friend's book. How did it all actually work? Did Hitler and Stalin have some all-powerful insight that allowed them to manipulate others to join their insane plots? Were they the demon heirs of Plato's philosopher who left the cave of shadows, stared at the sun, and then returned to rule based on his superior knowledge of reality (*BF* 2)? Who writes the plots of totalitarianism, Hannah? she asked.

Nobody was Arendt's answer. This is why totalitarianism was profoundly anti-political: in the end, there were no opinions, no debates, no agency, no . . . people. Political principles had been replaced by pure ideology. You want people to stop starving? Stalin asked in 1932. Then the counter-revolutionary Ukrainian peasants need to starve—the logic of the man-made famine known as the Holodomor that killed millions. You think the world is run by unaccountable financial organizations? Hitler asked. Then you must work with us to eliminate the Jews. *You can't say A without saying B and C and so on, down to the end of the murderous alphabet,* was how Arendt put it (*OT* 609). You didn't even need Hitler or Stalin to follow this logic. They had succeeded, she added, in *contaminating their subjects with the specifically totalitarian virus* (*OT* 408). The plots had started to reproduce themselves.

Mary McCarthy wasn't only worried about the plots of totalitarianism. I suspect she was also alluding to Arendt's own compelling, maybe too compelling, "underlying plot of ideas." Both Karl Jaspers and later the French political philosopher Claude Lefort pointed out that in telling the story of totalitarianism, Arendt's own arguments sometimes came dangerously close to reproducing the logic she was describing, leaving no space for an alternative anti-totalitarian history of resistance and contestation. In fairness, Arendt would go on to write some of that history in *On Revolution,* but there is a claustrophobia about *The Origins of Totalitarianism,* an awful inevitability about events as they are retold, and you could (as political scientists have) describe Arendt's genius for plotting as the book's flaw. It is a very driven book about a very driven historical phenomenon. But you could also (as I do) read Arendt as giving brilliant expression to a sense of powerless vertigo in a world that seems to be in the grip of a relentlessly awful plot. *Nothing which was being done, no matter how stupid, no matter how many people knew and foretold the consequences, could be undone or prevented,* she wrote. Many observing world events between the election of Donald Trump in America in 2016 and the invasion of Ukraine in 2022 would have understood exactly what she meant.

Hannah Arendt finally finished a complete draft of *The Origins of Totalitarianism* in the summer of 1949. That autumn she returned to Germany for the first time since 1933. She stayed in Europe for the next six months. Just a few months later, on July 14, 1950, Adolf Eichmann crossed the ocean in the opposite direction and arrived in Argentina. For a brief period, they had both been in Germany at the same time. Eichmann had been lying low in the far northeast of Lower Saxony, relying on disinformation that he had escaped to the Middle East to keep his whereabouts undetected. Unlike Arendt's, his final escape from Europe had not been particularly difficult to organize or execute. "A chain of German helpers, Argentine public officials, Austrian border guards, Italian records offices, the Red Cross, men from Vatican circles, and influential shipping magnates" willingly helped him and other Nazis, explains one of his biographers.[7]

It was a horrible time. Exhausted, but still feverish and driven, she had spent the latter part of the 1940s studying mass death and now death was stalking her closer to her new home. Back in New York, two of her closest refugee friends were dying. Arendt had first met the Austrian poet and writer Hermann Broch in 1946. By that point in her life even the paternal substitutes needed to be replaced. Broch's strange sweetness resembled Walter Benjamin's, as did the otherworldliness of his writing which, she wrote in a review, spanned *the abyss of empty space between the no longer and the not yet*.[8] Broch died eighteen months later in May 1951.

Another close friend, the *erotic genius* Hilde Fränkel, had cancer and was also dying. She had first met Fränkel back in Frankfurt and they had picked up the threads of friendship in New York after her lover, the philosopher Paul Tillich, had brought her into the Blücher-Arendt circle. Ten years Arendt's senior, gorgeous, all easy charm, grace, and great fun, Fränkel was the woman who had kept her grounded in the early New York days. Their friendship was one of teasing, confession, indiscretion, and hopeless laughter, usually directed at the men in their lives. Away from home, Arendt was missing Fränkel in an awful prelude to the absence she knew was soon to follow.

In Germany, the rubble had been swept clean and the bodies

buried but the imprints of totalitarianism remained. People still lived in a fiction, but it was a new one in which Nazism, the Holocaust, and the destruction of everything had somehow not really happened. They sent one another picture postcards *still showing the cathedrals and market places, the public buildings and bridges that no longer exist,* as though their lives were still stuck on those pieces of cardboard and not forever defined by the previous ten years.[9] The war was over but the sense of unreality had not dissipated. Arendt was not so much returning home as entering a new space of statelessness between worlds and times, between fact and fiction; *the no longer and the not yet.*

She was in Europe to finish the work of reclaiming stolen goods that she had begun with the Jewish Cultural Reconstruction organization in 1944. Archive fever had driven her work on *The Origins of Totalitarianism* but now she mourned. Each library retrieved brought with it the ghost of the scholar or the rabbi it had once belonged to. Each piece of Judaica came with the image of a razed synagogue. Each menorah evoked the memory of a family who would never eat together again. By the time she and her colleagues had finished, they had reclaimed more than 1.5 million books, thousands of objects, and hundreds of scrolls.[10] In Berlin, she met her old boyfriend from Königsberg, Ernst Grumach. A scholar and archivist, Grumach had been captured and put to work in the Reich Security Main Office. His job was to archive the books, texts, and manuscripts stolen by the Nazis from across Europe. When the stock was bombed, the "Grumach Group" were forced into hard physical labor. He wrote her a poem to mark their reunion: "For if we didn't cling to these old bonds / we would long have roamed in unknown terrain, lost souls in a strange land."

You see, she wrote to Blücher, *in East Prussia people believe in continuity* (*WFW* 135).

She kept moving, walking past the skeleton cathedrals, through the empty marketplaces, knocking on the doors of libraries without roofs to inquire about indexes, records, and manuscripts, curling up uncomfortably on cold trains, cadging lifts from the Allied forces, and typing up her field reports alone in hotel rooms. From her headquarters in Wiesbaden, she traveled to Frankfurt, Würzburg, Nuremberg, Erlangen, and then, crossing back over her student itineraries, Freiberg and Heidelberg, finally up to Berlin. She wrote home to Heinrich in New York often. *Berlin: Snubby, from Spandau to Neukölln is one big field of rubble; nothing recognizable, only a few people in the streets . . . Alexanderplatz, Lützowfuer, Tiergarten (what's most eerie are the upright statues, like ghosts in an empty field)* (*WFW* 133). *When I get tired, I feel completely lost.* Being back in Germany unleashed a primitive existential *fear of total abandonment,* she told him (*BFW* 104–105). What had been abandoned was reality; hers, everyone's. *And one wants to cry out, but this is not real—real are the ruins, real are the past horrors, real are the dead whom you have forgotten,* she despaired. *But they are living ghosts, whom speech and argument, the glance of human eyes and the mourning of human hearts, no longer touch.*[11]

Alone amidst the ghosts and the denial, in Freiberg she wrote to Heidegger to tell him that she was back. This was their first contact since she had left in 1933. Heidegger had been dismissed from Freiberg University in 1945 (he was readmitted in 1951). In his deNazification hearings, he claimed that he had stepped back from National Socialism after the Night of the Long Knives in 1934; since then, he had been out of favor with the regime and so had returned to philosophizing. That might have been so, but he remained a party member until 1945, and while he acknowledged that errors had been made, usually in a self-serving way, he never once acknowledged the victims of the Holocaust—nor would he for the remainder of his career. The deNazification hearings had only ended in March 1949, a few months before Arendt had arrived back in Germany. The commission had concluded that Heidegger was a Nazi "fellow traveler" and temporarily banned him from teaching.[12] When Arendt arrived back in Freiberg he was poor, alone, and not a little indignant and self-pitying. I don't know why she wrote to him. It would have been easier for me and countless other Arendt scholars if she had never seen him again but had continued to read and use his philosophy to pull existentialism in a different political direction. But as is often the case, there are plot twists in Hannah Arendt's life and writing that are not always easy.

So, they met again and after they had walked through the woods up to the *Schlossberg* and stared down at the ruins and through the gothic lattice of the Minster spire which had somehow survived the Allied bombing, he took her back to his house to meet his wife, Elfride Heidegger-Petri. Frau Heidegger was a teacher, a National Socialist, and an unrepentant anti-semite. "We are struggling by word and deed, using every means at our disposal against the Jewish-Marxist spirit," she once wrote in a propaganda essay.[13] Elfride Heidegger was hardcore. As well as having an understandable problem with the fact that her husband brought the love of his life home for coffee, she was upset to discover that that love was still as Jewish as she had ever been. The two women argued. It was one thing for Hannah Arendt to know that anti-semitism had not left Germany with Hitler's death, but it must have been another to feel its breath on her face.

Letters, passionate letters and poems (many poems) followed from Heidegger, including one written for the dying Hilde Fränkel ("For the Friend of the Friend"), whom he had never met, and which he called "Death." Arendt sent him an essay, "On Organized Guilt and Universal Responsibility," that she had first published in *Jewish Frontier* in 1945.[14] In the essay, she had argued that the complete takeover of Nazi totalitarianism in the latter stages of the war made it difficult to claim that all Germans were guilty Nazis without buying into the very Nazi logic that said of course all Germans were Nazis. *You can't say A without saying B.* Nazism *had* rendered everyone complicit in the war machine and mass murder; all were indeed responsible to different degrees, including those (such as Heidegger, although she did not mention him by name) who had supported and abetted Hitler's rise. But what needed to be understood was not how all Germans were as evil and guilty as their leaders: clearly, they were not. More troubling was how the ordinary bourgeois German had turned executioner not because there was a gun at their head, but because they had persuaded themselves, with remarkable effortlessness, that a job was a job and feeding the family came first. How had evil been organized so that it became so commonplace? That was the question.

Heidegger thought the essay was bold and commendably brave in its desire not to condemn all Germans, as well he might. A "merely moral attitude is not enough," he wrote back. Humanity must "rise to the call of Being, and save itself in it" (*AMH* 64–65). But existential salvation from unspeakable crimes was not exactly what she had had in mind.

What were the consequences of living in a world where men had created a crime so monstrous it was far from certain that it could ever be addressed? If we can no longer tell what is real from what is fake, how can we judge what is right? How can you ground a new political reality when common sense itself has been blitzed? These were the questions in Hannah Arendt's mind after 1945 and she would not stop asking them until her dying breath. Totalitarianism had sucked moral responsibility out from human affairs. Kant's world was dead in Königsberg/Kaliningrad. Judgment was now a matter of neither reason nor imagination but scripted in advance. There were enemies (but few friends), victims and executioners, but nothing to tell who was which save the "cool reason" of insane ideologies. Nazism was not just immoral, lawless, and evil. It had shattered the categories by which moral distinctions could be made at all. *In their effort to prove that everything is possible* totalitarian regimes had committed *crimes which men can neither punish nor forgive* (*OT* 591), she concluded. How could history—politics, moral life, and human community—possibly move on after this?

Searching for answers, she'd followed preparations for the Nuremberg trials carefully in the summer and autumn of 1945, pulling the newspapers, her coffee, and her cigarettes toward her each morning before she uttered a word. Thinking, with which she always started her day, required smoke, silence, and, most importantly, solitude.

Earlier that summer, Adolf Eichmann had disappeared from the American prisoner-of-war camp he was staying in under an alias. His real name, however, was mentioned frequently by his former comrades in the cramped dock at Nuremberg that November. One of his underlings, Dieter Wisliceny, was particularly forthcoming. Wisliceny remembered hearing Eichmann boast about his execution of the Final Solution at the end of the war. "I will jump into my grave laughing, because the fact I have the death of five million Jews on my conscience gives me extraordinary satisfaction," he liked to repeat to anyone who would listen.

In August, Arendt wrote Karl Jaspers a long and anxious letter about the forthcoming trial. *The Nazi crimes, it seems to me, explode the limits of the law; and that is precisely what constitutes their monstrousness. We are simply not equipped to deal, on a human, political level, with a guilt that is beyond crime and an innocence beyond virtue . . . That is the abyss that opened up before us as early as 1933 (much earlier, actually, with the onset of imperialist politics) and into which we have finally stumbled. I don't know if we will ever get out of it* (*AKJ* 54). Radical evil, she called it then.

Jaspers's reply turned out to have a hugely significant slow burn in Hannah Arendt's imagination. "I'm not altogether comfortable with your view, because a guilt that goes beyond all criminal guilt inevitably takes on a streak of 'greatness'—of satanic greatness—which is for me, as inappropriate for Nazis as all the talk about the 'demonic' element in Hitler and so forth," he cautioned. Why mythologize the master mythmakers? Hermann Göring, who relished his reputation for theatrical evil, underscored Jaspers's point at the end of the trial by dramatically poisoning himself with cyanide the night before his execution. Before he decided that it was in his interest to perform the part of a guiltless functionary at his trial, Eichmann, too, very much enjoyed playing to his reputation as an obsessive Jew killer, swishing about in his long leather coat, imagining a frisson of notoriety that he believed he could feel as he entered a room, "as feared and mysterious as a film noir villain."[15] More melodrama was no answer to Nazi melodrama, said Jaspers. Don't give them what they crave.

Jaspers had another suggestion: "It seems to me that we have to see these things in their total banality, in their prosaic triviality, because that is what truly characterizes them. Bacteria can cause epidemics that wipe out nations, but they remain merely bacteria" (*AKJ* 62). It was not until sixteen years later, as she sat in the courtroom in Jerusalem in an unseasonably cold April and finally heard Adolf Eichmann speak, that Hannah Arendt began to understand what her *Lieber Verehrtester* had meant. An evil as banal as bacteria.

On her return from Europe, she and Blücher spent the summer of 1950 in Manomet, a pretty seaside village in Plymouth, Massachusetts. Hilde Fränkel had died in the spring. Alfred Kazin and another friend, Rose Feitelson, arrived to help work on the English (her *Denglish* as she called it) in the final proofs of what was now titled *The Origins of Totalitarianism*. The landscape reminded her of the countryside around Königsberg, where families would vacation on the Samland Peninsula by the wooded lakes or on the coast with its world-famous amber mines and sweeping views of the endless gray-blue sea. *The sea, dunes, forest, a bit like the coast of Samland, where I grew up,* she wrote to Jaspers. *Very pretty, lots of lakes* (*AKJ* 152).

She had finished her book, but it had not quite finished with her. In a part of America that resembled what was now Kaliningrad, as she finally relaxed back into her companiable, lovely life with Blücher and her close friends, she began to pull again at the threads of the book she had just written with the bleak experience of her visit to Germany in mind.

Among the attacks on democracy in the twentieth century, totalitarianism stood out for the extremity of its assault on not just political but existential meaning; it was less a system than a force. No institution, law, tradition, could stand in the way of the relentless movement of its mad logic. She began to see more clearly how dangerous this made the totalitarian precedent.

In free societies laws create boundaries in which liberty can operate. But totalitarianism was a law unto itself, enforced by state violence and a terror that pressed people together like a *band of iron*. Gone were the spaces between people, and gone, too, was *the living space of freedom*. Plurality *disappeared into One Man of gigantic dimension* (*OT* 600). But the big man was a fake (it's hard not to think of Trump here). In reality, he was made of millions of atomized and bereft men and women. Terror was the driver, but the true existential experience of totalitarianism was loneliness. This was not the gentle ennui of the disaffected bourgeois of the late nineteenth and early twentieth centuries, but a soaring terror of total isolation so overwhelming that its sufferers would do anything not to acknowledge it. Was loneliness, she now wondered, the *true predicament of our time*—was this totalitarianism's most pernicious legacy?

Loneliness is inescapable. Faced with the knowledge of death, everyone feels alone in the end. Suffering and pain can never be communicated fully. But now modern uprootedness and social atomization had democratized existential abandonment. *What prepares men for totalitarian domination in the non-totalitarian world,* Arendt wrote in an essay that she began that summer, *is the fact that loneliness, once a borderline experience usually suffered in certain marginal social conditions like old age, has become an everyday experience of the evergrow-ing masses of our century* (OT 615). *The Lonely Crowd,* as her friend, the sociologist David Riesman, had described it in his 1950 co-authored book of that title. Riesman had read the proofs of *Origins* and noted the similarities between the social and existential condi-tions he and his colleagues found in America and those she found in Europe.[16] Was loneliness perhaps the *authentic form* of modern experience that totalitarianism had just made visible? Less cruel, obviously, than state terror, but nonetheless profoundly inhuman for all that? I think of her looking at the eerie upright statues alone in Berlin's war-scorched *Tiergarten,* and of that arresting image in her letter to Blücher of *ghosts in an empty field.*

Deprived of true contact with others, *men lose the capacity of both experience and thought* (OT 620). A common sense of the world's reality, which Kant taught was so vital not just to political but to all sensible communal life, vanished. People no longer knew if they were looking, hearing, tasting, sensing, or experiencing the same world. This is the context in which post-truth politics takes hold. Unchallenged, the lies continue; they grow bigger and more ridiculous. The spaces where it is possible to object, to say, "but this is self-evidently ludicrous," contract, and with them go the opportunities for genuine civic life.

Everyone is abandoned by everybody else. As for the child alone in the playground, joining in the populist and authoritarian games, however cruel and repellent, is preferable to total isolation. Loneliness is the bully that coerces us into giving up on democ-racy.

The threat, she thought, was that loneliness might come to supplant the altogether different experience of solitude. Loneliness is that feeling you get in a crowd or group when you cannot quite trust people not to be hostile to you. Solitariness is the much nicer experience of being alone with yourself, with your thoughts and quietly busy cogitating. Without solitariness it is impossible to think at all. And if we cannot think, we cannot exist—either with ourselves or with others.

Solitary thinking, in this sense, is the prerequisite for thinking about others. Among other things, thinking is the exercise of representing the views of other people in one's mind, of testing perspectives, experimenting with possibly new or alien ideas. By contrast, loneliness is crushing: it dulls thought and makes contact with others appear too perilous to hazard. As Arendt eventually wrote, in quite possibly the saddest sentence in *The Origins of Totalitarianism: What makes loneliness so unbearable, is the loss of one's own self which can be realized in solitude, but confirmed in its identity only by the trusting and trustworthy company of my equals* (OT 614).

As she came to see, the loss of self and mutual trust was not confined to totalitarian regimes, but was becoming a feature of Western consumer societies, too. When Václav Havel wrote about "post-totalitarianism" in his sublimely courageous 1978 essay "The Power of the Powerless," just three years after Arendt's death and nearly thirty years after the first publication of *The Origins of Totalitarianism,* he pointed out that while Czechoslovakia by that point was no longer dominated by the "boisterous" Bolshevism of the immediate post-war period, an awful existential and political impoverishment persisted which, he also argued pointedly, was by no means confined to Eastern Europe but present in capitalist democracies, too. Arendt would have recognized both Havel's argument and its political urgency: the powerless—wherever they

Hannah Arendt,
Manomet, Massachusetts,
1950.

were—were not as helpless as they feared, but to grab political power meant first seizing back the thinking self.

Mary McCarthy observed that Hannah Arendt was one of those people who you could actually *see* thinking. She would lie on a daybed in her Riverside Drive apartment, eyes closed, cigarette in hand, ashtray nearby, sometimes for over an hour while others would tiptoe around her.[17] "Where's Hannah?" "Thinking." "Still?" In Manomet in the summer of 1950, her first major book completed, she lay beneath the pines, sea salt in the air, listening to her thoughts, thinking about thinking, companionship, loneliness, and everything she had lost, and what might be lost to the world still.

The essay she wrote that summer was called "Ideology and Terror: A Novel Form of Government." Two years later she returned to Germany to deliver the paper as a lecture, first in Marburg and then in Heidelberg. When the first German edition of *The Origins of Totalitarianism* (*Elemente und Ursprünge totaler Herrschaft*) appeared in 1955, she added the essay as the book's final chapter, where it has remained in all subsequent editions.

Like all tyrannical regimes, because totalitarian governments were based on fear and terror, they carried with them the seeds of their own destruction. They would fail, never soon enough, but this is one plot from history that is pretty reliable. The atomized condition of the contemporary life, however, and the failure of modern democracies to respond to that condition, is another matter.

The publication of *The Origins of Totalitarianism* confirmed Hannah Arendt as a rising star of intellectual life in America. "With this book, Hannah Arendt emerges as the most original and profound— therefore the most valuable—political theoretician of our times," wrote Dwight Macdonald in *The New Leader*. "I can compare her only with one other woman: Simone Weil." He did not think to compare her with any men, despite her profundity. The English poet and critic, and later a regular at her New Year parties, Al Alvarez called the book "the only work of real genius to have appeared in this decade" in America, with the snobby caveat that Arendt was really European, so her genius should not be taken as indicative of American creativity in the 1950s. Many praised her moral and historical clarity, others complained that she was difficult to understand. "Hm . . ." she wrote next to a line from a review that began: "Hannah Arendt is not easy reading."[18]

Invitations and accolades followed. The days of living pen-to-mouth were over. In 1953 she was invited to give the prestigious Christian Gauss Seminars in Criticism at Princeton University, the first woman, she was told repeatedly, and to her great irritation, to do so. Six years later, Princeton offered her the position of Full Professor, the first woman to be given such a role, she was again told repeatedly. After her appointment was reported in *The New York Times,* under the headline "FACULTY ADDS WOMAN," she threatened to withdraw. *I am not disturbed at all about being a woman professor,* she informed a journalist, *because I am quite used to being a woman.*[19] Deadpan wit was Hannah Arendt's preferred idiom for dealing with questions about gender. Asked by younger women about feminism, apparently she would reply: *Vive la petite difference!* Some have interpreted this as evidence of her conservatism, but I have always thought *la petite* in that sentence hilariously eloquent.[20]

In the Gauss seminars she warned of *a state of apolity . . . or what we today would call statelessness.*[21] The stateless people of the 1930s had become the lonely and empty people of the 1950s. How might human existence be reclaimed? Politics? But what kind given the failure of democracy in Europe? The lectures were intended as a first foray into an unfinished study of Marx, Marxism, and its twentieth-century mutation into Soviet totalitarianism. How had the moment for promised political freedom been so catastrophically blundered? she asked. And what could be learned from that blunder for a future anti-totalitarian politics? These questions would preoccupy her throughout the 1950s and would eventually find their way into *The Human Condition, On Revolution,* and a (never completed) study called *Introduction to Politics.*

In the spring semester of 1955 she went to Berkeley, traveled as far west as she had ever been, and discovered, as she frequently did when she thought America was at its most attractive, a corner of Europe. San Francisco, she wrote to Heinrich Blücher, is *very, very, nice, like a vastly enlarged Lisbon (WFW* 224). Alongside the advanced course on totalitarianism where she met Julius Gikonyo Kiano, she taught a course to politics undergraduates called "Contemporary Issues." Her syllabus is notable today for the near absence of much actual political science. Instead, she set her students to read fiction, poetry, philosophy, personal testimony, and political history. They read William Faulkner and Ernest Hemingway to help them think about the experience of the First World War. Bertolt Brecht introduced them to the revolutionary imagination. Czesław Miłosz, David Rousset, and George Orwell plunged them into the unbelievable worlds of totalitarianism. Albert Camus and Jean-Paul Sartre coached them in existential rebellion and David Riesman brought them closer to home with his *The Lonely Crowd.* The Berkeley-based nuclear scientist J. Robert Oppenheimer concluded the course with his stark warnings about the growing prospect of technological world destruction.

Oppenheimer's security clearance had been revoked one year earlier, in 1954, during Senator Joseph McCarthy's "Red Scare" purges. Arendt was appalled by McCarthyism's explicit threat to American democracy (and fearful for Blücher and herself). Here again was the bogus identification of enemies, the imputation of plots, the manufacturing of fear. In America, it seemed, you could do all that without concentration camps and pounding jackboots.

The experiences you're going to read about, she told her sunny Californian students in their first class together in the spring of 1955, are nothing remotely like your own—although a bit like her own, she admitted in her thick German accent and behind her trademark mask of cigarette smoke. But I don't want you to empathize, she added, even though the experiences described are often horrible and deserving of great sympathy. I want you to understand. *Imagination,* she told them, and I'm quoting directly from her teaching notes here, *is the perquisite of understanding. You should imagine how the world looks from the point of view where these people are located.* The stakes of this imagining could not be higher. *The assumption is: It is the common world of all of us and that is what is between you and this other location,* she explained. Arendt was using her texts to put a common world back on the table. Actually, the common world was the table. She did not want her students to empathize because she wanted them to see what separates human experiences as well as what we have in common, what is different as well as what is the same. *It is the common world of all of us and that is what is between you and this other location,* she said, *like the table* (and at this point I imagine her knocking the table before her in the classroom), *like the table that separates and binds you to him at the same time. That,* she concluded, *is the meaning of ONE world.*[22] The table we sit around discussing books, listening, sharing, disagreeing.

It was Kant's "enlarged mentality" that Hannah Arendt was bringing with her to California from Königsberg. The ability to represent the experience of others in one's mind—even though we have not actually perceived that experience for ourselves.

Time and again, Arendt would insist that totalitarianism had defied traditional forms of comprehension. How do you make sense of the camps without somehow conceding that they might actually make sense? What kind of thinking was that? You need a different kind of imagination to comprehend the incomprehensible, she argued. Her response to totalitarian thinking was to advocate more understanding, more thinking, in the hope that we can create new modes of moral and political judgment. Hers was not a call for a return to political reason (such as you often hear today) but for a kind of emergency thinking that may, she said, in the end, be all we have. *The manifestation of the wind of thought is no knowledge,* she wrote in 1971; *it is the ability to tell right from wrong, beautiful from ugly. And this indeed may prevent catastrophes, at least for myself, in the rare moments when the chips are down (RJ 189).*

Toward the end of her California stay, she took a trip to Stanford University to visit a new center for the study of behavioral sciences. She was not impressed. "You act in A-way, so B will follow and then C. . . ." The logic looked familiar. The *problem with modern theories of behaviorism is not that they are wrong but that they could become true,* she later remarked (*HC* 322). The thought that future governments and big businesses would routinely use behavioral science to predict and manage the lives of their populations and customers would have confirmed her worst nightmares about the *problem solvers (CR* 11).

Hannah Arendt found something else in Stanford too. In the Hoover Institution Library Archives she came across an account of the final days before Königsberg fell to the Soviets. On January 27, 1945, the SS had driven three thousand Jewish women from Königsberg to the seaside village of Palmnicken. They were the survivors of the approximately thirteen thousand who had already been death-marched to the city from concentration camps in the Nazi-occupied east. The SS drafted in old men and teenage boys from the city to help and the women were ordered into a disused amber pit and shot. Four days later, those who remained were driven into the winter sea under gunfire.

In the archives she discovered that the Nazi recruitment drive in her home city had not been particularly successful. The SS had summoned two thousand boys and men, but only one thousand turned up, and of those, only eighty-two were fit to be drafted (*WFW* 251). It might well have been the case that the men were too scared or too exhausted to show up. But to Hannah Arendt, those numbers also suggested a possible resistance—a disobedience maybe. The iron grip had lost its hold. Something else was beginning in Königsberg—for some, at least, the chips had come down.

CHAPTER SEVEN

What Are We Doing?

> What I propose, therefore, is very simple: it is
> nothing more than to think what we are doing.
>
> —*The Human Condition*

In October 1955, just short of her forty-ninth birthday—successful, secure, loved, and at the height of her intellectual powers—Hannah Arendt visited the National Archaeological Museum in Athens and stood before a striking grave stele relief dredged up from the Ilissos River in the late nineteenth century. Its subject is a beautiful, ballsy young man who stares directly at the viewer, oblivious to his own disappearance from the world. At his feet, a small slave boy rests his head in his hands in misery while a dog despondently sniffs out traces of his lost master. To the right, an older man, possibly his father, possibly his lover or teacher, stares intently at the figure, perplexed at how his gorgeous boy can be both strikingly present and absent at the same time.

Athens was part of a tour of three classical cities that Arendt had promised herself while teaching at Berkeley in the spring of

Photograph of the Stele of Ilissos,
National Archaeological Museum, Athens.

1955. *Rome-Athens-Jerusalem,* she had written to Karl Jaspers: *Then in one year I'll have taken in the whole western world. And that presumably will put my heart at rest again. The world is just so lovely* (*AKJ* 253–54). Rome had been grand, if austere; Venice, where she had stayed with Mary McCarthy in her rented apartment on the Campo San Lorenzo, was *indescribably delightful,* but Athens, Athens was captivating.

There are many reasons why Arendt might have been drawn to

the marble stele in particular. The museum is littered with the gravestones that became popular when a plague in 420 BCE created a new market for the sculptors who had previously been working on the Acropolis. It is likely that she would have first read about the reliefs as a student in Adolf von Hildebrand's influential study of classicism, *The Problem of Form in Painting and Sculpture* (1893). Hildebrand saw in Greek classic form the coming together of Kant's distinction between how we perceive and imagine things—based on what we see before us with our eyes—and how we understand them—based on what we actually know about the form that things take in the world. He claimed that classical reliefs do this amazingly well by combining the two-dimensional outline that we usually see when we look at things from afar with the three-dimensional forms which we understand that dogs, boys, and quizzical old men actually have: imagination and understanding coalesce.

But there was another reason why the stele reliefs appealed to Hannah Arendt. Unlike the self-standing and commanding statues of the big men, the gods, or the funerary monuments to warriors and great notables elsewhere in the museum, the stelae depict the lives and households of the ordinary citizens of Pericles's Athens. The figures portrayed, writes the American art historian Richard Neer, are "enmeshed in *polis* society just as surely as [they are] enmeshed in a block of stone."[1] Enmeshed in the *polis* and yet distinct, equal yet different, collective yet singular, one of us and yet unique: in a word, plurality. Arendt was drawn to the gravestones of Athens because they gave her a picture of what she understood to be the human condition.

She bought Karl Jaspers a disappointingly inadequate postcard reproduction of the Ilissos stele and sent it to him. *The actual grave stela is incredibly beautiful and impressive,* she assured him. But it was not the aesthetics of the relief she really wanted to tell him about: *the dead youth looking off into the distance, the little slave and little dog mourning at his feet; and then the old man—not mourning but his whole form a single question mark incarnate,* she writes (*AKJ* 269). Why is the old man not mourning? What has he *not* got to lose? Is this you? Arendt could be asking Jaspers. Or me perhaps?

There is so much that Arendt loved about the Greek world in the Ilissos stele. The private, inconsolable grief of the slave boy, visible but tucked under the stairs to one side, not a central part of the image, but necessary to its sense of completeness. Nobody had more to lose upon the death of an Athenian citizen than the dependents in his household.

The youth seemingly so present in the world despite his death; the confidently crossed ankles, that indifferent stare. This young man knows he's here to be seen, his courage to be shown, his actions judged, his deeds remembered; and he's so at ease with all this that he just stands there, as though propped up at a bar in the *agora* over a glass of wine. He looks every inch a man of the *polis;* prepared to pit his opinions against others, ready for a bit of *agon.* The sad dog suggests that he was a hunter or he might be a fallen warrior, one of the heroes of the Peloponnesian Wars who Pericles promised would always be remembered by the existence of the *polis* itself. The words and deeds of men acting freely in concert, he declared, would be a living memorial to the courage of those who gave their lives so that there could be a free politics at all—at least among the men whose absolute rule over the household and the endless labor of slaves and women in it gave them the time and leisure to be fully participating democratic citizens.

And then to the side of it all, and for Arendt the most arresting character in this Greek tableau, the contemplative figure who is not just an old man thinking but a person whose entire body is a single question mark incarnate. He is there because none of this, the life, the death, the home, the appearing in the world, or the courage would make any sense at all were it not thought about, worked over, and given form and presence in the minds of men.

One could almost believe that the philosopher has thought the whole scene into existence, so perfectly does the stele represent the moment when for Arendt, as for many modernist Hellenists of her generation, Being, as in the full glory and potential of *human* being, was born. Except that this would be to miss the crucial Arendtian point that the philosopher is not above or outside this scene, making it all up out of his fine and superior thoughts, ordering and mastering the world with his mind, but right there in the picture itself, perplexed, with a sad little dog sniffing at his feet.

He could be Socrates, that's what I think Arendt was thinking, who used to hold court in Simon the Shoemaker's shop on the borders of the *agora,* a popular hangout for the restless young men he would provoke into thinking dangerously. "It isn't that, knowing the answers myself I perplex other people," Socrates confessed: the "truth is rather that I infect them with the perplexity I feel myself."[2] He did this so successfully that the Athenian elite lost patience and demanded he state his loyalty to the *polis* by drinking hemlock. In obliging, Socrates demonstrated both his obedience to the state and his loyalty to his own thinking. Acting freely to engineer his own death, he exercised his freedom from the state. It's easy to see why the Athenian establishment didn't want this catching on. Athens was a democracy of the elite, of fixed ballots and dodgy lotteries, of men keeping power. Socrates was goading people into discovering freedom in acts of thoughtful resistance.

After his death, Socrates' pupil, Plato, stepped out from behind him and argued that henceforth it might be better if political life were ruled by ideas, not by everyday citizen-thinkers. The truth behind these ideas would be gleaned by a team of super philosopher kings fearless enough to look at the sun and crafty enough to persuade those in the shade to assent to their rule. Governance by ideas with the aim of making politics something that ordinary people did not really have to bother themselves with began at this

Hannah Arendt in Greece, 1955.

point, which is why Arendt thought that Socrates' death marked the beginning of the end for the true Athenian promise of politics.

Socrates would almost definitely not be mourning. He would have been examining all of it: the boy's beauty, his death, the miracle of human presence as it exists in the world and in the thought of others, the love that makes the absent present. The sheer fact that there was a human world there to be mourned at all would have been enough to keep him muttering to himself happily for days. But was Hannah Arendt mourning?

On the one hand: absolutely not. *I've begun so late,* she had written to Jaspers from Berkeley shortly before her trip, *really only in recent years, to truly love the world [. . .] Out of gratitude, I want to call my book on political theories "Amor Mundi"* (*AKJ* 264). There is a photograph from her visit which shows her with her friends in front of the Parthenon (I think it is the Parthenon but am not absolutely sure) looking slightly down the hill at the Temple of Athena Nike. She has, naturally, a cigarette in her hand and she is quite clearly enraptured. *Everything here means more to me than I ever knew. I can't, I simply can't tear myself away,* she wrote to Jaspers. Everything meant more than she ever knew.

On the other hand, Arendt knew that she was gazing into a lost world. Modern life had pushed any promised freedoms of the Athenian *polis* out of reach. By the mid-twentieth century, many women, slaves, and workers had been "emancipated" from the labor of providing the necessities of life for privileged male citizens, only to discover that they were not very free at all, at least not politically. People were still toiling away, but now in the service of a consumer culture that exploited not only their labor but the intimacies of their most private lives. Coaxed out of the shadows by promises of autonomy and self-determination, all that modern social life had delivered to the marginalized, so she thought, was the freedom to try and be yourself in a world that dictated the terms upon which that freedom was acceptable. Women and slaves have learned the hard way to be suspicious when they are finally invited to the party.

The moment that democracies began to open up in the late nineteenth and early twentieth centuries, power moved further and further into the shadows. Social life, with its conformities and strictures, its busy visibility and chatter, got bigger and bigger until people began to believe that this was where all the power really lay. This is how we end up with the kind of politics—although Arendt would balk at calling it an actual politics—where we are endlessly asked to perform our private identities in public while politicians and the super-rich appear to have absolute rights to privacy. Tell us who you are loving right now and how, show us the shape of your body and the goodness of your soul, consent to socially prescribed ways of living and dying, but don't think you are going to get a public account of the terms under which you are being governed (or the tax records of politicians), because that is not what you need to concern yourselves with.

Arendt knew that the Athenian promise of a more potent political freedom was gone, but she was not about to give up on it either. *The Greek polis will continue to exist at the bottom of our political existence—that is, at the bottom of the sea—for so long as we use the word "politics,"* she later wrote in an essay on Walter Benjamin.[3] So long as we accept the very little that the word "politics" means now, the example of Greece will remain lost. But, like Walter Benjamin, Hannah Arendt was a pearl diver; she liked to descend deep to the bottom of history and tradition to find what pearls from the past had been left on the seabed. And Greece has a lot of sea. *Whenever I can, I go swimming,* she wrote to Jaspers; *swimming always gives me a sense of being at home (AKJ* 269).

In September 2021, in the second year of the Covid pandemic, I went to the National Archaeological Museum in Athens to retrace Arendt's steps. The museum, like Athens itself, probably contained as many tourists as there would have been in 1955, which is to say, not many. Most of us luxuriating in the near-empty rooms that morning were middle-aged or older Europeans, determined, having made it through this far, to see Athens once or perhaps one last time. We moved silently through the halls, masked culture raiders quietly joyful about being out in the world. I strode around rather breathlessly, anxious to find Arendt's stele, worried that it might not be there and that I would not get to stand where she stood, her whole body a question mark incarnate, and work out whether I should be happy and joyous or sad and in mourning. After ten minutes or so of this foolishness, I showed a guard a picture of the Ilissos stele on my phone and she kindly led me to room twenty-two which I presume is much the same as it was when Arendt visited.

I stood in front of the stele for a while, experimented with Adolf von Hildebrand's game of walking backward and away so that the figures looked two-dimensional and then forward again to confirm their three-dimensionality to see whether I could get my perception and understanding to coalesce.

It wasn't until I walked around the room a few times that I

really began to comprehend what I was looking at. There are approximately twenty stelae in room twenty-two of the National Archaeological Museum and they all, in various ways, show the living saying goodbye to the dead. There are men saying goodbye to men, women to men, women to women, babies and children to their mothers, boys to old men, and pets to their owners, including dogs, birds, cats, and a rabbit. I was surrounded by the grief of all life. Yet the sorrow depicted on the stelae was not one of bottomless despair. Looking at each one after the other, I realized that what ran through all of them was an acceptance that this grief had to be endured—an acceptance of a bitter reality. And what made that acceptance feel so real was the human connectedness conveyed on each slab of marble because, as Arendt saw, these were not monuments to the lives and actions of individual men, but to plurality itself.

As I circled the room, one of the most common motifs I noted was a handshake between the dead and the living: a last touch between hands that had labored and worked, that had put things into the world and taken them out again; a last touch between friends, lovers, and family. On the wall just to the left of the Ilissos relief was the "Farewell Stele" which depicts a final grasp between two women. Their hands were so strong, so present, so real that you wanted to reach out and touch them with your own. I could not take my eyes off it. It helped that the women were incredibly beautiful, at least the equals of Arendt's young man. She must have seen it too. But maybe there was no picture postcard of this goodbye between women to send in 1955, no memento of their extraordinary courage in grief.

It was because of a plague, scholars tell us, that we can look at so many of the stelae today; several rooms in the museum are given over to them and there are even more in the basement, apparently. I was not only looking into the deep past in room twenty-two in the National Archaeological Museum, I was looking at the present.

There is a sentence in *The Human Condition* that I always circle back to. It's a long and complicated sentence, but it flows quite smoothly when you hear it in your head, and I heard it very clearly in Athens that morning. Arendt writes:

> *The human sense of reality demands that men actualize the sheer passive givenness of their being, not in order to change it but in order to make articulate and call into full existence what otherwise they would have to suffer passively anyhow.* (*HC* 208)

We cannot change human suffering because it is the condition of our existing at all. But we can make it articulate. We can make loss, death, and therefore life, present, discernible, real, and in that way turn something unbearable into something human. That is only possible with others though; hence the touches, the hands, the quizzical looks, the being together, and the being separate. That is what the stelae were showing me.

The absence of a response not merely to reality, but to what Arendt calls *a human sense of reality* is a feature of our currently impoverished politics. The pandemic made this newly obvious. Across the world, policies were implemented to save human lives that explicitly prohibited a farewell human touch. Meanwhile, thousands of other lives were sacrificed to keep economies moving because, we were often told, dying and suffering would not pay for themselves. Rarely in recent times, and certainly in the West, had people felt so powerless. The first sense of powerlessness was existential: a plague is an extreme situation; we can respond to it, but we cannot control it. The second was political: our most intimate lives—where we could go, who we might touch, and how we might die—were being managed, over-managed some would say, economized, and rationalized. People complied because they wanted to live but also, and much more fundamentally, because they recognized the one thing that seemed to be so glaringly absent from the policies of many governments: a shared vulnerability, a human condition that demanded a human response.

Human frailty is at the heart of *The Human Condition,* the book that was chasing Arendt's thoughts as she traveled through classical Europe in 1955. After writing, and to an extent living, the dark history of *The Origins of Totalitarianism,* she stripped everything back so that she could look at the world again, cleansed of ideology, history, and master narratives. The book is a cultural phenomenology of human existence as it appeared to her in Greece and Rome, as well as elsewhere, from the vantage point, as she put it, of *our newest experiences and most recent fears (HC* 5). She was going back to basics to try and think the world anew.

The Human Condition is a book about the spaces we live in: private life, public life, social life, and about how we move through those spaces: labor, work, and action. It is a book about the life we must live to survive, the world we make between us that will endure across time, and about the plurality that defines us, and which just might, one day with care and a good eye for pearls, give us a politics fit to be human in.

Arendt works with categories and definitions. *The human condi-*

tion of labor is life itself; she tells us. *The human condition of work is worldliness.* Action *corresponds to the human condition of plurality* (*HC* 7). But these categories are not in a hierarchy. This is not a book that will tell you how to get from labor to action, from the invisibility of the home to the splendor of the public realm—although Arendt will insist again and again that spending too much time fretting about conforming to society will stop you enjoying the freedoms or pleasures of either. Still less does she attach absolute values to the things we do: labor is a chore, but it is also the essence of life; work is valuable because we can make tangible things that give permanence to the world, but destruction is also part of creation; action is the best thing we can do but always hazardous, always risky, because we can never know what will follow from our actions.

If we really want to be free, she says, we cannot, indeed must not, second-guess ourselves with theories and grand political philosophies because, ever since the death of Socrates at least, these have so very clearly been part of the problem. The *conditions of human existence* cannot explain who we are or tell us how to be *for the simple reason that they never condition us absolutely,* she writes (*HC* 11). If we want to remain human, we must first learn to relinquish the desire to totally know, control, or escape the world around us— and that includes knowing, controlling, or escaping ourselves.

On October 4, 1957, almost two years to the day after her visit to the National Archaeological Museum, Hannah Arendt looked up at the night sky from her window on the Upper West Side and wondered whether she could catch a glimpse of *Sputnik,* the first satellite to orbit the earth, which had been launched by the Soviet Union earlier that evening. Had the Americans been the first to shoot a satellite around the globe, the mood in New York that evening might have been more jubilant. This was the age of the space race, of big men and big science, rockets, stars, and sky's the limit. But Arendt spotted something more deeply troubling than mere disappointment in the lack of triumphalism from those around her. There was a palpable sense of relief that it was now possible to leave the earth behind. This was mad, she thought. The *earth is the very quintessence of the human condition*. The world that men wanted to escape was the one which they had made themselves. Hannah Arendt looked up at the starry skies above her, formed her body into a single question mark incarnate, returned to her desk, and typed in the preface to *The Human Condition*: *What I propose, therefore, is very simple: it is nothing more than to think what we are doing* (*HC* 5).

Athens was rapidly being industrialized when Arendt visited the city in 1955. Following the war, people had moved to the city from the countryside in search of work and prospects. The narrow streets were already beginning to swell with concrete and traffic as she walked them. Later, the children from that first group of migrants yearned for a return to the pine trees and the sea, so new developments and beach resorts were built around the city. Yet the building was unsustainable. As the planet heated up, the fires that were once part of the regular ecology of the pine forests intensified. The Greek economy also accelerated, and more building and more development followed. Then there came the economic crash of 2008 and devastating cuts to essential services, including forest husbandry and fire services. In 2018, the resort of Mati, outside

Athens, was turned into a fireball. One hundred and eight people were killed.

One month before I arrived in Athens, thanks to yet another unprecedented heat wave, fires had reached the forests to the north of the city, moved up the slopes of Mount Parnitha and surrounded the shoreline of Lake Marathon, Athens's principal reservoir. Ash rained down on the city whose inhabitants, once again, retreated indoors. There was more than one reason to wear a face mask in Athens in the summer of 2021.

The lessons about firefighting and evacuation had been learned so that the death toll from the fires that year, thankfully, was lower. Other lessons have not, however, been learned. Reforestation is being contracted out to private firms, genetically modified trees that have no place in the Mediterranean are being planted where the pine forests once stood, and local people feel politically powerless to intervene. Apparently, the governance of their home is not something that need concern them.[4] What, indeed, are we doing?

In his "Wood Thieves" essays, the young Karl Marx described how the privatization of the Rhineland's forests in the early 1840s meant that the people who had lived in and around them for centuries, gathering wood from the forest floor for fuel, suddenly became "wood thieves." "We are only surprised that the forest owner is not allowed to heat his stove with the wood thieves," Marx commented on the new laws that protected the rights of the forest's owner rather than the people who lived in and around it.[5]

In this new world, Arendt commented on Marx's essay as she began her uncompleted study of his work, *it is no longer two people who need wood who stand face to face but a wood owner and a wood thief (human needs are not the crucial point any more)*. Nor is the actual wood crucial anymore. *In the eyes of the law, it could just as well be plastic.* The *de-naturizing of nature*—the turning of wood into a commodity—and *the de-humanizing of man* coincided at precisely the same moment (*AKJ* 167). Wood and people are no longer wood and people, but abstractions refigured in social relations. Arendt didn't much care for Marx's solution to this alienation, but she absolutely agreed with his diagnosis of its cause.

The day after my visit to the Archaeological Museum, I climbed up to the Acropolis with friends. The first time I had visited, over twenty years ago, I met a chemist, named Georgios, at dinner the night before who had explained to me how the monument had come to endure over time. While working on the Temple of Athena Nike, the original architects realized that simply joining together slabs of marble with mortise and tenon could not support the large bronze acroteria on top, so they inserted steel rods into the pediment to keep them upright and stop the roof from caving in. When British archaeologists arrived in the 1920s, they discovered the empty sockets left by the rods and filled them with Birmingham steel, but these proved less durable than their fifth-century BCE prototypes and crumbled into ashes within a few years. The Greeks knew something that British industrialists did not. As a young man, in his spare time, Georgios began to analyze the traces of the rust left by the original rod. In fact, he probably began to do this just as Arendt visited (he often spent his lunch hour looking for clues in the basement of the National Archaeological Museum, he told me). After many years of work he discovered that zinc had been added to the steel and that this was why the iron rods had kept the roof up for so long. The ancient Greek architects had rust-proofed the Acropolis and preserved its glory for the future.

Works and deeds and words, Arendt wrote in *The Human Condition,* are the only things that give us frail humans a home *in a cosmos where everything is immortal except ourselves* (*HC* 19).

It is still all there at once in Athens as it was to Arendt in 1955. The brilliance, the courage, the endurance of the human condition and the works, deeds, and words by which we make homes for ourselves that stretch across time. And also the destruction, the carelessness, the loss, and the damage, the wood that is no longer just wood and the human needs that are no longer the point. The glory and the frailty, the joy and the unutterable sadness.

Eight years after her first visit to Greece, in late April 1963, Hannah Arendt leaned over the railing of a ferry, eager to catch a first glance of Aegina, the small and intensely pretty island just an hour by boat from Athens's port of Piraeus. She breathed in the salt from the spring wind, listened to the sound of the rattling chains as the boat prepared to dock, and smiled. Her reports from Eichmann's trial had just been published in *The New Yorker;* the first back in February, the last just a month before she had left New York. The ensuing controversies that would consume so much of her life in the early 1960s had begun. The trip to Europe was her treat to herself, Heinrich Blücher, and the friends that joined them along the way and was paid for with the insurance money from her 1962 car accident in Central Park.

She had left Blücher behind in Athens to enjoy his daily walk between the *agora* and the Acropolis, taking the long way past the Pnyx and the Areopagus. On the boat with her was their old friend Charlotte Beradt. A blacklisted journalist in Nazi Germany, Beradt had turned her hand to hairdressing when she had arrived in New York, running a unique kind of intellectual salon in exile where she expertly colored hair (including Arendt's). Beradt also had expert knowledge of the inner workings of fascism and anti-semitism. In the mid-1930s she had started to collect people's dreams and carefully recorded seventy-five of them in an extraor-dinary book, *The Third Reich of Dreams,* which she would publish in 1966. It was Beradt who produced the first draft translation of *The Human Condition* into German before Arendt got to work re-fining and, in some cases, expanding her text. It was also Beradt who gave Arendt the Greek typewriter which is responsible (to the irritation of many readers) for the high frequency of untranslated Greek words in her published work from about this time onward.[6]

Arendt patted her friend's hand to signal over the sound of the engine that they were approaching the port and should get ready for the ritual scramble to disembark. Beradt lifted her hand to gently pull one of Arendt's graying locks back over the scar on her forehead where her hair had been slow to grow back after her ac-cident (it would never grow back completely). *Have you seen pictures of the Aphaia temple on Aegina??* she later wrote to the Jasperses, *it sits on the peak of a mountain,* which *affords a view all around the island and [is] perhaps the most beautiful experience of all (AKJ* 502, 503).

She had left Blücher back in Athens, as she would when she flew out to Crete for a few days later, because he did not share her passion for pre-classical thought and culture. Following Nietzsche and Heidegger, Arendt believed that it was in the writings of the early Greeks that you really got a sense of what being—in the sense of *Existenz,* an authentically human life—meant for the an-cients. After Socrates, Heidegger once wrote, philosophy was little more than "the narcotization of anxiety" by reason.[7] Almost a year to the day that Arendt made her trip to Aegina, he would retrace her journey to the island with his wife, Elfride, for a two-week holiday.

Excavated in the nineteenth century by a German and an Englishman, the Temple of Aphaia was first assumed to be dedicated to Athena and dated as being built around the time of the Peloponnesian Wars, and so roughly contemporary with the Acropolis. Sculptures from the pediment commemorating the wars had been taken from Aegina to Germany at the same time. There they were restored in neoclassical style by the Norwegian sculptor Bertel Thorvaldsen and put on display in the Glyptothek in Munich close to Königsplatz where the Nazi Party later built its headquarters in the mid-1930s.

Later it was discovered that the Temple had much older origins and foundations and that, in fact, it was not originally dedicated to Athena but to Aphaia, a goddess of fertility, life cycles, children, and childbirth—I'm calling her the goddess of natality—worshipped only on Aegina and in Crete.[8] The Temple had appeared classical, but in reality it was archaic, which is exactly why both Martin Heidegger and Hannah Arendt had been so eager to see it.

Where other philosophers and thinkers push birth far away from the business of the world, from politics, morality, from sight, in *The Human Condition* Arendt put it right at the center. Natality, she argued, may even be *the central category of political thought* (*HC* 9). Each time a new person comes into the world, they come with a capacity to act, to begin something new. A culture that worships birth is one that is essentially at ease with the idea of change, unpredictability, and the new; not for change's sake (Arendt is not interested in monstrous political births) but because the human condition will always require new responses to a shifting and porous reality. This is why natality and action are so crucial to political plurality. We are not born to make the world in our image or bend it to our will but to inhabit it with others, to act "in concert" with, and between, one another.

And this, at heart, is what also makes us frail, not just as individual bodies attempting to survive, but frail as people who must exist together. Nobody acts alone, even when they believe that this is what they are doing. It is the nature of all human action to cut across limits and boundaries and to get in the hair of other people (as every parent knows). We have laws and frameworks to contain action, but they can never completely *withstand the onslaught* with which each generation inserts itself into the world. In this matter, it is the laws and institutions, indeed, all political matters that involve us living together, that are also frail. We talk a lot these days about "strengthening" democratic institutions against authoritarians and populism, and with good reason. Arendt's insight is more radical and perhaps, at this juncture, particularly helpful: What if we recognized the frailty of human affairs as the condition of politics to begin with? What if we reckoned with human vulnerability as a starting point and not as some political afterthought?

On this question in *The Human Condition,* she leaves Greece and, completing her classical tour, takes her reader to Jerusalem and Rome. If we are no longer to submit to being governed by the imagination of our Platonic overlords, and if we want a politics that can respond to a human sense of reality, we need some guiding principles, she says. These are not the traditional political principles of power, honor, or virtue. Arendt's two principles are forgiveness, which she finds in the example of Jesus of Nazareth, and promising, which has been a feature of political contract theory since the Roman Republic.

Forgiving circumvents the hazard of acting without ever knowing what the results of that action might be. When others forgive us, the deed is undone, which is helpful to know when I decide to act in good faith but still worry about the outcome of my actions. It is a mistake to believe that Arendt is simply advocating for a kinder politics here. Forgiveness takes courage, disobedience even. She reminds us that Christianity was originally practiced by small groups of people *bent on challenging the public authorities in Israel* (*HC* 239). The sentiment here is very similar to Socrates' resistance to the Athenian state by passively disobeying while appearing to obey. Christian forgiveness is subversive because it rejects the idea that only one power—God, the king, the sovereign, or the state—can forgive. Arendt seizes on this democratization to make the point that forgiveness assumes plurality. Forgiving yourself is not a political act. We forgive others to give one another the freedom to act without fear, which is political. Mutual respect, she adds, is how we might get forgiveness to work for us all.

Promising is how we bypass the unreliability that Arendt calls the *dark heart* of human affairs. Nietzsche once described promises as being a "memory of the will." Arendt, indebted to Nietzsche's observation that promising things for the future is what makes us human not animal, saw what the author of *The Will to Power* could not quite: that the drive to create worlds out of the strength of the imagination alone led to tyranny. In Arendt's version, when we make promises we are affirming our vulnerability to others too.

This is why she likes constitutions which are promises between people that also stretch into the future. Mutual promising is *the alternative to a mastery which relies on domination of one's self and rule over others*. Forgiving and promising may sound like frail principles upon which to bind a political community together but this is the point. The recognition of human frailty is the price we pay for freedom, she says, *for plurality and reality, for the joy of inhabiting together with others a world whose reality is guaranteed for each by the presence of all* (*HC* 244).

Joy, natality, birth: writing *The Human Condition,* in despair that things had got to the point where the only good option seemed to be leaving the planet itself, Hannah Arendt had turned her entire form into a question mark incarnate—and she was, defiantly and joyously, *not* mourning.

The sculptures from the Temple's pediment remain in the Glyptothek, a fact that rankles on Aegina. But they are not as they were when they stood alongside Nazi monuments in the 1930s and early 1940s. At roughly the same time as Martin Heidegger retraced Arendt's journey to Aegina in 1964, the Aphaia sculptures were undergoing an important transformation. Munich's Königsplatz was bombed during the war and some of Thorvaldsen's neoclassical figures had been badly damaged. In the 1960s, the museum took the opportunity to "de-restore" them and so sever the aesthetic connection with the Nazi monuments and institutions that they had once resembled. The smooth bodies and limbs of the warriors were dismembered, and prosthetic steel rods were used to join the original and the remaining fragments, leaving space and absence in the place of the firm presence of nineteenth-century marble. No longer tributes to the virility and splendor of total Greek Being, the sculptures now look like what they were in fact all along: man-made objects given meaning and presence, imagined and damaged by human history.[9]

Warriors from East Pediment's Group of the Temple of Aphaia after de-restoration, Munich Glyptothek.

Arendt, and possibly Heidegger, would have appreciated the "new" sculptures. The "de-restoration" gave them back the otherness that both thinkers identified with Greek thought. All life has an incongruity to it, something that belongs just to it and that we cannot grasp. The warriors still look brave and courageous; they carry the essential human trait of wanting to be distinct and unique; they very much remain epitomes of Greek Being. But now, between the gaps, rods, and missing limbs, the rocky historical road that took the fighters from being an idea in a sculptor's mind, to marble, to Aegina, then to Nazi Germany, and now to somewhere in our own culture, also reveals the groundlessness of the project of *Existenz*. This groundlessness is what Heidegger taught Arendt about all those years ago in Marburg. Thirty years later in *The Human Condition,* she gave her response.

The only way to protect and nurture human distinction, she argued, is to let plurality flourish. This means letting reality and human frailty in. In 1936, Heidegger had claimed that the Greek *polis* was a "world-disclosing artwork."[10] Arendt thought this was entirely the wrong emphasis. Myth, art, storytelling, and history are fine, brilliant, and human ways of remembering and interpreting the world, of making it a place fit to live. But you cannot make politics into an artwork without breaking eggs, that is, people. It was action that made political existence meaningful, not idealism or worse, an absolute idea about how the world should be. *With word and deed we insert ourselves into the human world,* she wrote. In this second birth, we confirm our vulnerability, our passive naked givenness, *and* the fact that we owe our uniqueness—our distinction—to the *paradoxical plurality of unique beings* (*HC* 176).

Arendt owed so much of *The Human Condition* to Heidegger's thought, even though she failed to name him once in all of its pages. Had things been different between them—*and I mean between, that is, neither you nor me*—she wrote in a letter, she would have dedicated the book to him (*AMH* 124). Since that first meeting in Freiberg in the 1950s, the two had renewed their intellectual closeness. A nostalgia for the earnest poignancy of their youth, as for many former lovers, gave their friendship an enduring intimacy. In her study of Arendt and Heidegger's relationship, Elżbieta

Ettinger tells us that Arendt had written a verse in lieu of an actual dedication, but decided not to include it in her letter:

> Re *Vita Activa*
> The dedication of this book is left out.
> How could I dedicate it to you,
> my trusted friend,
> to whom I remained faithful
> and unfaithful,
> And both in love.[11]

The Human Condition is a book about how to attend to what is most precious about existence by making it human between us. With her silent dedication she was also telling Heidegger that his philosophy harbored a very different kind of politics from the fascism that so attracted him, that she had found out about that, and that she wanted to share it with him. It was her faithful but unfaithful book, an act of forgiveness and of love. Heidegger never acknowledged this letter or his receipt of the copy that she had arranged for her publisher to send to him or its contents. He ghosted her gift.

"Give me a place to stand on, and I can move the earth," Archimedes, the Greek mathematician and scientist, once said. If, his thought ran, he could reach a point sufficiently distant from the earth and a long enough fulcrum, then he could actually lever the planet—move it, change it, master it. Archimedes' point promised to put man in a position of maximum power over the earth by developing the right science and technology, a lever in this case.

But the catch was that to find that point he must first leave the earth itself.

In the final chapter of *The Human Condition,* Arendt argued that modern man had now found the Archimedean point, but that this was not entirely good news. As Kafka put it in one of his aphorisms: "He had found the Archimedean point, but he used it against himself; it seems that he was permitted to find it only under this condition."

The moment that Galileo pointed his telescope up at the sky, a gap had emerged between the way that the physical and natural world appeared and the scientific and objective reality that his new technology revealed. Things were not as they appeared. The sun did not revolve around the earth. Henceforth, reason and doubt would come to define human existence. Viewed this way, René Descartes's famous "I think, therefore I am" was at once a declaration of the power of thought and reason to determine existence and an acknowledgment of our alienation from the earth. *If everything has become doubtful, then doubting at least is certain and real,* as Arendt put it (*HC* 279). Heisenberg's uncertainty principle, with the anxiety that how science might look at the physical world might actually change life itself, was not far behind. Thinking became the primary way that we knew the world. Remember Kant walking the bridges of Königsberg and Euler, the mathematician, writing his theorem to explain why you could not move around the city without crossing at least one of its seven bridges twice.

The Human Condition, by contrast, is not a book that theorizes the world, but an exhortation to think about what we do in it. The *Vita Activa*—the active life—was her original title (and remains the German title). In *The Origins of Totalitarianism* Arendt had taken on the death cults of Nazi and Bolshevik totalitarianism. In *The Human Condition* she asked what happened when reason and science combined with Western consumerism. *The modern age which began with such an unprecedented outburst of activity,* she wrote, *may end in the deadliest, most sterile passivity history has ever known* (*HC* 322). As the 1950s closed, she found a receptive audience for her fears. The book was hugely popular, nominated for the 1959 National Book Award and reviewed extensively, not only in the United States but across the world, which was quite something for an anti-philosophical book of philosophy. Reprints and translations followed quickly after its first publication in 1958 to the surprise of both Arendt and her publisher, an academic press unused to esoteric bestsellers on quite this scale.

To an extent though, it was exactly the anti-philosophy philosophy that readers were responding to. Above all, Hannah Arendt wanted to bring people back to earth so that they could appreciate what they had—and what they had to lose. In *The New Yorker,* Mary McCarthy described *The Human Condition* as being like a lost property office. Arendt was not seeking to impose new truths, merely to write about those we had left behind.[12]

In this matter, Arendt's second major book is every bit as much of an accurate prediction of the present as was *The Origins of Totalitarianism,* with its warnings of loneliness and a chronically apolitical existence. She worried that technology and overconsumption were alienating us from the earth. In the twenty-first century, the worry now is that we have destroyed it entirely. Arendt was too much of a humanist to think about natural life on the same terms as human life. When she wrote about the sterility of laboring simply to consume more, she was concerned that the specifically human element of work had been sacrificed to an economy of dis-posables, ready-mades, and waste. With that, too, went the sense of permanence created by the craftspeople, the artists, historians, makers, and poets who catch the fleeting nature of human experi-ence and give it a permanent home. But Arendt also saw that there was an intimate connection between the ability to cultivate a human home and care for the natural environment. In a 1960 essay, she picked up on the Roman origins of the word "culture" to explain that the word derived *from colere—to cultivate, to dwell, to take care, to tend and preserve—and it relates primarily to the intercourse of man with nature in the sense of cultivating and tending nature until it be-comes fit for human habitation. As such it indicates an attitude of loving care and stands in sharp contrast to all efforts to subject nature to the domination of man.*[13]

Four years after the publication of *The Human Condition,* the biologist and writer Rachel Carson, another woman who refused to accept the modern world on the terms offered to her, published the first installments of the book that would ignite the modern environmental movement, *Silent Spring,* in *The New Yorker.* "If we are living so intimately with chemicals, we had better know some-thing about their power," read the strapline to her first article. This understatement did nothing to prepare readers for Carson's devas-tating opening description of the torment of a dying population of a small American town poisoned by the pesticides that had been sprayed on their land. "No witchcraft, no enemy action had snuffed out life in this stricken world. The people had done it themselves," she wrote. "One species, man, has acquired significant power to alter the nature of his world," unleashing a "chain of evil" in "the world that must support life."[14] I have not found any evidence that

Arendt read Carson's book, but toward the end of her life, she would describe the *recent sudden awakening to the threats of our environment* as offering *the first ray of hope* in resistance against the *"going is the goal" culture of waste, obsolescence, abuse, misuse, and throw away.*[15]

Just eight months after the publication of Carson's *Silent Spring, The New Yorker* published the first installments of *Eichmann in Jerusalem* in February 1963. Between Carson's and Arendt's epoch-defining articles, the magazine published a third in November 1962, James Baldwin's "Letter from a Region in My Mind," the text that would become *The Fire Next Time,* and that so deeply impressed Hannah Arendt that she was moved to write to him about love. "We human beings now have the power to exterminate ourselves; this seems to be the entire sum of our achievement," Baldwin wrote in words that directly echoed Arendt's own dire warnings.[16]

Several contemporary readers wrote to *The New Yorker*'s editor, William Shawn, to comment that something extraordinary seemed to have happened to the quality of truth-telling in the magazine's pages (some also wrote to reject the truths that all three told). With a stunning moral, political, and historical clarity that now looks nothing less than visionary, between them Carson, Baldwin, and Arendt laid out the threats to the human condition on earth: endemic and violent racism, reckless greed, overconsumption, unthinking technological change, and environmental catastrophe—the poisonous masterplots of modern life.

"It is the responsibility of free men to trust and celebrate what is constant," Baldwin wrote. Life, natality, struggle, love, the human condition, and the planetary condition: these were the constants that all three writers celebrated and defended. The constants are right here, they all said, in this world, on this earth, and right now. The very different revolutions each called for were not about creating new realities but about articulating those that already existed: for Baldwin, the "suffering and dancing country" of Black America; for Arendt, the *sheer givenness of life;* for Carson, "the wonders and realities of the universe about us."

There is a reason why James Baldwin, Hannah Arendt, and Rachel Carson are three of the writers from the last century whose voices speak to us most urgently in our own. They show us, yet again, possibly because people did not pay sufficient attention the first time, possibly because the very things they feared have indeed got much much worse, the beauty and fragility of existence.

Hannah Arendt was an expert at inhabiting moments of wonder—the experience the Greeks called *thaumazein*. Remember her on the cliffs of Portbou frantically searching for Walter Benjamin's grave but pausing to note the *fantastic beauty* of the blue sea and the green-white coastline that stretched out below her, or drawing on her cigarette as she stared across at the sea from the Acropolis. Even as her priority was always the human, the sensual world was not simply divided into subjects who think and objects to be used. All life forms are meant to be seen, heard, touched, tasted: *they are never mere subjects and can never be understood as such: they are no less "objective" than stone and bridge,* she wrote in her final book, *The Life of the Mind* (*LM* 19). This interchange between appearance, the wonder of the otherness of all life, as James Baldwin might have said, is one of the constants.

During the 1950s and early 1960s Hannah Arendt found her feet in America, but she barely paused to let them touch the ground. It was in this period that Robert Lowell wrote his pigeon poem for her. By now she had made the "flight's lost moment" her own and trained her bird eyes on the globe as she shuttled between America and Europe on the new Pan American Airways, and on the landscape of her newfound land as she whizzed past it on trains over to the West Coast and up and down the Eastern Seaboard. Heinrich Blücher had conquered his imposter syndrome by working out that the best way to explore ideas was not by writing them down but by teaching, and like Socrates in Simon the Shoemaker's shop in the *agora,* he was subverting young minds at Bard College in upstate New York. The former refugees now led the life of permanent commuters.

The months between 1956 and 1957 that she spent writing up *The Human Condition* were exhilarating and exhausting. In the spring of 1956 she presented the book's arguments as the Walgreen Lectures at the University of Chicago. She liked the smart and interesting students who attended her classes and the experimental interdisciplinary ethos of the Committee on Social Thought, which had been established in 1941. The following spring, she returned to teach Hans Morgenthau's "Recent Political Theory" course, with its impossibly long reading list ("I haven't read all the books, and don't expect the students to read them," he reassured her). Morgenthau's opposition to the Vietnam War would get him kicked out of President Johnson's administration around the same time as the controversy that followed her reports on Eichmann meant that she, too, was ostracized. The two became close. After Blücher's death in 1970, they became very close, but that was for later.

As she worked on the book's final chapter, she corresponded with an old friend from her student days in Freiberg, the political philosopher Alexandre Koyré. Koyré was just finishing his ground-breaking history of modern science *From the Closed World to the Infinite Universe* (1957), in which he shared Arendt's anxiety about the direction of twentieth-century technology. "*Sur notre situation climatique et politique . . . En bref:* the worst since at least a hundred years," he wrote to her from Paris in March 1956. "Yet *la vie* continues as usual."[17]

In September 1956, she went to the Netherlands with Mary McCarthy to see the Rembrandts in Amsterdam and also visited The Hague, Delft, Haarlem, and Rotterdam. Rembrandt's intensely human faces—generous, frail, suffering, and compassionate—had openly defied the narrow capitalist spirit and dry Protestant asceticism of his age. Arendt, out to preserve the human condition in her own, found much to enjoy about them.

In Amsterdam, she followed the footsteps of Baruch Spinoza who, with his generous pantheism, also flouted the imaginative restrictions of the seventeenth century. Arendt loved Spinoza for his fearless teaching about reality, but thought that he probably did not laugh much, as she herself did in these months, with the wide smile that came to characterize her later years. On her return from Europe that October, she bought herself a record player to celebrate her fiftieth birthday, because *ultimately the power of music is the greatest there is* (*AKJ* 272). From now on, there would be music at her parties.

In the late spring of 1957, she spent an intense evening of serious drinking with the poet Elizabeth Bishop (Mary McCarthy's former classmate and a friend of Robert Lowell) and Bishop's lover, the Brazilian landscape architect Lota de Macedo Soares. Eighteen years later, after the publication of Arendt's eulogy for

W. H. Auden in *The New Yorker,* Bishop wrote to thank Arendt for her attentive evocation of the poet and for her readings of the poems which, said Bishop, were exactly those she would have chosen to remember him by. "You may well not remember me," she wrote, "but you may remember my Brazilian friend, Lota de Macedo Soares. She enjoyed her conversation with you so much and talked about it for years afterward." *What an idea that I won't remember you*, Arendt replied: *I remember every minute of that remarkable evening with you and your Brazilian friend and to tell you the truth I was always disappointed that I never heard from you again.*[18]

Elizabeth Bishop wrote some of her most powerful nature poetry when she lived in Brazil with Lota de Macedo Soares. She wrote poems about the landscape's "monster ferns," "lichens, gray moonbursts," "sooty dragons," and scarcely breathing lizards; about how colonialists "ripped away into the hanging fabric" of the rainforest to consume its treasures; about the alienating gaze of visiting tourists whose "lack of imagination" makes them journey to "imagined places"; and the squatter children reasserting property rights "in rooms of falling rain."[19]

I do not know whether Arendt knew the poems from Bishop's 1965 collection *Questions of Travel,* which contains her most stunning nature poetry, but I do know that she owned a copy of the collection for which Bishop had won the Pulitzer Prize in 1956, *Poems: North & South—A Cold Spring.*

Like the book that Arendt was completing when they met that evening in 1957, an early poem from that collection, "The Man-Moth," is an acute meditation on the cost of the separation of appearances from reality in the modern age. Bishop's fictional creature, the Man-Moth (inspired by a newspaper misprint of "mammoth"), imagines the moon to be a small hole through which he might escape the earth. After all, he lives in a world of appearances only, so how is he to know any different? Up he climbs to investigate, only to fall back to earth, scared but unhurt, to resume his days of lost fluttering on "the pale subways of cement he calls his home." The Man-Moth does not know the physical properties of the universe he inhabits. Like the inhabitants of Plato's cave, he sees only queer lights, and senses, not measures, the temperature around him. "Man, standing below him, has no such illusions," writes Bishop—because, Hannah Arendt would have added silently to herself, smiling with recognition as she read the poem, of course man has his telescope, his instruments, and his Archimedean point, and knows full well what the moon is and how it travels. Man knows all, but at what cost?

Catch the Man-Moth, Bishop writes in the final stanza, and if you really pay attention, he might hand you one of his tears:

> *If you catch him,*
> *hold up a flashlight to his eye. It's all dark pupil,*
> *an entire night itself, whose haired horizon tightens*
> *as he stares back, and closes up the eye. Then from the lids*
> *one tear, his only possession, like the bee's sting, slips.*
> *Slyly he palms it, and if you're not paying attention*
> *he'll swallow it. However, if you watch, he'll hand it over,*
> *cool as from underground springs and pure enough to drink.*

Poetry, Arendt wrote in *The Human Condition, whose material is language, is perhaps the most human . . . of the arts* because *it remains closest to the thought that inspired it* (*HC* 161).

. . .

Hannah Arendt came home in the late 1950s, home to the world that she had learned to love and which she was committed to protecting from inhuman political forces. Meanwhile, Adolf Eichmann had settled in Argentina. As she worked on the final drafts of *The Human Condition* in 1957, he spent his weekends proudly recording his central role in the extermination of the Jews with a group of exiled Nazis, including the Dutch collaborator, Waffen-SS member, and journalist Willem Sassen. For these men, Nazism was an incomplete project. Extracts of the "Sassen Tapes" appeared in *Life* magazine in 1960 as Eichmann awaited trial in Jerusalem. The pandemic may have been over, but the *totalitarian virus* had by no means disappeared.

CHAPTER EIGHT

How to Change the World

> The revolutionaries are those who know when power is lying in the street and when they can pick it up.
>
> —*Thoughts on Politics and Revolution*

C atching the sparkle of the sea light on the dust of its streets, loved for its bookshops, cafés, and ice-cream shops, creative and hospitable, the Hamra district of Beirut exudes a calm confidence about humanity even as, as is often the case in Lebanon's history, the grounds for that confidence can seem thin. In the late spring of 2019, a new mural appeared in Hamra on the wall of a parking lot on Cairo Street. It showed a woman wearing a red dress, sitting on a bench, absorbed in reading. Behind her shoulders, men opened their mouths and raised their fists demanding to be seen, heard, and reckoned with. The book the woman was reading was the Arabic translation of Hannah Arendt's *On Revolution*. Just five months after the mural first appeared, the people of Lebanon took to the streets and the 17 October 2019 Revolution— Lebanon's *thawra*—began.

When the mural's artist, Diana Al-Halabi, began thinking about what she wanted to depict on the walls of Hamra's main street, she told me that she had just one idea in mind: to paint a picture of a woman reading in public. She was inspired by the common experience in Beirut of having your bag searched. What if a woman had a book in her bag? she wondered. And what if that book was on revolution? What if that was her dangerous secret? Al-Halabi had not read any of Arendt's work before three friends advised her separately that the book in her mural had to be *On Revolution*. She has now. During the first months of Lebanon's revolution, images of Al-Halabi's mural went viral.[1]

There are no dangerous thoughts. Thinking itself is dangerous, Arendt teaches famously; but thinking by women, which she rarely men-

Woman reading On Revolution, *by Diana Al-Halabi, on Cairo Street, Hamra, Beirut.*

tioned, is perhaps especially dangerous; and not least when the subject of their thoughts is revolution.[2]

Working on *The Human Condition,* Arendt had begun her study of the tradition of political philosophy in earnest. Cicero, Machiavelli, John Locke, Thomas Hobbes, Edmund Burke, Montesquieu, Thomas Jefferson, John Adams, Thomas Paine, Jean-Jacques Rousseau, Alexis de Tocqueville, Karl Marx, Vladimir Lenin, Rosa Luxemburg: she read and reread them all at her desk in New York and in libraries across the United States and Europe, typing up neat pages of quotations, diligently and carefully, tracking the development of the mindset that had led, at worst, to totalitarianism and, at best, to insipid democracy and, just as determinedly, digging for evidence that another politics might still yet be possible. In the end, she concluded that it might be.

That conclusion owed as much to the wide-eyed attention of the twelve-year-old Hannah who had clasped her mother's hand as they marched together over the bridges of Königsberg on their way to a public meeting called in response to the Spartacist uprising of early January 1919, as it did to political philosophy. After the end of the First World War, the November Revolution had briefly suggested another future for Germany. Soon, however, the movement was divided. On one side was the Social Democratic Party of Germany which, bidding to preserve power, wanted reform within a parliamentary framework. On the other was the German Communist Party which urged complete and immediate revolution. Caught between them was the woman who Martha Arendt had brought her daughter out onto the streets to support,

Rosa Luxemburg; economist, former SDP member, communist, co-founder of the Spartacist League, the Polish-Jewish outsider, who had only recently been released from prison where she had been held for her implacable and vocal opposition to the war.

Luxemburg was not afraid of violent action. She believed that capitalism itself was a daily and continuous act of violence—the "monstrous" and "abnormal" conditions of poverty, servitude, hunger, and suffering—and had supported the Russian Revolution of 1905 on those grounds. Yet, before anything else her revolutionary impulse was rooted in the reality of people's lives, which she examined with the same attention as she had the bird- and garden-life that she famously cultivated during her prison years. *What mattered most in her view,* Arendt wrote, *was reality, in all its*

Rosa Luxemburg (1871–1919) addressing a meeting after the
Seventh International Social Democratic Congress, Stuttgart, 1907.

wonderful and all its frightful aspects, even more than revolution itself.[3]
The commitment to spontaneous revolutionary action for which
Luxemburg is famous begins with the reality of the ways that people act—real people, not political parties, ideologues, or even great
political philosophers—when they decide that enough is enough;
the slow violence, the intrusion, the struggle simply to survive.
"You know I could sense that something was coming," Diana
Al-Halabi said to me about how Lebanon felt in the summer of
2019, "the way animals can sense earthquakes."

Luxemburg cautioned that Germany's revolution was too
soon; it was not yet a people's revolution; more bloodshed, more
suffering would follow and, like the war that had just ended, it
would all be for nothing. She was overruled by her own party and
proved grotesquely correct. On January 15, 1919, the *Freikorps,*
veteran misogynistic thugs, who would later supply the emerging
Nazis with muscle, captured Luxemburg along with the Communist Party leader Karl Liebknecht. One smashed his rifle butt into
her skull, others then piled in, very probably beating her to death,
although when she was found five months later in the Landwehr
Canal she was also discovered to have a bullet wound in the back of
her head, just for murderous measure.

In the sham trial of the man wielding the rifle ("*attempted* man-
slaughter," sentenced to two years and two weeks) and the man in
charge when she was thrown into the canal ("illegal disposal of a
corpse," sentenced to just four months), a photograph showing the
men celebrating her murder the next day was presented as evidence, whereupon the defendants and their supporters burst out
laughing. In 1966, nearly fifty years after she and her mother had
marched together, Arendt would report this scene in a long review

of the first full-length biography of Rosa Luxemburg by British historian J. P. Nettl: *"Accused Runge, you must behave properly. This is no laughing matter,"* said the presiding judge. *Forty-five years later,* she added, during the trial in Frankfurt of the officials who had worked at Auschwitz, *a similar scene took place; the same words were spoken.*[4]

Arendt was an enthusiastic but cautious revolutionary. Enthusiastic, because along with Luxemburg, she believed that revolutions are the ultimate political new beginnings. Cautious, because she also understood how easily the most extraordinary collective action, which she prized, could turn into mass movements of violence and tyranny, which she despised. Too many revolutions ended with bodies floating under bridges and empty benches where women had once sat and read. Following Luxemburg, Arendt's challenge was to discover another kind of revolutionary history, one that might better instruct us in the politics of the future.

In the eighteenth century, revolution became an existential as well as a political event. This wasn't always the case. People have always rebelled, but only in modern times did the idea of perpetual change link up with a sense of the potential development of the self, and its dependent relations with other selves. Arendt talks about revolutions acquiring a pathos in the eighteenth century that they did not have before. "Pathos" comes from the Greek word meaning "to suffer." In the late seventeenth century, "pathos" slipped into also meaning any quality that aroused extreme pity: there was your suffering and the suffering of others; what was new was how the two got entwined. Historically speaking, human suffering turned politically theatrical.

People have always acted against oppression but with the

French Revolution, Arendt claimed, a powerful new historical narrative with the suffering of humanity at the center emerged. According to this revolutionary story, suffering is intolerable, change *has* to happen and will have to *keep* on happening in the name of humanity. The momentum of revolution was unstoppable: history, justice, and the human spirit itself demanded it. This was worldly love to be sure (it was her love of the world that led Arendt to study revolution in the first place) but she also thought it was love grotesquely perverted.

For Arendt, there was a grim paradox involved in setting a powerfully motivational idea—zero tolerance for suffering humanity—to run in human affairs. All at once, men and women became actors and agents in the history of revolution. Instead of the more stubborn tangles of public freedom, the necessity of history, Hegel's dream of the inevitable dialectic of human freedom, now drove the narrative. Rather than citizens in a new politics, revolutionaries started to see themselves as players in history; judging, acting, and making decisions *from the standpoint of the spectator who watches a spectacle* (OR 42).

In the case of the French Revolution, the theater was one of pure terror. A "spectacle that has fallen under the sign of Saturn," Georg Forster reported from Paris in 1793. But it was the Girondist Pierre Victurnien Vergniaud's words which were to scream down to the twentieth century with the most penetrating echo: "The revolution devouring its own children" (OR 39).

What had emerged was a kind of revolutionary thinking which—and a kind of revolutionary who—is fundamentally grandiose and narcissistic: lethally so, Arendt thought. Rosa Luxemburg was right to be more afraid of a cruelly *deformed revolution* than of a failed revolution, she wrote in her 1966 review. *Haven't events proved her right?* Hadn't Stalinism done more harm to the cause of revolution than any *honest defeat* might have done?[5]

As new calls for revolution went up in the 1960s, Arendt feared that Luxemburg's lesson had yet to be learned. Why? At least partly because Rosa Luxemburg was not only a brilliant theorist of imperialism and revolution but also a woman. Each generation of the "New Left" rediscovers Rosa Luxemburg, she observed in her review, finding hope in the nostalgic image of a woman who could charm revolutions into being the way she once famously charmed the birds off the trees. *But side by side with this glamorized image, there survived also the old clichés of the "quarrelsome female," a "romantic" who was neither "realistic" nor "scientific."* By the time they were forty, her fans invariably found a reason to drop Luxemburg in the same lazy sexist stereotypes in which they had rediscovered her.[6] The men of the Left also lined up to denounce Arendt's own book on revolution (the Marxist historian Eric Hobsbawm joined that rather long list of critics unable to spell Hannah in his lofty denunciation of her "preference for metaphysical construction or poetic feeling over reality").[7] She was *always out of step,* Arendt wrote of Luxemburg. So was she, but maybe that's just the way some revolutionaries walk?

For a brief twelve days in the autumn of 1956, it looked to Arendt like history might actually be shooting rainbows under the sign of Rosa Luxemburg. On October 23, students in Budapest protested against Hungary's Stalinist puppet government and its disastrous economic policies. Later that day, a few broke into the national radio station where they were then detained. When protesters gathered outside to demand the students' release, the secret police (ÁVH—Hungary's loathed State Protection Authority) arrived and opened fire, killing and wounding several. The Hungarian people responded and within twenty-four hours a student demonstration became a revolution.

Arendt, who was in Europe at the time, was ecstatic. It *is the best thing that has happened,* she wrote to Karl Jaspers from Münster, Germany (*AKJ* 306). The first images from Hungary published on the front pages of Western European and American broadsheets showed the toppling of the ridiculously large statue of Stalin from his concrete plinth in front of the national theater and smiling crowds surrounding the empty tanks stilled by the army's refusal to fire on their fellow citizens. It was as though the very concept of mass power itself was under attack. *If there was ever such a thing as Rosa Luxemburg's "spontaneous revolution," this sudden uprising of an entire people for the sake of freedom and nothing else,* she told a rapt student audience in Bremen when she returned to Germany a year later, then this is what they had seen in Hungary.[8]

Arendt is often criticized for the way that she idolized the American Revolution which, she believed, unlike the French version, kept the democratic promise of politics active. Yet this was nothing compared to how the Hungarian Revolution captured her imagination in 1956. America's revolution was history—*And when you look at what's left there now,* she once remarked: *What a come down!* (*AKJ* 357). Hungary's, like the Cuban revolution, which was also ongoing, was now: in the present. Far more than the anodyne social conformity of contemporary American democracy, Hungary suggested a genuinely new anti-totalitarian future.

Gloriously, in her view, people had taken a haphazard moment in Soviet history and turned it into a grab for freedom. The immediate political context for the uprising was the farce that followed the death of Stalin (Arendt would have appreciated the 2017 film of that title and judged its portrayal of the regime's ludic morbidity entirely accurate). Stalin's successor, Nikita Khrushchev, had given his famously not-so "Secret Speech" denouncing his predecessor in a closed session of the 20th Party Congress in February 1956. This was never intended as a dramatic *volte-face,* Arendt claimed, but was consistent with the traditions of self-criticism and inner purging that had characterized Communist Party politics since Lenin's death in 1924. But once the speech had been leaked to the West and then, by the backdoor, to Eastern Europe, that was how people in Hungary decided to interpret it: at face value; *against the speaker's intention,* Arendt reported delightedly, in a *catastrophic misunderstanding* they seized the words from another plot, took them as their treasure, and began something new.[9]

There was no grand historical narrative propelling Hungary's revolution. *The question was not how various freedoms should be approached,* she wrote—*it was how to stabilize a freedom that was already an accomplished fact.*[10] "The unity of the people did not express anything artificial, but rather expressed a fact in many forms," echoed activist Maya Ezz El Din in her description of Lebanon's 2019 revolution over sixty years later.[11] That revolution, like those of the Arab Spring in the early 2010s, Tiananmen Square in 1989, Hong Kong in March 2019, and Maidan, Ukraine, in 2014, also began with students and activists demonstrating in a public place (Martyr's Square, Beirut) and escalated rapidly when secret government security forces responded violently. Like the protesters in

Hungary, the Lebanese were fed up with economic policies dictated by foreign powers for the benefit of the country's elites. Wildfires had recently devastated a residential area to the south of Beirut and the Lebanese Civil Defense simply didn't have the resources to fight them. The government promptly and foolishly announced a new tech tax on WhatsApp, Facebook, and FaceTime calls in yet another attempt to bolster the country's catastrophic finances which was just as quickly interpreted as a tax on the freedom of speech, free expression, and communication.

Hungary's students occupied a radio station; three generations on, students in Beirut used their smartphones to light up the night sky in defiant concert. "The demonstrations are spontaneous and the intervention of parties in this movement is an insult. The protests must remain with the citizens," the footballer-turned-politician Pierre Issa announced on October 18, 2019.[12] Ironic selfies captioned with the words "I am the leader!" flashed across social media. "All of them means all of them," *"Kellon ya'ani kellon!"* went a popular slogan targeting all of Lebanon's political elites, including Hezbollah.

Freedom of speech is not a demand of these revolutions; it is their essence. What is being claimed is the *right to have rights*. Less a case of bread first then ethics, as in Bertolt Brecht's chilling dictum, the political ethos expressed in the discussion tents that sprang up in Beirut and Tripoli, as with the workers' councils in Hungary, was about speaking freely together to establish how best to get bread to all—and, in Lebanon's case, regular electricity, rubbish off the streets, and something like a functioning economy. "Electrification *and* Soviets," said Lenin of the 1917 revolution: end poverty *and* produce a new form of down-top, people-focused government. Arendt never tired of repeating Lenin's demand. Electricity and self-governance also pretty much summed up the basic demand on Lebanon's streets in 2019.

Political action is *fun*! Hannah Arendt declared, aged sixty-four, laughing, in a 1970 interview with the German journalist Adelbert Reif, referring to the student activists of the late 1960s. She was quite serious. Active, participatory, public political life opens up *a dimension of human experience that otherwise remains closed* to us, she explained.[13] Bad political systems are not only unjust and cruel: because they deny us the right to make our own rights, they also deny us an essential part of our existence. Fun, "public happiness," as it was called in the eighteenth century, the joy of genuine political participation, connects us with an experience which, until we encounter it, is felt only as a dull absence—a waiting. It is not (or not simply) rage which is let loose in revolutions but something more precious: the opening up of human experience, of a life lived amidst the voices and echoes of others, where change is always possible. Have fun, Arendt urged the students of the 1960s; have as much fun as you possibly can.

Real freedom—and I have come to think this is Hannah Arendt's central political insight—requires the presence of others so that we can test our sense of reality against their views and lives, make judgments, probe, and learn. As for Nietzsche who she follows in this matter, for Arendt, courageous agonism, conflict without resolution but with mutual respect for one another, should drive politics. This kind of freedom does not happen in the dark but needs a place *where people could come together—the agora, the market-place, or the polis, the political space proper* as equals, to object, protest, imagine (*OR* 21). The revolutions she dreamed of shone a new light on these places, allowing people to take their own shapes as they emerged from the darkness.

The Hungarian Revolution failed. On November 4, Soviet tanks entered Budapest. In New York, Arendt read the reports with dismay: 2,140 people executed, 55,000 put into Hungarian prisons, and 75,000 deported to the east.[14] The biggest European refugee crisis since the war followed. The councils, the freedom, and the bid for a fully political life were all crushed. On August 4, 2020, a confiscated cargo of ammonium nitrate exploded in Beirut's docks, killing 218 people and leaving at least 300,000 more homeless. The blast nearly killed off what little hope a long battle of attrition and Covid-19 had left untouched: Lebanon's *thawra* is unfinished.

Arendt was devastated by the suppression in Hungary but also more politically excited than she had been for years. The United States and Western Europe had been happy to give their enthusiastic support to Hungary's revolutionaries, but only from a distance, and in the end so far away as to be useless. The only *intervention that could have really aided the Hungarian Revolution could have come from those battalions of volunteers all over the world who are genuinely prepared to fight for nothing but freedom itself,* such as was attempted with Spain in 1936, she told her student audience in Bremen a year later. Solidarity without borders, urged the former refugee from fascism, was what was needed, but was absent. When governments fail, people must step in.

The essay in which she finally gave her account of the Hungarian Revolution was one of her most impassioned and revealing pieces of political writing since *The Origins of Totalitarianism*. The revolution had been crushed, but just as Kant had argued that the

French Revolution should not be judged on its immediate consequences but by the way its example would resonate across history,
so, too, did Arendt believe that Hungary would remain significant
for how it was remembered. The image with which she chose to
illustrate this thought was one of women in the streets. On October 23, 1957, one year after their defeat, the people of Budapest
defied the government's prohibition against public demonstrations. *We still see the silent procession of black-clad women in the streets of
Russian-occupied Budapest, mourning the dead of the revolution in public,*
she wrote. We *still see* and will keep on seeing, she meant; the
women were ensuring that *memory kept circulating* even as the revolution had failed.[15]

Writing on October 19, 2020, Rima Majed, an activist and
professor of sociology at the American University of Beirut in
Hamra, refused to commemorate the first anniversary of Lebanon's
revolution: "we need not become prisoners to the concepts of time
and date that are imposed upon us," she wrote.[16]

Arendt wanted to dedicate her essay on Hungary to Rosa
Luxemburg—to keep her memory circulating—but her German
publisher, Klaus Piper, was nervous about how that might appear
to readers in West Germany and suggested a few words to distance
Luxemburg from the current Soviet regime. She pushed back: if
you needed to explain why Luxemburg was different from the Soviets, the whole point of the dedication would be ruined—you
can't qualify a gesture. *Poor Rosa! She has been dead now for forty years,
and still falls between all stools,* she concluded.[17] The time was still not
right.

Arendt was naïve about the Hungarian Revolution and she
knew it. She initially added an epilogue on Hungary to a new edition of *The Origins of Totalitarianism* to show how it might be pos-

sible to beat the terror and the loneliness but later withdrew it. The public beatings and gruesome hangings of ÁVH members were neither as just nor discriminate as she had first imagined. Nationalism and anti-semitism had played their part in the revolution too. Yet by the 1950s, she also understood that disappointment was the better part of political hope. Far better in the end, she would have reminded herself, a failed revolution than a deformed one.

In the bitter cold of early January 1919, Martha Arendt clasped her daughter's gloved hand as they ran laughing through the streets of Königsberg. "You must pay attention, this is a historical moment!" she shouted to her child. Hannah Arendt did—and then she never stopped.[18] Her biographer, Elisabeth Young-Bruehl, speculates that the 1966 essay on Rosa Luxemburg was also a belated love letter to Martha, who had died in 1948 on a ship sailing for England leaving an America that had made her miserable.[19] Try as she might, Arendt could not compensate for the losses that her mother had endured. Sad and guilty, she arranged for the Jewish prayer of mourning, the *Kaddish,* to be recited in England—far away from Königsberg and their past life. Young-Bruehl suggests that in her essay Arendt wanted to honor both women's capacity for loyalty, but I don't think it was just that. In their different ways, both Luxemburg and her mother taught her to grab life as it was really lived; not to dream in the abstractions of others, but seize those rare moments when, as you run out into the street, you realize that something is happening, something that could change absolutely everything.

In 1788 James Madison argued that America's new federal government needed a national capital to secure its authority. Two years later, President George Washington sent surveyors onto the lands of the Piscataway people to map out ten square miles in the mud marshes of the Potomac River. Revolutions, Arendt remarked, are frequently built on quicksand (*OR* 154). Lying in crisp snow or crystalline against that apparently ever-sharp blue sky, to the foreigner from a distance Washington, DC, often appears too shiny and white to quite be true. Once you get there, it takes about a minute to realize that the capital is far smaller than the image it projects to the world.

On Revolution was published in 1963—the most tumultuous year so far in the civil rights movement's struggle in the United States. The year began with protests against segregation in Birmingham, Alabama, and the imprisonment of Martin Luther King Jr. In the late spring, the Children's Crusade marched through the streets and up to the doors of schools and universities blocked by Dixiecrats. On August 28, more than 200,000 people came to Washington to demand "jobs and freedom" and King delivered his "I Have a Dream" speech. In September, four children, Addie Mae Collins, Carol Denise McNair, Cynthia Dionne Wesley, and Carole Rosamond Robertson, were murdered in a white supremacist terrorist attack on the 16th Street Baptist Church in Birmingham. The Civil Rights Act would follow in 1964.

This should have been the exact moment to make a new case for the American Revolution, or even better perhaps, a new American Revolution. But in 1963, Arendt was living in another time and place. Eichmann's trial in 1961 had sent her spinning backward through history to Nazi Europe. The backlash against her reports from Jerusalem had left her feeling bruised and alone. Her best friends remained close, but others, such as Hans Jonas from Mar-

burg, had fallen silent. She was almost fifty-seven, still tired after
her accident and worried about Heinrich Blücher's health following his aneurysm in 1962. With the exception of her return to Europe and visits to Italy, Athens, and Aegina in April, 1963 was
quite possibly the worst year of Hannah Arendt's life since she was
herded onto a train in Paris and sent to Gurs camp in 1940.

Revolutions are built on quicksand for the best and worst of
reasons. The best reason is that they arise from the spontaneous
actions of people which may—or may not—build new foundations for living on. Contingency is built into Arendt's version of
an enduring revolutionary republic. The survival of any political
community is only as good as the contracts and promises that people make between one another and as powerful or flimsy as those
might be at any given moment. America's *constitution worship,* she
observed, was a historically novel and admirable way of keeping
the memory of its revolutionary foundations in active political cir-
culation (*OR* 196).

The worst reason is that the same revolutionary promise might
be swept away by narratives made from empty, but lethal, abstractions. What, Arendt frequently asked, is the "will of the people" if
not a collective noun with the potential to eradicate plurality? Pay
attention.

Revolutions are storytelling events; in modern history they are
perhaps the ultimate political storytelling events. The story Arendt
told about America in *On Revolution* was pretty much a whites-
only story. "It is a strange phenomenon in all American writing,"
wrote the Palestinian writer Khayri Hammad, in a note on his
1964 translation of *On Revolution* into Arabic: "They talk about
their land as if it was empty and not inhabited by indigenous peo-

ples," as though the foundation of Washington were the second coming of Rome ("The general feeling is that the Vandals are coming to sack Rome," reported the *Washington Daily News* ahead of the Freedom March in August 1963).[20]

In Arendt's story, America's revolution (unlike that of France) was spared the horrors of bloody absolutism because the colonies were also spared the horrors of immiseration that plagued Europe in the eighteenth century. *The women on their march to Versailles,* she said, quoting British historian Lord Acton, *played the genuine part of mothers whose children were starving.* Because *stark naked poverty* was so extreme in France, so, too, were its solutions. *"Les malheureux sont les puissance de le terre"* cried the young Louis Antoine de Saint-Just, Robespierre's right-hand man; "the wretched are the power of the earth." The power of sheer human necessity became sheer terror in the effort to *regulate economic questions by force.*[21] The suffering would stop or it would be made to stop. Arendt never claimed, as she is sometimes misread as saying, that poverty or economics were unimportant to progressive politics. She simply understood that you have a better chance of establishing a republic based on public reason and not violence if people are not living in a constant state of physical and mental pain. Suffering has a way of canceling out argument. Bread first and then ethics.

In Europe, the "wretched" became the multitudes in whose name the nation became a new political absolute. The more fortunate America, in Arendt's somewhat partisan telling, was spared this fate. The apparent abundance of land kept wealth in prospect and so poverty in check. The colonial settlements contained the embryonic federal system that would eventually put political power into communities. If this all reads like a founding mythology of white freedom, this is because that is exactly what it was. Arendt knew this, but also consistently understated the racial violence of America's founding moment. We *are tempted to ask ourselves,* she wrote in *On Revolution, if the goodness of the poor white man's country did not depend to a considerable degree on black labor* (*OR* 60). Tempting indeed.

She knew perfectly well that it was not true that there was no extreme suffering in America. *Abject and degrading misery was present everywhere in the form of slavery and Negro labor,* she also wrote. However, this misery did not figure in her account because she assumed that it did not really figure in America's sense of its revolution either. Up to a point, she criticized this omission. Elsewhere, modern revolutions had made human suffering the theater in which they were performed. By contrast, slavery, which she described as the *primordial crime* on which *the fabric of American society rested,* did not appear to be part of the spectacle of the revolution at all. *From this, we can only conclude that the institution of slavery obscurity is even blacker than the obscurity of poverty; the slave, not the poor man, was "wholly overlooked"* (*OR* 60–61). America's revolution was deformed from the beginning.

But Arendt was also content to leave slavery in historical obscurity. Just as she did not see Elizabeth Eckford in 1957, nor the Khoikhoi people in South Africa in 1946, neither did she account for the impact of the thirteen long years of the Haitian Revolution (1791–1804) in her history of modern revolutions, nor, indeed, any number of slave rebellions that showed men and women fighting their way out of *dark obscurity* to take the shape of the courageous and active citizens she so prized.

By 1963 it was impossible to overlook the consequences of

America's deformed revolution any longer. That autumn she returned to the University of Chicago where she took refuge from
the Eichmann affair by teaching the smart students on the Committee on Social Thought program. The ever-solicitous Hans
Morgenthau had arranged her accommodation in the Quadrangle
Club. He had opted for an elegant suite which, while lacking a sofa
on which visitors could sit, had a large desk resembling Arendt's
own in her Riverside Drive apartment. "I took the one with the
nice desk assuming that your interests are more likely to be intellectual than social," he wrote to her.[22] It was a safe assumption.
Several colleagues appeared to snub her in the wake of her Eichmann reports, including the novelist Saul Bellow, who she had
previously counted as a friend. Morgenthau made sure he was
around at lunchtime so that she did not have to eat alone.

As she sat behind her desk, across America citizens were doing
the thing she most valued about the legacy of the American Revolution: acting to secure the authority of the constitution by
insisting—yet again—that it align with the democratic demands
and aspirations of the republic. Throughout the autumn semester
of 1963, tens of thousands of people, including her own students,
were boycotting Chicago's public schools in protest against the
segregationist dumping of Black children in overcrowded and inadequate classrooms, including freezing tin huts in playgrounds.
(Just a year earlier, a University of Chicago student named Bernie
Sanders had organized a student sit-in to protest the same.) The
promise made by *Brown v. Board of Education,* along with the Fourteenth Amendment, must be kept.

Chicago's own Freedom Day was held on October 22, 1963.
Two days later, Arendt stepped out from behind her desk to de-

bate the meaning of revolution with her colleague, the historian Louis R. Gottschalk, at a special event organized by UNESCO. Gottschalk was an expert on the French Revolution and Lafayette, who had fought in the American Revolution before returning to France to play a key role in the French. *Freedom* was the word missing from Gottschalk's history of revolution, she began. You could not open a newspaper, move through the corridors of the university, let alone the city's streets, without seeing the word *freedom* that week in October. Freedom was screaming in Chicago, and she knew it. Freedom to participate in your own government, she continued, to have dignity, to be a citizen and not a subject; that was the essence of revolution and that was precisely why now, she added, across the South, Black revolutionaries were schooling their fellow citizens on the true meaning of 1776.

A pause, perhaps to light that cigarette, which had by now become her first line of public defense when she knew things were about to get tricky.

But it was different in the North, she went on, where the revolution was less political than social, and where the demand for an end to extreme inequality risked turning revolutionary power into violent force. She named the formidable Cecil B. Moore, a criminal lawyer and president of Philadelphia's NAACP, who had no problem with meeting the organized violence of the city authorities with the organized violence of the unions. Moore was untapping something, she suggested, something that resembled the same lethal pathos that had turned the French Revolution into a bloodbath.

Arendt would repeatedly associate Black activism with revolutionary violence in the 1960s and early 1970s. *Hatred and love belong together, and they are both destructive; you can afford them only in private and, as a people, only so long as you are not free,* she had written to James Baldwin a year earlier in 1962. But she had missed Baldwin's real point in *The Fire Next Time:* Black action was always framed by whiteness in the United States. How was it possible for anybody to be free so long as white people projected their own dark fears about themselves (the most unspeakable darkness of all in America's history) onto Black people? That was Baldwin's challenge.

In the end, Arendt concluded that America had not lived up to its revolutionary promise. There was always a fateful ambivalence about the kind of freedom at stake in the republic. Was its legacy the liberty to pursue happiness *free from* governance? Or was the happiness of *collective* self-governance to be its true treasure? If you really believed that America was the land of natural wealth and endless opportunity you could take this question at face value, indeed it is one of the oldest questions in political philosophy. But if you define freedom chiefly as economic prosperity, which she argued was what swiftly happened in America, then the horizons of freedom quickly turned dull. The noble idea of public freedom withdrew *into the inward domain of consciousness,* she wrote in *On Revolution* (*OR* 131). Individualism and the *monstrous* (her word) belief that capitalism produces unbridled freedom had led to *unhappiness and mass poverty*. These were the *ravages with which American prosperity and American mass society increasingly threatened the whole political realm* (*OR* 209).

By the early 1960s, American society resembled the situation she had left behind in Europe twenty years before: social atomization and political purposelessness had expanded a void ready to be filled, or rather refilled, with racist fury. For it was not, of course, the social revolutionaries of the North who were blowing up children, lynching university students, spitting in the faces of clergy, and declaring themselves the "multitude" whose ethnic rights overrode the constitution, but American fascists in the South. We must perhaps worry about the political virtues of the grassroots organizations that keep America non-authoritarian, she admitted two years later, when we remember that the Ku Klux Klan is also one such association.[23]

On the evening of January 6, 2021, I sat down for a regular lockdown Zoom chat with the historian Sarah Churchwell. Minutes before, news of the mob breaking into the Capitol had started to come through. "You seem to be having a coup in your country, Sarah," I said. "That we do," she replied, not sounding surprised. Churchwell had devoted a lot of time to studying the cultural legacies of American fascism since the election of Donald Trump in 2016. Our eyes flickered to the CNN live feed we both had running in the corner of our screens and then back again to our faces, attempting to lock gazes. The inability to know when you are looking directly at one another on Zoom has literalized the screwed optics of our current politics: do you see me, we ask, and, more urgently, are we looking at the same damn thing?

What we were looking at that day at first seemed like a violently drunken Halloween party at which the parents had dressed up—as revolutionaries, Confederates, one very un-cute jackalope—and left the kids, along with their sanity, at home. "Despite its violence," Jamelle Bouie noted in *The New York Times* two days later, "the mob on Wednesday was, in many respects, very silly . . .

But a lark can still have serious consequences."[24] Washington, DC, may always have been smaller than the image it liked to project, but now it looked achingly vulnerable. The doors of the Capitol crashed as though they were made of balsa wood on a B-movie horror set; for the longest time it looked as though nobody was going to stop the zombies from finding their prey.

The lark turned out, in the words of political journalist Sidney Blumenthal, to be "the most serious sedition against the constitutional order since secession."[25] A month earlier, on December 12, 2020, the Proud Boys, Donald Trump's own army of misogynist thugs, had rampaged through Washington, DC, looking to incite the kind of violence that would give him the pretext to invoke the Insurrection Act as a prelude to a far from spontaneous but carefully planned coup to overthrow the patently legitimate election of Joe Biden. "Seventeen seventy-six!" cried the man-children repeatedly, "our house!" as they swaggered out of their comfortable hotels into the bright winter sun in what *The Washington Post* described as a "falsehood-filled spectacle," flashing knives, attempting to march in step.[26] Somehow, they did not exactly look as though they were having fun.

I don't accept fascist revolutions as revolutions, Arendt said in her final remarks in the UNESCO talk of October 1963; *because [the] element of freedom is altogether lost. But also because the notion of founding something new and stable, a new house, has been lost.* "Our house!" they screamed, but in reality, all America's pseudo-revolutionaries had to offer was their destructive outrage. If it's not our house, then we'll tear it down. *A permanent revolution,* Arendt concluded, *is either a contradiction in terms or totalitarianism.* She had so very much wanted the quicksand of America to be less viscous than the mud that had sunk Europe. But it never was to begin with, it certainly was not in 1963, and, perhaps, is even less so now.

A woman reads a book alone on a bench, thinking about revolution. Behind her, an actual revolution is taking place. She could be Hannah Arendt at any moment of her life. How to think in solitude while responding to the events happening around us was one of her abiding questions.

Just before she left for Jerusalem in 1961, Arendt published a collection of six essays, entitled *Between Past and Future*. It was her personal favorite of her books and, scholar Jens Hanssen tells us, alongside *On Revolution,* was also the only other of her works to be translated into Arabic before the end of the Cold War coincided with the end of Lebanon's civil war in 1990.[27]

The preface to that book, "The Gap Between Past and Future," is a short, dense, experimental piece of prose, and is one of my favorites among Arendt's writings. Each time I read it I feel both as though I am back in the twentieth century with Hannah Arendt, battering against its darkness, and as though I have never read this text before in my life, as though its words are pulling me into a future we are perhaps only now on the brink of imagining.

She begins by quoting an aphorism written by a friend from her refugee years in Paris, the poet René Char. It reads: "*Notre héritage n'est précédé d'aucun testament,*" which Arendt translates as *our inheritance was left to us by no testament* and describes as *strange* and *strangely abrupt* (*BPF* 4). Char had spent the war fighting with the French resistance. Freedom, Arendt says, is what is so strangely condensed in his words. "At every meal we eat together," Char wrote in another aphorism, "freedom is invited to sit down. The chair remains vacant, but the place is set" (*BPF* 4).

Does something exist, not in outer space but in the world and in the affairs of men on earth, which has not even a name? she asks next. What is this strange kind of freedom we are waiting to join us at the table? Freedom has not one but many names. In America in 1776 it was called "public happiness," in 1789 the French called it "public freedom." They called it "*Kellon ya'ani Kellon!*" in Lebanon in 2019. In 2022 it was called "*Jin, Jiyan, Azadi*" (Woman, Life, Freedom) in Iran and Kurdistan, and "*Slava Ukraini*" in Ukraine. When activists shouted, "I can't breathe," quoting George Floyd's dying words in 2020, they were also putting the demand for freedom into new words.

Arendt's point is that there is no one form or name for freedom that can easily be passed down through the generations. *Our inheritance was left to us by no testament.* There is no *testament,* says Char, no testimony, no narrative form for this experience. There is no freedom manual. Freedom lands differently each time, or it does not land at all.

But there is still our "inheritance." Freedom does not happen in a historical vacuum. The dead leave their "wills"—they want us to act, by using our wills. When we act for the future, we are also meeting our obligations to the past. This sense of being within a long political tradition of freedom was also very important to Hannah Arendt.

Sixty years ago, a woman, a refugee from totalitarianism, wrote a book on revolution. Hannah Arendt is now part of our inheritance. Now another woman carries that book in her handbag. She is in Beirut, but she could also be in Iran or Afghanistan.

She could be in Minsk, Belarus, Moscow, or Texas. She could be anywhere in the world where women have had enough. The book is her secret. In its pages she reads about how the most unexpected events can suddenly prompt people to step out of the shadows. She cannot put the book down. She takes it out into the streets, through the security checkpoints, and sits reading on a bench in the sunlight. Hours later, she looks up from her reading to find that her city is different; something is happening; a rainbow shoots across the sky. This is a historical moment, she whispers to herself: pay attention!

CHAPTER NINE

Who Am I to Judge?

> Best of all will be those who know only one thing
> for certain: that whatever else happens, as long as we
> live we shall have to live together with ourselves.
> —*Personal Responsibility Under Dictatorship*

O n May 23, 1960, the prime minister of Israel, David Ben-
Gurion, announced in the Knesset (Israel's Parliament) that
"one of the greatest of the Nazi war criminals, Adolf Eichmann,
responsible together with the Nazi leaders for what they called the
final solution of the Jewish question, that is the extermination of
6,000,000 of the Jews of Europe," had been caught by Mossad and
was now in the country where he would be tried under Israel's
"Nazi and Nazi Collaborators (Punishment) Law" at a yet to be
specified date.[1] At that point it was not widely known that Eichmann had been captured in Argentina, although as the prime minister spoke, the Argentine government was making its displeasure
about that fact known in diplomatic circles.

Straightaway, the rumors and counter rumors that had been a
characteristic of his life began. Eichmann was a pure-blooded Nazi

born in Germany, "Aryan" to the tips of his fingers. No. He was actually born near Tel Aviv which accounted for his intimate knowledge of the "Jewish question." He spoke Hebrew and Yiddish fluently. He was sophisticated, a student of theology and well-read in philosophy. No. He was a violent brute, an ignorant, cynical drunk, and an inveterate womanizer. He was now diminished, a small man who had been living an unassuming and hard-working life as a devoted husband and father in constant terror of capture for the past fifteen years. He was now a "baby-faced" goon, with a sinister curled lip, who had had plastic surgery to alter his features. One of his many mistresses had betrayed him.[2] He had been hiding in Kuwait, Cairo, Germany, Austria, South America . . .

Hannah Arendt read everything she could find on the case while she waited for the diplomatic wrangling between Israel and Argentina to conclude and for the announcement of a trial date. Three weeks later, she made her offer to William Shawn to cover the trial for *The New Yorker* and began preparations for her trip to Jerusalem in the April of the following year. When they were eventually published, her five reports on the trial transformed Hannah Arendt from a political theorist and noted public intellectual into a figure of notoriety. To this day, the Eichmann affair hovers like a brown cloud over her writing and reputation. Why?

The Eichmann trial was not just about the man Adolf Eichmann; indeed, for all his notoriety and vain self-importance it was perhaps only minimally about Adolf Eichmann. It was *the* Holocaust trial of the century. Since Nuremberg, Nazi atrocity trials had been organized across Europe. Yet no country or international organization had directly addressed the Third Reich's biggest and most monstrous crime: the genocide of the Jewish people.

Screened nightly on American television (Israel was still too poor for a television in every house) and reported on regularly across the world, the Eichmann trial was the global media event that finally pushed the Holocaust under the nose of public opinion. For survivors and relatives, the trial was devastating. Each family had its stories, many had their private terrors, memories, and secrets, but the suffering and violence of the genocide had never been represented publicly on this scale before. In Israel and the United States especially, people were floored by what they heard, not only those, like Arendt, who had had direct experience of the Third Reich, but second-generation survivors and others whose immediate lives had so far been untouched by events. A "great collective dirge was acted out," Susan Sontag wrote. "Masses of facts about the extermination of the Jews piled into the record; a great outcry of historical agony was set down. There was, needless to say, no strictly legal way of justifying this. The function of the trial was like that of the tragic drama: above and beyond judgment and punishment, catharsis."[3]

From the very beginning, Arendt distrusted the trial's theater. Adolf Eichmann's murderous policies had pursued her across the borders of Europe. Without his monstrous example, she would never have been the anti-totalitarian thinker she was. Now it was her turn to pursue him; she did so with a deliberate and studied detachment. She would always maintain that she went to Jerusalem as a reporter. Her job, as she saw it, was to collate the facts from the mountain of court transcripts, witness statements, historical records, and legal judgments that bulged out of her suitcase in Jerusalem and spilled out onto her desk on Riverside Drive upon her return to New York. Had that been all that she had done, however, *Eichmann in Jerusalem* would hardly have caused the scandal it did. Far from being a straightforward piece of reportage, the reports were Hannah Arendt's most audacious experiment yet in political imagination.

Eichmann in Jerusalem is a portrait of a new kind of criminal, and a history of the political and historical context that allowed him to kill. Eichmann's crime was not just against the Jewish people, but against the human condition itself, its rich plurality, complexity, and enduringness. The problem, as Arendt came to see it, was that neither the court nor Eichmann himself understood that a new kind of murderer stood in the dock. Back in 1945, she and Karl Jaspers had discussed whether Nazi totalitarianism had ripped apart moral and legal categories irreparably. Sixteen years on, it seemed that the world was no closer to comprehending that a new category-defying kind of evil had insinuated its way into history: a banal kind of evil, as she famously put it.

As historians have shown, Eichmann had decided that playing the part of a mindless bureaucrat, an ordinary man who was guilty only ever insofar as he was following orders, was his best chance of appearing innocent. It is often claimed that because she saw him as banal, Arendt had fallen for this performance. Worse still, that she had also taken at face value some of his most grotesque self-exculpating stories: about how he admired Zionism, hated violence, and had even worked with Jewish leaders to mitigate (his own) murderous policies. The collaboration point was particularly sensitive. It was not that collusion was news, certainly not in Israel where, in 1954, Rudolf Kastner, the former chairman of the Jewish Rescue Committee in Hungary, unsuccessfully brought a libel case against a survivor who accused him of doing a deal with Eichmann to exchange war materials for the lives of the Jews of his hometown (Kastner was assassinated not long after). Arendt was unsparing, and not always accurate, in her accounts of collaboration. When she charged the much-respected progressive rabbi Leo Baeck of misleading his congregation in Theresienstadt about what awaited them, many readers thought, with good reason, that she had gone too far.

Arendt *did* think that Eichmann was banal. She also believed it was important to understand that Nazism had corrupted everyone it touched. Crimes against humanity, in her view, were not just against bodies, but against everybody's morality. Mass murder on this scale can only work by disabling moral choices. But not for a moment did she believe Eichmann was innocent. Because he was banal it did *not* follow that he was not evil. What astounded her in Jerusalem was the breathtaking thoughtlessness with which Eichmann described his crimes. *He merely, to put the matter colloquially, never realized what he was doing,* she writes in the postscript to *Eichmann in Jerusalem*. It is an outrageous sentence if read at face value (*EJ* 287). Of course Eichmann knew what he was doing! Arendt meant that he never grasped *morally* or, what amounts to the same thing for her, *imaginatively* the *reality* of what he was doing. He executed the obscenest crime of the century without even giving his victims the courtesy of being invested in their murder. That was the true horror.

The scandal caused by her book partly came from how Arendt chose to present her thesis. A critical, cutting, and consistent irony was her response to Eichmann's murderous thoughtlessness. There is a tradition of ironic writing in post-Holocaust literature. Commenting on the prose of the survivor Jean Améry, W. G. Sebald noted that irony "operates on the edge of what language can convey."[4] When words fail, simply repeating what *was* said marks the point where the moral imagination can go no further. Remember Arendt quoting David Rousset's exchange with a guard in Auschwitz in *The Origins of Totalitarianism:* "For what purpose, may I ask do the gas chambers exist?" "For what purpose were you born?" (*OT* 579). Lifted from their first context, the meanings of words can be interrogated, made to echo and resonate, judged. Irony in this sense is a kind of two-in-one conversation on the page. But what many read, or heard, in *Eichmann in Jerusalem* was not moral irony, but ironic contempt.

You lack *Herzenstakt,* Hannah, Gershom Scholem complained, "tact of the heart" (*AGS* 202). *It's really not my fault if you didn't understand the irony of my language, which through indirect speech I made crystal clear,* she responded (*AGS* 207). Arendt's irony did not land with readers in the way she assumed it would. Instead, the echoes created a space for doubt and something else slipped into view, something that many found intuitively repulsive. "Your wording reveals that you are accusing the victim, even though you are only intending to describe," wrote Robert Weltsch, an old friend from her days campaigning for a binational Palestine, in a long and careful letter.[5] As Robert Lowell put it after her death, "Hannah's rage against Eichmann's mediocrity was itself enraging."[6] Hannah Arendt wrote *Eichmann in Jerusalem* in the way she did because she wanted to force an encounter with the moral and political wreckage of the Holocaust. The tragedy was that few were ready for that encounter, at least not on her terms, and her boldest experiment in political imagination was in many respects her least politically successful.

Bezalel Street, Jerusalem, by Stahv Shayo, 2021.

Her rage began the moment she entered the city of Jerusalem. It was unusually chilly in April 1961, but to Arendt everything was hot and bothersome. The hotels and bars were crammed with Germans, one of whom threw his arms around her sobbing loudly: "We are the ones who did this" (*WFW* 355). *Outside the courtroom clustered an oriental mob, as if one were in Istanbul, or some other half-Asiatic country,* she fussed in appallingly racist haute européene to Karl Jaspers. *Everything is organized by a police force that gives me the creeps, speaks only Hebrew and looks Arabic. Some downright brutal types among them* (*AKJ* 435). She had come in search of her German-

Jewish past, the law, and a reconciliation with history. What she found was poverty, emotional excess, and her own demons.

She moved from her hotel in the city center as soon as she could, up the hills and into the trees, clear air, and wider streets surrounding the Hebrew University. Her friend Judah Magnes, with whom she had worked in the 1940s in the campaign for a binational Palestine, had been one of the university's founders, its first chancellor, and from 1935 its president. He had died in New York in October 1948. The campus suburb in which she found refuge in the spring of 1961 was not the one he had helped found in East Jerusalem in 1918. That had been closed by the Jordanians in 1948 after the war. Like her hotel, the new campus, completed in 1958, was built on fields that had once belonged to the Palestinian village of Lifta.

The courtroom was also a new building. There was no suitable national court in Jerusalem at that time. But you could not try Adolf Eichmann in Tel Aviv or Haifa. Historical symbolism and Israeli nationalism demanded Jerusalem. A courtroom specifically designed to accommodate cameras, microphones, and the press, as well as Eichmann's iconic bulletproof glass box, was constructed at the newly completed *Beit Ha'am,* or People's House, on Bezalel Street. This was Jerusalem's new cultural center. Eichmann's courtroom *was* a theater. Three days after the trial commenced, *Life* magazine ran a series of intimate photographs showing Eichmann in his prison cell, washing, reading, eating, talking with his guards, and walking in the small, improvised exercise yard outside in his slippers. No European Jews were permitted to guard him for fear that they would take justice into their own hands. The *downright brutal types* had been commissioned because they could be trusted not to be downright brutal. Among them was a Yemenite named Shalom Nagar who would eventually draw the lot to become Eichmann's hangman.

The trial began on April 11, 1961. The three judges, Benjamin Halevi, Moshe Landau, and Yitzhak Raveh, sat behind a long desk on a dais at the front of the room, the prosecution, defense, and defendant before them. The camera lights glared. The world's press had gathered, headphones clamped to their ears as a team of translators busily traded words in the wings. The court's official language was Hebrew, which Arendt, again irritated, thought was absurd given that nearly all participants spoke German flu-

Nazi war criminal Adolf Eichmann pacing in exercise yard outside his cell at Djalameh Jail.

ently. *It was not the language that went crazy,* she said in an interview with Gunter Gaus in 1964, explaining her lifelong attachment to German.[7] But as she was soon to discover, in Eichmann's case, it had.

The court's official language was abandoned on two occasions. First, when a survivor insisted on speaking the language which the new State of Israel associated with the timidity and vulnerability of Jewish Europe, Yiddish. Second, when the judges, exasperated with having to listen to Eichmann's torturous self-justifications, addressed him directly in German. "We know that in German, the predicate comes at the end of the sentence, but it takes too long to reach the predicate," Judge Moshe Landau quipped despairingly at one point.[8] Eichmann liked to pretend that he was fluent in both Yiddish and Hebrew. He wasn't, of course, but as the historian Bettina Stangneth in her superb biography, *Eichmann Before Jerusalem*, demonstrates, shameless self-fashioning was Adolf Eichmann's greatest, perhaps his only real, talent.

And then, there he was before her, the cunning architect of what Arendt had once described as *radical evil,* sitting in his glass box and shuffling his papers self-importantly in front of him (conspicuous paper shuffling was central to his performance as the guileless bureaucrat) *like a ghost that happens to have a cold, in his glass cage . . . nicht einmal unheimlich*—not even uncanny, she wrote to Blücher (*WFW* 355). There was a mismatch between the man's appearance and the monstrosity of his crime.

The first week of the trial was bogged down by wrangling over matters of jurisdiction. The press became restless. They had come for historical drama but what they got was lawyerly procedure conducted in an airless concrete building. Some went home. Then, on April 17, Eichmann stood up in his box to enter his pleas. He was charged with fifteen crimes against the Jewish people and crimes against humanity. He pleaded "not guilty in the sense of" to every indictment he was charged with. It never would become clear exactly in what sense Eichmann did think he was guilty. He would variously claim: to have a clear conscience because he had no choice but to obey his superiors' commands; to be a zealous Kantian who tenaciously clung to the categorical imperative (even as it unfortunately appeared to be misplaced as Hitler's will); to be a model repentant for a crime of which he was only just beginning to realize the scale; and on the gallows, a committed Nazi, defiantly and pompously unrepentant. He told the judges he planned to write a book on the tricky philosophical and historical nature of his guilt. He didn't, thank goodness, get the opportunity, and Hannah Arendt wrote it for him.

Later that same day, Gideon Hausner, the state attorney general, opened for the prosecution. "When I stand before you here, judges of Israel, in this court, to accuse Adolf Eichmann, I do not stand alone. With me stand six million prosecutors," he began, and then over the ten sessions that followed, detailed the persecution of the Jews in a sweeping narrative arc that began with the pharaohs and concluded with the man in the glass box. *Bad history and cheap rhetoric,* Arendt bristled (*EJ* 19). If anti-semitism was the main story, what was it exactly that was specific to Eichmann's crime? Was Eichmann *only an innocent executor of some mysteriously foreordained destiny* decreed by a timeless hatred of Jews (*EJ* 20)? The weather turned, and the courtroom began to heat up.

The witnesses for the prosecution began the next day. These included experts, such as her friend Salo Baron, the eminent historian of Jewish history, as well as documentary and witness testimony from abroad. This evidence, detailed, meticulous, and comprehensive, showed how Eichmann had moved from arranging the deportation of Jews out of Europe in the late 1930s to arranging their mass murder after 1942. The prosecution introduced a crucial legal innovation to the trial and to legal history: the spoken testimonies of survivors. Only a handful of Jewish witnesses had been heard at the Nuremberg trials. There was enough anti-semitism in the Allies' legal backrooms to worry about the testimonies of "vengeful Jews" undermining the prosecution's case. There was also the anxiety that the Nuremberg court might find it as hard to comprehend the horror of the death camps as had those who survived them. In the Eichmann trial, witness testimonies took center stage. Over the weeks the air thickened as survivor after survivor took the stand. It was these accounts, given by middle-aged people in neatly pressed suits and summer dresses like their own, that American audiences would watch each night on their televisions after dinner. It was indeed, as Sontag said, theater in its profoundest sense.

But as she listened, Arendt grew increasingly skeptical about the legal value of these testimonies. Where others were gripped, appalled, and shaken, she spotted a legal anomaly. Few of the witnesses seemed to link Eichmann to the specific crimes they spoke of. Instead, the prosecution asked that his criminality be inferred from the agonized memories that poured from the stand. Arendt thought that this missed something essential about his moral turpitude. In his previous life, Eichmann had enjoyed playing the role of the Nazi brute, but his real crime was administrative. This did not make it any less of a crime or less of an evil than had he person-

Hannah Arendt at the Eichmann trial.

ally murdered thousands with his bare hands. His sadism was in the detail of the paperwork. She started to wear sunglasses to court to cut out the glare from the television lights.

Only the words of one witness punched through Arendt's skepticism. They belonged to Zindel Grynszpan, the man who had been marched through the streets of her place of birth, Hannover, put on a train, and then beaten across the Polish border; father of the wretched Herschel, who had walked into the German embassy in Paris on November 7, 1938, and shot Ernst vom Rath, providing the false pretext for *Kristallnacht*.

So we were on our way to Poland. When we had been going for two kilometers, the SS started whipping us— over the heads—hitting us, those who fell behind—those unable to walk were dragged on the road—blood was flowing on all sides. The bundles we had in our hands were torn away from us and thrown aside. They acted most barbarically; that was the first time I saw the barbarity of the German people.[9]

Grynszpan spoke for just ten minutes, blinking slowly into the television lights and the silent auditorium. So much of the history being documented in the trial was condensed in his few plain words: forced expulsion, trauma, violence, the disappeared (Herschel's fate remains obscure), unspeakable loss, and grief. The old man opened the hole of oblivion and then spoke clearly from deep within it. Almost despite herself, Arendt was moved. *This story took no more than perhaps ten minutes to tell, and when it was over—the senseless, needless destruction of twenty-seven years in less than twenty-four hours—one thought foolishly: Everyone, everyone should have his day in court* (*EJ* 229).

The warmer it got in Jerusalem, the more irritable she became and the less the trial seemed to be making sense. *The whole thing is so damn banal—stinknormal,* she moaned to Blücher (*WFW* 357). On the evening of April 26, she got into a fight until one in the morning with Golda Meir, then Israel's foreign minister and later the prime minister. She liked Meir a lot; *since she's American* (Meir was born in Kyiv and raised in Milwaukee), she reported to Blücher, their quarrel *was almost amicable* (*WFW* 361). The argument was about Israel's national law of the rabbinical injunction against mixed marriages and the refusal to legitimize the children of mixed marriages made outside of the country. This would be bad enough for any state, Arendt judged, even if the motivation was genuinely religious. Meir appalled her by replying that as a socialist she was an atheist, but that she did "believe in the Jewish people" and it was on that basis that she had no problem at all with race laws, and in fact thought them necessary. There *certainly was something breathtaking in the naïveté with which the prosecution denounced the infamous Nuremberg Laws of 1935, which had prohibited intermarriage and sexual intercourse between Jews and Germans,* Arendt later wrote, in one of the many passages in *Eichmann in Jerusalem* that people, for a variety of reasons, found difficult to hear (*EJ* 7).

After a month she had had enough. On May 9 she took a break and traveled to Italy and Sicily, back to classical Europe and away from Israel and the present. Then she returned to Germany. She was due to teach an introductory politics course at Wesleyan that autumn. The course director, Sigi Neumann, wrote to her in Munich to ask whether she would be prepared to teach Jean-Jacques Rousseau. She would not, she replied. The last thing she needed after weeks of encountering totalitarian ideology face-to-face was to be reminded of how the author of the "will of the people" had helped to unleash political absolutism into the world. *God knows he is important enough, but I don't like him, and right now I am in no mood to deal with somebody whom I personally dislike.*[10] One intensely dislikeable man was enough for Hannah Arendt in the early summer of 1961. She was not in the mood.

Away from the courtroom she missed the most harrowing testimony of all from those who survived the death camps. One was the writer Yehiel De-Nur who had adopted the camp slang name for inmates, Ka-Tzetnik, and who wrote science fiction based on the other "planet" of Auschwitz. When De-Nur spoke, it was as though the boundaries between Poland and Israel and between the past and present had evaporated. He was still trapped in his hole of oblivion. He could not stop talking about theological systems, aliens, unspeakable violence. Nobody knew quite how to respond. The prosecutor, Gideon Hausner, gently interrupted him, where-upon De-Nur collapsed on the stand. When she came to write up her reports, Arendt seized upon this scene as evidence of the trial's excessive theatricality. The traumatized mind had no place in the courtroom, she objected. The law had to be permitted to do its work of creating clear distinctions between fact and fiction, right and wrong, and standards of thought and judgment.

Arendt was not simply being a legal purist. A lifetime studying totalitarianism had convinced her that freedom was best served when the law was clear about boundaries. Neither pity, terror, pa-thos, nor trauma should govern judgment when it comes to mat-ters as grave as crimes against humanity. It is a persuasive argument, up to a point. Since the Eichmann trial, the use of witness testi-mony has helped produce new and more capacious understandings of justice in atrocity trials. But it was undoubtedly easier for Han-nah Arendt to make that argument with such confidence because she was not in the courtroom when De-Nur collapsed, and nor, more significantly, when a hundred entirely lucid and articulate witnesses spoke during the six weeks she was away.

She returned to Jerusalem in June to hear Eichmann's own tes-timony and to look him in the face one last time. Eichmann had fashioned himself as an unimaginative bureaucrat for his trial, a role for which, as Bettina Stangneth demonstrates, he had been preparing for years. As her book shows, this was a complete fabrication. In truth, Eichmann was the same driven ideologue and anti-semite as he had always been. Hannah Arendt was no more fooled by this performance than anyone else in the courtroom. Of course, Eichmann wanted to pretend that it wasn't him on trial but the system, and that he was being scapegoated for something he couldn't help. In this sense, his defense was itself commonplace and banal. Obedience under tyranny *was* the moral and political problem raised by the trial, but for Arendt it was never an explanation in itself. Eichmann's lack of depth was indiscriminate. He was not so much the demon behind the bureaucrat as a man so detached from reality that *neither* role had any real meaning. The true moral obscenity lay in the fact that such mind-numbing thoughtlessness— *Gedankenlosigkeit*—had enabled the Holocaust. That was what was so outrageous.

In the event, Eichmann protested his evil as banally as he protested his innocence. Arendt first picked up on this in his speech. His language was dead, repetitive, detached, and yet invested with pompous self-regard. He was full of himself, but his words were empty. Whether explaining detailed bureaucratic procedure, repeating the hideous abstractions of Nazi circumlocution, discoursing on his tortured soul, or indeed boasting about his Nazi brilliance to his comrades in Argentina on the Sassen tapes, when words came out of Adolf Eichmann's mouth they turned to ash on the air.

> *The longer one listened to him, the more obvious it became that his inability to speak was closely connected to his inability to think, namely to think from the standpoint of somebody else. No commu-*

*nication was possible with him, not because he lied but because he
was surrounded by the most reliable of all safeguards against the
words and the presence of others, and hence against reality as such.*
(*EJ* 49)

His words were empty because his mind was without resonance.
Eichmann was thoughtless to the point that he no longer inhabited
the real world—which was partly why he could wreak such terror
upon it.

He talked mainly in clichés, many of them made up by himself.
One of his favorite sayings at the end of the war was the one first
related by Dieter Wisliceny at the Nuremberg trials: "I will jump
into my grave laughing, because the fact I have the death of five
million Jews on my conscience gives me extraordinary satisfaction." Eichmann's self-satisfaction is probably the most salient part
of that sentence. In Jerusalem he liked to say, solemnly: "I shall
gladly hang myself in public as a warning for all anti-Semites on
this earth," which was also very satisfying. *In his mind,* Arendt
wrote, *there was no contradiction between "I will jump into my grave
laughing," appropriate for the end of the war, and "I shall gladly hang myself in public as a warning for all anti-Semites on this earth," which now,
under vastly different circumstances, fulfilled exactly the same function of
giving him a lift* (*EJ* 53–54).

Finally, in June 1961, Adolf Eichmann took the stand to plead
his case. He put his glasses on his nose and blinked through the
double glass at the three judges as though they were his equals; as
though it were possible to calmly discuss how he came to plot,
design, and execute the murder of millions; as though, bizarrely,
he hadn't been there, hadn't been the crime's most lethally effective

executioner. He was, appallingly, absent. On the surviving video-tapes of the trial, Eichmann never looks at the spectators in Jerusa-lem and gazes over the heads of survivors as they speak. When a film showing documentary footage from the death camps is screened, he ostentatiously scribbles in his notebook, noting down details of facts he is pretending to learn about for the first time while conveniently not seeing, because he never in fact really saw, the consequences of his actions. *Eichmann was not stupid, but rather intelligent,* Arendt explained. *But it was his thickheadedness that was so outrageous, as if speaking to a brick wall. And that was what I actually meant by banality. There's nothing deep about it—nothing demonic! There's simply resistance ever to imagine what another person is experi-encing.*[11]

Eichmann was judged and sentenced in the second week of De-cember. By then, Arendt was back in New York. She had lost some of her original fury to exhaustion and anxiety in the intervening months. She had been teaching Machiavelli, not Rousseau, to stu-dents at Wesleyan that autumn. Eichmann might have once fanta-sized that he was as cunning and clever as a Machiavellian villain, but in fact, he was the opposite. Machiavelli's electric accounts of the artistry and virtuosity that went into making the Florentine Republic reveal a world in which people act to make power visi-ble. His heroes (and his anti-heroes) are those who understand that to be human is to be free to act, to risk, to show oneself, and to create. A master "theorist of beginnings," Machiavelli would have fallen off his horse laughing at the idea that the grossly unimagina-tive Adolf Eichmann was anything like him.[12] For a few quiet weeks that autumn Arendt enjoyed the contrast. In October, Heinrich Blücher had the stroke that would prefigure his eventual death just under ten years later and she felt the walls that had kept her safe for the past twenty-five years begin to tremor. The judgment against Eichmann was a welcome respite from the anxiety of balancing teaching with caring for the man she loved more than anything in her well-loved world.

Eichmann was convicted of four counts of committing crimes against the Jewish people, seven counts of crimes against humanity, and a final three counts of belonging to Nazi criminal organizations (the SS, the SD, and the Gestapo), and was sentenced to hang. His lawyer, Robert Servatius, began the appeal procedure. This generated another controversy. Some, such as the Jewish philosopher Martin Buber, argued that the better ethical and political course of action would be to show clemency, and so not allow Germans to believe that Eichmann's death was their expiation. Arendt did not agree. Given that Eichmann had decided that he did not want to share the world with other kinds of people, there was no reason why people should be expected to share their world with him. He was finally hung just after midnight on June 1, 1962. *He was completely himself,* she wrote of Eichmann's last minutes:

> *Nothing could have demonstrated this more convincingly than the grotesque silliness of his last words. He began by stating emphatically that he was a Gottgläubiger, to express in common Nazi fashion that he was no Christian and did not believe in life after death. [Instead, the Nazis fervently believed in the god of Aryan manhood.] He then proceeded: "After a short while, gentlemen, we shall all meet again. Such is the fate of all men. Long live Germany, long live Argentina, long live Austria. I shall not forget them." In the face of death he had found the cliché used in funeral oratory. Under*

the gallows, his memory played him the last trick: he was "elated"
and he forgot that this was his own funeral.

    It was as though in those last minutes he was summing up the
lesson that this long course in human wickedness had taught us—
the lesson of the fearsome, word-and-thought-defying banality of
evil. (EJ 250–51)

She did not know that shortly before his death Eichmann had
asked his brother to petition Martin Heidegger for his views on
last rites: "Not that I would presume to liken myself to this great
thinker in anything, but it would be important to me with regard
to my relationship with Christianity" (the same Christianity that
he dramatically repudiated on the gallows). There is no record of a
reply.[13] Nor would she ever know that Eichmann's hangman, Shalom Nagar, profoundly disturbed by his role in the violence of justice, would become a kosher slaughterman.[14] Three months later,
Arendt was knocked unconscious in a car accident and her world
went black.

Nine of the ribs that encased Hannah Arendt's heart were broken
when a truck hit her taxi in Central Park in March 1962. Her face
was so badly pulped by the impact of the crash that when Mary
McCarthy walked into her hospital room the next day she burst
into tears. *At first I looked like a Picasso that turned out wrong,* she wrote
brightly and bravely to Karl Jaspers. *When I go out, I put on a black*
veil and pretend that I'm Arabian or a heavily veiled lady. Then, too, I lost
a tooth, which doesn't exactly add to my beauty (AKJ 474). She wore an
eye patch over one of her eyes for weeks afterward. When she had
recovered enough to begin work, Hannah Arendt did so with a

renewed and now fearless fury. She was damned if she had survived the Holocaust, exile, learned to love the world, sat in that *stinknormal* courtroom for weeks and weeks, then had her accident for Adolf Eichmann to have the last word.

She began writing up her reports that summer in the rented bungalow in Palenville in upstate New York where she and Blücher holidayed each year. Her room resembled a smoking battlefield, strewn with mimeographed sheets of the trial's transcripts (running to approximately 5,000 pages), Eichmann's interview transcripts (3,600 pages), newspapers, magazines, drafts, and notebooks. She wrote in a rapture, mining documents and submitting facts to her control as she struck her fingers down hard on her typewriter, cigarette ash falling between the keys. Once again, she was writing to destroy; this was more archive fever and her last effort to throw off the virus that had infected her entire life. *I wrote this book in a curious state of total euphoria,* she later confessed to Mary McCarthy. *Is it not proof positive that I have no "soul"?* (*BF* 168).

She had pricked the totalitarian balloon and revealed it to be full of air. But that did not make it any less dangerous. If thoughtlessness, as much as intent, was a characteristic of modern evil, then the book of horrors could not be closed with the fall of the Third Reich or Eichmann's death.

In 1945 Karl Jaspers had written to her about a fast-spreading bacteria, a deadly pandemic. The virus had escaped into the world. *The fact is that today I think that evil in every instance is only extreme, never radical: it has no depth and therefore has nothing demonic about it,* she explained to Gershom Scholem. *Evil can lay waste to the entire world like a fungus growing rampant on the surface. Only the good is always deep and radical* (*AGS* 209).

Robert Lowell described *Eichmann in Jerusalem* as "a new kind of biography, a blueprint of a man flayed down to his abstract moral performance."[15] Arendt was not alone in seeing in Eichmann's vacuousness an aesthetic as well as a moral challenge. Susan Sontag compared him, sitting in his bulletproof glass cage, to "one of the great shrieking but unheard creatures from the paintings of Francis Bacon." Because she too thought Eichmann could not hear his own voice, Arendt inhabited it with her ironic ventriloquizing, like a parasite determined to destroy its host. She wanted to catch the disembodied meaninglessness of Eichmann's words and return them and him to Earth—so that both could be judged.

But it was she, not he, who was judged. That same ironic tone, her coldness, the lingering suspicion that she was, after all, out-rageously, blaming the Jews for their own murder, cut deep and hard. The backlash, when it came, was brutal. Much of Jewish in-tellectual New York turned against her. The old *Partisan Review* crowd were openly hostile. Leon Abel published a long and damn-ing critique of *Eichmann in Jerusalem* in the spring issue of that year. Irving Howe, from *Dissent* (which had published her "Little Rock" essay), organized a town hall meeting in New York. Her support-ers Alfred Kazin, Daniel Bell, and Raul Hilberg were shouted down. "The meeting was like a trial," Lowell recounted: "Any sneering overemphasis on Hannah, who had been invited but was away teaching in Chicago, was greeted with derisive clapping or savage sighs of amazement." In Israel, the dying Kurt Blumenfeld, one of her few remaining ties to Königsberg, refused to respond to her letters. Letters—hurt, pained, reproachful, and furious—landed daily in her mailbox. She replied to many of them as best she could. She knew she had upset people, and Hannah Arendt, of all people, was hardly going to deny the existence of other people's perspectives.

Some "of the criticisms made of you are based on the tone in which many passages are written?," the writer and journalist Günter Gaus pressed her on German television. In the video of their interview, Hannah Arendt pauses, takes off her glasses, rubs her injured eye, and replies:

> *I'll tell you this: I read the transcript of his police investigation, thirty-six hundred pages, read it, and read it very carefully, and I do not know how many times I laughed—laughed out loud! People took this reaction in a bad way. I cannot do anything about that. But I know one thing: Three minutes before certain death, I probably still would laugh. And that, they say, is the tone of voice. That the tone of voice is predominantly ironic is completely true. The tone of voice in this case is really the person. When people reproach me with accusing the Jewish people, that is a malignant lie and propaganda and nothing else. The tone of voice, however, is an objection against me personally. I cannot do anything about that.*

You are prepared to bear that?

> *Yes, willingly.*[16]

One of the myths about *Eichmann in Jerusalem* is that Arendt exculpates Eichmann by presenting him as a mindless bureaucrat who was only following orders. But this really wasn't the story. On the contrary, the book is a broadside against moral relativism and an early attack on the culture of ethical posturing. Arendt was worried about guilt, and she was worried about the trivialization of guilt. In the face of crimes against humanity, it simply wouldn't do to *speak in generalities according to which all cats are gray and we are all equally guilty* (*EJ* 297). What needed to be understood was exactly how we *are* morally culpable, and to act on that knowledge.

Who am I to judge? That was the question that the Eichmann affair raised. Hannah Arendt's answer was that I am nobody unless I do in fact judge. It was an existential answer to a new political question. Arendt judged *against* Eichmann's thoughtlessness. She went against prevailing moral sentiments—she called out collaboration, refused to allow the traumatic grief of his victims to be made to work for either weak law or bad politics, and insisted on Eichmann's prosaic triviality, because to do anything else would be to concede to living in a world where not only did facts cease to matter, but how we personally responded to those facts did too.

When her reports were first published in *The New Yorker* in February 1963, she also became part of that story. Even those who hadn't read her had strong opinions; hurt righteousness spread and the outrage was contagious. As the opprobrium piled up, she realized with horror that far from nailing facts and re-creating a reality where Eichmann's evil could be seen and understood, her own words were now swirling in a maelstrom of preconceptions, misreadings, and, on occasion, outright lies. She was judged for having dared to judge. How did she know? She wasn't there. She had offended. How dare she!

It was judgment itself, she concluded, that was now lacking in the world. At its most extreme, there was Eichmann's lack of judgment, his monstrous inability to connect with the reality of what he had consented to with such vapid enthusiasm. Yet what was also now insidious was a culture that was very happy with sweeping concepts of collective guilt and innocence, of absolute badness and a virtue beyond signaling, but conspicuously resistant to the complex difficulties of real human experience.

Is our ability to judge, to tell right from wrong, beautiful from ugly, dependent upon our faculty of thought? Do the inability to think and a disastrous failure of what we call conscience coincide? she asked in a 1971 essay, "Thinking and Moral Considerations," which would eventually become the first chapter of her final book, *The Life of the Mind.*[17] She concluded that it was—that thoughtlessness created the conditions for evil. And nor could the stakes be higher. Those who resist, be it dictatorships, totalitarian regimes, or the sly bullying that comes with the groupthink and performative politics in democracies, are the people who listen to the voices in their head, the other "I" in the "I am" that says with Socrates: I cannot live with myself if I go along with this, no matter what the cost. I simply cannot be. *Best of all will be those who know only one thing for certain: that whatever else happens, as long as we live we shall have to live together with ourselves.*[18]

The image of a few thoughtful souls hedging their existential bets, and sometimes their lives, on turning their solitary thoughts into judgments to live by is flimsy ground on which to build an opposition to thoughtlessness, tyranny, and lies. It may not be all we have, as we will see in this book's final chapter, but for Hannah Arendt, resistance always begins with those who cannot live with themselves and suffer violence toward others—*whatever* the circumstances and however powerless they are.

"There was nothing I could do about it" was not only Eichmann's (pitiful) defense but that of many since who consent to bad things but who are far from being vicious political ideologues. Yet as Arendt knew from her own experience, it is often from the position of powerlessness, when it seems as though there is nothing left to do, that reality reveals itself most starkly—at least to those who have the moral courage to see it. *Impotence or complete powerlessness is, I think, a valid excuse,* she said in a 1964 radio talk: *Its validity is all the stronger as it seems to require a certain moral quality even to recognize powerlessness, the good faith to face realities and not to live in illusions. Moreover, it is precisely in this admission of one's own impotence that a last remnant of strength and even power can still be preserved even under desperate conditions.*[19] This experience of impotence is the opposite of what she would describe a few years later as the *impotence of bigness* (*CR* 33). She was writing then about the empty might of an America that had just been defeated in Vietnam. There is an alternative to going along with the big lies, was her message after Eichmann. When you see clearly that you have nothing, existentially and politically speaking, to lose, you have everything to fight for.

Hannah Arendt would have recognized the extremes of the twenty-first century from those of her own. At one extreme, we too witness the sublimity of people literally fighting for their existence from points of absolute powerlessness. At the other, there is the self-important outrage, the bullying, and the conspicuous resistance to complex realities that has come to mark our political culture over the past twenty years. *I don't know if we will ever get out of this,* she'd written to Karl Jaspers in 1946 when he told her that it was the banality of evil that she really needed to pay attention to. She was right to worry.

CHAPTER TEN

What Is Freedom?

> We are *free* to change the world and to start
> something new in it.
>
> —*Crises of the Republic*

It was called the Carnation Revolution, and it was to be Hannah Arendt's last. On April 25, 1974, senior army officers moved against Portugal's dictatorship. Anti-colonial resistance in Mozambique, Angola, and Guinea-Bissau was wearing the army out. The brutal treatment of conscripts had confirmed that Portugal's *Estado Novo,* and the big family corporations it supported, was less interested in the country than in maintaining its own wealth. In February, a senior general, António de Spínola, had published a book, *Portugal and the Future,* in which he urged that the country cease fighting in the colonies (unthinkable under Salazar, who had died in 1968). In March he was fired. In April, Spínola, along with other officers and large numbers of the conscript army, made his move against the regime: a military coup began, and the tanks rolled into Lisbon.

And then something extraordinary happened. The dissenting army had ordered Lisbon's citizens to stay inside for their own safety, but they disobeyed and came out onto the streets too. An activist and restaurant worker named Celeste Caeiro brought a basket of red and white carnations with her and began to hand them out to the soldiers as a gesture of support. The artistry of her gesture caught on. Soon, the sellers in the flower market were giving away carnations in the thousands. Flowers blossomed in the guns of tanks and in the barrels of rifles. They nestled behind the ears of generals and in the lapels of military fatigues, carpeted the roads, and were thrown into the air. Political freedom is discovered in such actions, Hannah Arendt teaches. As in acting and musicianship, *the accomplishment lies in the performance itself* (*BPF* 154). Celeste Caeiro and the people of Lisbon turned the violent politics of a coup into street theater and changed the course of the revolution. Portugal brought down its fascist dictatorship with only four casualties (civilians who were shot by the regime's brutal and despised political police, the DGS, who shot into a crowd outside of their headquarters).

Hannah Arendt, then entering the last eighteen months of her life, watched the news reports from Lisbon alone in her Riverside Drive apartment. Heinrich Blücher had died in 1970. These were the same cobbled streets they had walked through together thirty-three years before, waiting for the boat to bring them to America. No more than the smiling young people now unexpectedly finding themselves at the beginning of a revolution, could they have willed the way their lives had turned out. But Heinrich wasn't there to talk with about any of this, and the room was empty. *How am I to live now?* her friends remember her asking the evening after his death (*BF* 266). It was a brutally genuine question.

Heinrich's death was made more painful by the loss of Karl Jaspers eighteen months earlier. Unlike Blücher's, Jaspers's death was expected. *I am sitting here thinking about you both and the parting that is before us,* she wrote to him and his wife Gertrud in her last letter: *But what is going through my mind and what I feel is beyond the grasp of language—among other reasons, because I am overcome by gratitude for all you have given me (AKJ 684). We don't know what happens when a human being dies,* she said in the speech she gave at his memorial service at the University of Basel. *All we know is that he has left us. We cling to the works, and yet we know that the works don't need us . . . Communication with the dead—that has to be learned (AKJ 685–86).*

She learned a lot about communicating with the dead in these years. Six months before the Carnation Revolution, W. H. Auden had also died. In her heart-stopping eulogy she called him up from his grave, poem by poem, as though she were continuing the conversation they had had over the fourteen years since they had first met. What made Auden a great poet, she said, *was the unprotesting willingness with which he yielded to the "curse" of vulnerability to "human unsuccess" on all levels of human existence.*[1] Hannah Arendt embraced human vulnerability too, but she never yielded to it.

Following the Eichmann scandal, she had taken a break from the sustained intellectual work required by book-writing and had gone into political response mode. There was much to respond to. World history was moving fast in the late 1960s and early 1970s. Portugal's revolution was the latest in what seemed to many to be a worldwide struggle for freedom. The year before, Chile's Popular Unity government had fallen to a right-wing coup (Arendt contributed to Mary McCarthy's fund for escaping leftists and refugees). The Prague Spring of 1968 reignited the torches first carried in Hungary in 1956. Across university campuses in France,

Germany, and, for Arendt most immediately, in the United States a new and militant generation of civil rights activists was in the ascent. She wrote long essays for *The New York Review of Books* and *The New Yorker* and spoke at town halls and public meetings. She debated violence with Robert Lowell, Conor Cruise O'Brien, and Noam Chomsky at the Theatre of Ideas in Manhattan in 1967. Arendt opened by decrying violence as a failure of politics. An exasperated Susan Sontag complained that she, along with the other speakers, had completely evaded "the issue that interests all of us: how to stop the war in Vietnam."[2]

Arendt did not believe in violence, but she did very much believe in protest, dissent, and disobedience. In 1966 she fought for the rights of occupying students at the University of Chicago who were protesting against their grades being handed over to the Selective Service System so that decisions could be made about who would be drafted to Vietnam. Universities were one of the few institutions in public life where free thinking was protected. The state, especially a violent state, had no business in the lives of those who studied in them.

With Blücher gone, her most intimate philosophical conversations were now mainly, although not exclusively, with herself. She began work on her final, unfinished, major book, *The Life of the Mind,* published only after her death and lovingly edited by Mary McCarthy in a last act of intellectual companionship. "Anti-Semitism—Imperialism—Totalitarianism" had been the three pillars of *The Origins of Totalitarianism.* Labor—Work—Action were the three actions that had organized *The Human Condition. The Life of the Mind* promised a final trilogy: Thinking—Willing—Judging.

As Portugal bloomed, she was busy preparing for the lectures she would give in Aberdeen, Scotland, the next month as part of the prestigious Gifford Lectures. Her subject was "Willing." This was her second visit. The year before, her theme had been "Thinking." *There are no dangerous thoughts; thinking itself is dangerous* is now probably the most quoted, and certainly most tweeted, of Hannah Arendt's sentences.[3] For Arendt, as we have seen, free thinking does not mean having fully formed opinions about everything and neither does it mean being a master of, or expert on, one's own thoughts. Thinking is an *activity,* a private performance which, like freedom, is significant mainly because we do it at all. *Hence the question is unavoidable,* she admitted in her lecture. *How can anything relevant for the world we live in arise out of so resultless an enterprise?* Quite. There are some heroes who have indeed summoned the courage to shout *Think!* down the barrel of a tank gun and have changed history in the process, but most people prefer to shout *Stupid!* into the void of social media which is not especially dangerous at all and is the very opposite of courageous. Thinking is not action.

Thinking matters, though, because when we do it, we move away from what we think we know because everyone else seems to know it. Thinking *means we have to trace experiences rather than doctrines. And where do we turn for these experiences? The "everybody" of whom we demand thinking writes no books; he has more urgent business to attend to.*[4] In other words, you, the person who has been generously taking time to read this book, even though you have more urgent things to do.

But this is also the problem with thinking: it requires that the thinker withdraw from the world. At what point do you withdraw so far that you can no longer see it clearly at all? Hannah Arendt had seen enough to know of the damage that distorted overthinking does to history. This is where the question of "willing" got interesting. On this issue she had, once again, been talking to Martin Heidegger.

In a 1976 obituary, Mary McCarthy painted a portrait of Arendt turning inward in her last years, like a Lear left to converse with her own inner fool overlooking the Hudson in a now permanent winter of the mind. But this was not the whole truth. Since Blücher's death, her relationship with Heidegger had become closer. She was shepherding the translation of his major works into English. The frequency of their letters increased. Another friend from later life, the philosopher J. Glenn Gray, whom she had met while teaching at Wesleyan in the autumn of 1961, became Heidegger's general editor at Harper & Row. Gray was a close intellectual companion in these years, as was Hans Morgenthau who, as Arendt scholar Samantha Rose Hill informs us, unadvisedly proposed to her on a short holiday to Rhodes in the spring of 1975.[5] She was too old, she told him firmly. ("I would love you if you were twenty, I would love you if you were ninety," he pleaded in response.)[6]

In October of 1971 she published a long essay on Heidegger in *The New York Review of Books*. It was her final reckoning with his work. With his Nazism Heidegger had, she conceded, made the disastrous philosophical error of trying to intervene to shape the world according to his ideas. Since then, though, his work had taken a new turn. Now he worried about how the will could set the self on a treacherous course in the world. We can't help but will (Nietzsche called this the "will-to-will"). You start with an impulse or an idea and before you know it your restless will is prompting you to inflict it on everyone else. "Non-willing"—not wanting to impose your will on the world for fear of damage, or more self-consciously, "I will non-willing"—Heidegger now argued, is necessary to keep both thinking safe and the world safe from thinking. Arendt approved of this active–passive solution to bad historical decision making. But the civil disobedient in her still wondered: where does this leave political freedom?[7] Was there not some way of carrying your will into the world—of changing the world—without all this endless internal self-regarding struggle? It was the former lovers' old quarrel. Why does not only what we think matter, but also what we do? Why is it not just me that is the problem, but us?

If men wish to be free, she had written in an essay ten years before called "What Is Freedom?," *it is precisely sovereignty they must renounce* (*BPF* 163). This is not an Arendt quote that you will find printed on many T-shirts, but in an era when so much hot air has been expelled into ideas about sovereignty—about taking back control, being great again, and shoring up borders—maybe it should be. At first glance, Arendt is doing little more with her criticism of sovereignty than rehearsing the point famously made by the English philosopher Thomas Hobbes when he argued that it is only by surrendering some power to a greater sovereign that people can be free from one another's violence. But in fact, it is the whole idea of freedom being achieved through sovereignty that she has a problem with. Once freedom is willed it ceases to be an action and becomes an abstraction, an idea, a fantasy even. And in the end, fantasies of total control or complete sovereignty are some of the most dangerous there are. *The famous sovereignty of political institutions has always been an illusion, which, moreover, can be maintained only by instruments of violence, that is, with essentially nonpolitical ends* (*BPF*

164). True political power comes only with the active assent of the people. The empty power offered by authoritarians, fantasy nationalists, and sovereignty fanatics, by contrast, can only be maintained by violence. In an essential twenty-first-century update of Arendt's argument, the British feminist critic Jacqueline Rose has argued that it is now women who are the main targets of this violence.[8]

But what then of *good*will? Is there a kind of will that does no harm? A will to nonviolence? What was it that willed Celeste Caeiro to pick up her basket of carnations that morning (the restaurant she worked in had bought them the day before to give to customers to celebrate its new opening, but the restaurant was closed) and take them with her out into the streets? On April 25, 1974, the problem of willing on her mind, Hannah Arendt packed her suitcase in New York and prepared to travel; first to Chicago and then on to Aberdeen.

Just ten days later, midway through her lectures in Scotland, she had her first heart attack; the second, in December of the following year, would kill her. Her longtime publisher and friend, William Jovanovich, who was staying at the same hotel, found Hannah Arendt standing in her room, wide-eyed, absent, surprised to discover, maybe for the first time in her adult life, that she was not present in her own mind. Mary McCarthy flew in from Paris to be with her in the hospital. Within days she was restless, impatient to get back into the world so that she could do the one thing that she knew really kept her in it—thinking about it.

For the past four years she had found a summer retreat in the Swiss Alps, near to the Italian border in a small recently built modern hotel, the Casa Barbatè, in the tiny hamlet of Tegna, ten minutes up the mountains by a one-carriage train from Locarno, a fashionable resort on Lake Maggiore. Like many former European exiles later in life, she sought a familiar landscape in the southern Alps which had the merit of having less of an atrocious history than those to the north and east. There, between the crisp early summer air, Swiss sheets, and the care of her friends, she recovered. She knew that you could not will a broken heart into fixing itself. *Active patience*—a title she first used for an article on the patience demanded of stateless refugees when she first arrived in New York in 1941—was required. She looked across the valley, noted the lizards hatching in the late spring sun, and, once again, waited.[9]

Portugal's was not a perfect revolution, but its first few months produced exactly the kind of political activity she approved of. Over one thousand workplaces were put under the management of councils of workers, *autogestão,* and housing co-operatives flourished.[10] Needless to say, this was not the kind of politics that General Spínola approved of. He was deposed after only five months and went to Brazil to set up a fascist paramilitary organization. After his departure there was a right-wing countercoup in September 1974, followed by another in the spring of the next year. By then, Arendt was back in Tegna, working again on "Willing." In the evenings, she would take the German and French newspapers up to bed with her to read about Portugal. She was also reading Kant in preparation for classes at the New School, where she had been given her first and last permanent academic position in 1967. She shared just the same sense of "wonder and enthusiasm" for Portugal's revolution as Kant once had for the French Revolution.[11] Like Kant, she recognized that she was watching one of those rare moments when, politically speaking, everything had been thrown up into the air.

For a few precious months in Portugal, it was not clear who was ruling and who was being ruled. What she saw resembled the ancient Greek political system of *isonomia* founded on the principle of equal freedom. Arendt wrote twice about *isonomia,* once in *The Human Condition* and again in *On Revolution* (*HC* 32, *OR* 23). The *isonomiac* societies were pre-democratic and had briefly flourished in settler and migrant communities away from established centers of power in ancient Greece. Neither authority nor tradition governed these communities. The principle was simply that each citizen had the right to act in the name of freedom of equality. Disobedience was built into daily political living since the only "rule" was that freedom was to be maintained for everyone. Responding to injustice was simply part of the political contract. In *isonomiac* societies, such as we might like to imagine them—and imagining them is probably as close as most of us are going to get to equal freedom in our lifetimes—citizens are made equal through their responsive commitment to one another's freedom. That's the theater, and that's the point.

When democracy was established in Athens, the unwieldy freedoms of *isonomia* were suppressed. Henceforth, majority rule would govern. In the last decade of her life, Hannah Arendt became increasingly convinced that the decline of opportunities for direct political participation was contributing to a genuine and perhaps terminal crisis in democracy. Eichmann had also taught her, yet again, about the importance of maintaining spaces where political action could also be moral action. (*Best of all will be those who know only one thing for certain: that whatever else happens, as long as*

we live we shall have to live together with ourselves.) But in the late twentieth century, the spaces in which this was possible were contract-
ing under the domination of big government and big business.
And as they contracted, the violence against those who wished to
claim those spaces back increased.

Nowhere was political disintegration quite so profoundly
heartbreaking for Hannah Arendt than in the United States. When
she had arrived from Lisbon in 1941, what had most impressed her
about America was *precisely the freedom of becoming a citizen without
having to pay the price of assimilation.*[12] Her new country seemed to
offer what Europe had so violently shut down: a plural politics of
active citizenship. But that was a long time ago now. She was, she
confessed in a long letter sent to J. Glenn Gray in August of 1973,
grief-stricken about the country.[13] The annual visits to Switzerland
were not just about nostalgia. Hannah Arendt had it in the back of
her mind that she might need to begin again.

In May 1975 Arendt went to a birthday party at which, striking a
distinctly uncelebratory tone, she gave a valediction. The Boston
Bicentennial Forum invited her to speak at its ceremony at Faneuil
Hall to initiate the celebrations for the two-hundredth anniversary
of America's revolution the next year. Few present were in any
mood for a party. *I fear we could not have chosen a less appropriate moment,* she opened by remarking.[14]

Three weeks earlier Saigon had fallen. Images of people scram-
bling onto the rooftop of the American embassy, their arms reach-
ing into the empty sky, confirmed what the rest of the world had
long suspected: the impotence of American power. More than a

decade of pointless war had brutalized and traumatized a generation. A new epoch of imperialist violence had boomeranged home
to the United States. The optimism of earlier civil rights and freedom movements had become tempered by cynicism. The release
of the Pentagon Papers in 1971 had exposed the lies that had gone
into making the war a fiction fit for other people's children to die
in. A year later, the Watergate tapes added insult to injury with the
revelation that it was not even cunning political minds who had
brought the country to this place, but ordinary, indeed, rather
second-rate crooks. It was as though, she said of Richard Nixon
and his cabal, *a bunch of con men, rather untalented Mafiosi, had suc-*
ceeded in appropriating to themselves, the government of the "mightiest
power on earth."[15] This looked familiar to Arendt (as it would again
for others between 2016 and 2020), but was all the more tragic for
what America stood to lose.

Arendt had become an American citizen in 1950 and took her
responsibilities as a citizen of the republic seriously. She loved
America for its love of beginnings, which she saw as embodied
in what, following Montesquieu, she called the "spirit of the
laws." "In the beginning, all the world was America," noted the
seventeenth-century philosopher John Locke, and Hannah Arendt
thought him absolutely correct to say so (*CR* 82). In the beginning, America's new citizens had *actively* consented to be governed
by its laws because they were, in effect, its authors. But lawlessness
was the spirit that threatened to take over America in the 1970s,
whether by its government, the failure of law enforcement to contain conventional criminal behavior, or by the conscious breaking
of laws by dissenters and activists. In May 1970 she took part in a
conference at New York University with the title "Is the Law
Dead?" No, it wasn't, argued Hannah Arendt. In fact, it was, in the

words of the clever headline with which Craig R. Whitney reported the event for *The New York Times,* "breathing hard."[16]

Acts of civil disobedience were neither the sheer lawlessness of criminals nor the rejection of law itself by anarchists and terrorists. Instead, in civil disobedience, Hannah Arendt saw how the moral act of individual conscience—I cannot live with myself if I consent to this—could sometimes also become a political act. Civil disobedience happens when people are not heard and when a significant number of people see that their government is clearly heading in a lawless direction. *The civil disobedient,* Arendt said, *acts in the name and for the sake of a group; he defies the law and the established authorities on the ground of basic dissent* (*CR* 75). The civil disobedient is not lawless, she is acting together with others precisely in the spirit of the laws—*breathing together,* Arendt says (*CR* 99).

Ten years on from her "Little Rock" essay in 1959, the civil-rights landscape looked different. It was not the law that had made change happen in the South: it was civil rights activists who had, in the end, put the Fourteenth Amendment to work. America could no longer ignore the crime of chattel slavery. *Not the law, but civil disobedience brought into the open the "American dilemma" and, perhaps for the first time, forced upon the nation the recognition of the enormity of the crime, not just of slavery, but of chattel slavery* (*CR* 81). In an idea whose time many would argue is long overdue, Arendt argued for a special constitutional amendment to be *addressed specifically to the Negro people of America* to acknowledge the enormity of that crime and *assuring them of its finality* (*CR* 91). America had worked (or perhaps it had simply hoped) because it was a nation created out of mutual promises. It was now time for those promises to be held to account and for new ones to be made.

It was a time, as she rephrased it philosophically in her Gifford

Lecture on willing, for the *I will* to become *I can*. Elizabeth Eckford had already grasped this when she walked up the steps of Central High, Little Rock, on September 3, 1957. So, too, did Darnella Frazier on May 25, 2020, when, aged seventeen, she stepped out of the Cup Foods grocery store in Minneapolis and took out her phone, knowing that she was in full view of armed police officers, and filmed Derek Chauvin murdering George Floyd. Frazier acted alone from moral conscience, but her courage transformed Floyd's dying "I can't breathe" into a movement of people breathing together—and breathing hard.

Arendt published her essay "Civil Disobedience" in *The New York Review of Books* in September of 1970. Five years later, on the eve of the bicentenary, her argument about America's exceptional political commitment to the living laws looked over-optimistic. Another exceptional quality of American political life had risen to the surface: violence. Violence was everywhere. Four of the country's most brilliant leaders, John F. Kennedy, Malcolm X, Martin Luther King Jr., and Robert Kennedy, had been murdered between 1963 and 1968. Student movements, too, had embraced violence. The Students for a Democratic Society organization which had been responsible for the mobilization of student activists at the beginning of the Vietnam War, and with which she had on occasion worked closely, had started to splinter by late 1969. Other more militant groups had emerged, such as the notorious Weather Underground organization which began a new bombing campaign in Washington and Oakland, California, in January 1975. In an event of spectacular pointlessness, three of the group had already blown themselves up in a bomb-making accident in Greenwich Village in March 1970. Violence is always a sign of the failure of politics, Arendt argued. By May 1975, she could judge the extent of that failure.

In Boston's Faneuil Hall, Hannah Arendt told her audience what many of them already knew but couldn't quite bring them-selves to say. Vietnam was an *outright humiliating defeat.* America could not reconcile itself to the *stark, naked, brutality* of that fact, upon which rested an even harsher truth: the power it imagined for itself was illusory. Read the Pentagon Papers carefully, she said, and they reveal that there was little real purpose in the war other than *the need for a super power to create for itself an image which would convince the world that it was indeed the "mightiest power on earth."*[17] This was America's *big lie* and it was as pernicious as any concocted in Nazi Germany or the Soviet Union. It turned out that you did not need state terror for a country to make up mur-derous stories about itself. PR-driven political maneuvering and the *hidden persuaders* of mass media could consign reality to obliv-ion just as effectively.

When Donald Trump audaciously invented the fiction that America's 2020 election had been stolen from him, commenta-tors evoked Arendt's *big lie* to warn of how close America was to democratic meltdown. Certainly, the resemblances are there, not least in what Arendt described as the *active, aggressive capability* to believe in lies (as compared to passive gullibility) that distinguishes modern political lying (*CR* 5). Modern political lying is not only shameless, it does not even bother to pretend otherwise. *The mod-ern political lies deal efficiently with things that are not secrets at all but are known to practically everybody,* she wrote, in another sentence that reverberates clearly today.[18] Political lying practically isn't even lying anymore. People are not duped. They are positively keen for deceit. The lies work because their authors know that in today's political culture it is not simply the case that people do not know what to believe, but rather that believing in anything with any degree of sincerity or authenticity has become all but impossible. To believe in the incredible and outrageous has become a kind of pseudo-action—a last lunatic lunge for political belonging.

Arendt would also point out that this active credulousness in the face of facts is only the latest chapter in the long history of politics and lying. Part of the theater of political life lies in the artistry with which politicians can conjure up an image of a world. To this extent, facts are always prey to the manipulation of opinion. The problem comes when the attempt to turn facts into matters of mere opinion goes too far. The total domination of fact-free opinion—what we now call post-truth politics—disturbs the fabric of the reality in which we live.

Conceptually, we may call truth what we cannot change, she wrote in an essay called "Truth and Politics," *metaphorically it is the ground on which we stand and the sky that stretches above us.*[19] Lying in politics is, of course, political, but in the end, the earth we stand on cannot be a matter of mere opinion. To even think that it might be is a mark of just how far we have traveled since Hannah Arendt exhorted us to get our feet back on the earth in *The Human Condition* more than sixty years ago.

We must render unto politics the sort of lying it needs to do its work and it should be possible to do this without a fatal collapse into cynicism, mendacity, or nihilism. Facts, after all, do not stand by themselves but need testimony, narrative, and witnesses; the kind of storytelling that can make facts appeal to people who do indeed have different opinions. The political storytellers we need the most right now, perhaps, are those who are most skilled at persuading us to share a world of facts.

There was another problem with America's *big lie* in the 1970s. The lies manufactured by public relations teams and policy wonks in Washington were so effective domestically because they rested on an image of America that many found all too plausible, indeed, that they believed passionately and were prepared to keep believing despite immediate and compelling evidence to the contrary. All political lies are also contingent truths, otherwise they wouldn't (usually) have a hope of getting a toehold on the public imagination. The image that the Pentagon lied in order to protect and propagate was one of America as a great and exemplary world power, incorruptible, democratically free, and morally fair. It was a lie that America still lived in. Some would say that it is a lie that America still lives in. *Let the chickens come home to roost,* Hannah Arendt pleaded in May 1975, let America see what it had truly become. *It was the greatness of this Republic to give due account for the sake of freedom to the best in men and to the worst*. If America really still wanted freedom, it had to renounce the fantasy of its own omnipotence. The country needed to reckon with its best and its worst.

Those were the last words she spoke in Boston and would be the last lines she would publish in her lifetime when her talk was reprinted in *The New York Review of Books* in June 1975 under the title "Home to Roost," a phrase that Malcolm X had first used after John F. Kennedy's assassination. Before that, Tom Wicker published an account of her talk in *The New York Times* and her mailbox was immediately flooded with letters requesting a copy of her typescript. One of these came from a young senator named Joe

Biden. "As a member of the Foreign Relations Committee of the Senate, I am most interested in receiving a copy of your paper," he wrote.[20] It is likely that Biden would have eventually read the published version of her talk. It remains an open question as to whether America has yet reckoned with its best and worst.

Hannah Arendt had started her thinking life with Kant in Königsberg and she would end it with him in America. In lectures at both the University of Chicago and the New School in the 1970s, she spoke about how Kant, perplexed by the events of the French Revolution, had turned himself into history's spectator, pivoting to look backward, identifying the historical particulars from the events that swirled about him and judging history from a distance; interested but also apart. In her final years she did the same. It was Kant who had first taught her that thinking was a moral consideration, that *how* we think has consequences for the world we live in. Fifty years later, she was still trying to work through how that thinking self could make judgments in a world that had so tragically lost its moral and political bearings.

In her 1974 lectures in Aberdeen, she had planned to pay homage to her hosts with a discussion of the medieval Scottish philosopher and theologian John Duns Scotus. Of all the philosophers of the will, she noted, Duns Scotus seemed happiest with the idea of a will that did not need to be in control of itself at all times. The choices we make, he argued, always have to reckon with the radical contingency of life, of how it is that things just happen to be, how they could have fallen one way but fell another. This recognition leaves us truly free to experience the world not as we would will it but as it is. This is not a surrender. Along with Kant, Arendt be-lieved passionately that we had free will and that living an ethical life would be unthinkable without it. Kant spoke of the power we have "of *spontaneously* beginning a series of successive things or states." The problem was that in the modern world it often seemed that Kant's will was neither free nor spontaneous. Adolf Eich-mann's absurd protestations about his reasoned and moral obedi-ence to Hitler's will had made this point all too grotesquely apparent.

Duns Scotus also thought that we have free will, but for him we can only truly experience freedom if we recognize that we ex-ercise it within a sea of contingency. Contingency is the price we pay for freedom, Arendt argued in *The Life of the Mind* (*LM* 213). It could have been otherwise, but we acted this way and then it was not. This was her final version of a refrain that had run throughout her political thought and life (as it has through this book). There is always a price to be paid for freedom. Contingency, plurality, the *sheer passive givenness of human existence,* the *best and the worst*. Free-dom cannot be forced; it can only be experienced in the world and alongside others. It is on this condition that we are free to change the world and start something new in it.

Accepting the randomness of freedom might be easier at life's end than at its beginning. Every new person with a moral obliga-tion to the world must believe that change will come; anything else is intolerable. Older people are often as, sometimes more, rest-less for change. Learning to love the world means that you cannot be pleasantly indifferent about its future. But there is a wisdom in knowing that change has come before and, what is more, that it will keep on coming, often when you least expect it; unplanned, spontaneous, and sometimes, even just in time. That, for Hannah Arendt, is the human condition.

At one point, she thought that once her heart had mended and she had completed *The Life of the Mind,* her final book might be on aging. In her research on the problem of will she had been reading Cicero's *Cato Maior de Senectute* (Cato the Elder on Old Age), in which the Roman Stoic philosopher and statesman cheerfully offers the consolations of thought, reflection, memory (and gardening) for those whose capacity for action must necessarily diminish. She had also been reading, with considerably less pleasure, Simone de Beauvoir's *La vieillesse* (1970), translated in the United States as *The Coming of Age* in 1972. She had never had much time for Beauvoir since Paris and had refused to write an endorsement for *The Second Sex* in 1952 on the grounds that Beauvoir treated sex as a social matter.[21] Age, too, she suspected, was a matter that went beyond sociology.

The book was never written. Her second heart attack killed her just six months after her Boston address. The brilliant theorist of new beginnings left us with only the promise of a book about the love of endings. After a good dinner with her friends Salo Baron and his wife, Jeanette, Hannah Arendt died sitting comfortably in an armchair on December 4, 1975. In her typewriter, she had left a blank sheet with the title of the yet to be begun third section of *The Life of the Mind:* "Judging."

I have no doubt that her study of endings and old age would have been every bit as joyous as *The Human Condition.* There is a photograph of Hannah Arendt taken in October 1971, just a year after Heinrich Blücher's death, in a car with another American icon, the artist Georgia O'Keeffe. As a young woman in New York in the 1910s, O'Keeffe would buy carnations from the street sellers and, paintbrush poised, would stare at them until they bloomed onto her canvases. Like Arendt, she resisted being defined by her gender and thought fiercely about freedom and the spaces which made it possible.

The two were together at Bryn Mawr, the women's college in Pennsylvania, where they were both accepting the M. Carey Thomas Award for Distinguished American Women. A small exhibition of each of their works had been set up for the event. Arendt had accepted her award in the afternoon, which had been followed by a celebratory tea. O'Keeffe's award ceremony then

Hannah Arendt and Georgia O'Keeffe at the M. Carey Thomas Award event, Bryn Mawr, Pennsylvania, October 1971.

followed. In the photograph they are either on their way to, or back from, dinner. Hannah Arendt is looking at Georgia O'Keeffe, eleven years her senior, the lines on each woman's face reflecting the pattern on the other's, and she is smiling and smiling with her eyes wide-open in pleasure. It is as though she has recognized a late ally who has confirmed that even after all the violence, the suffering, the loneliness, the lies, and the loss, there will always be women and men with their flowers and their determined and splendid goodwill, refusing to accept the compromised terms upon which modern freedom is offered and holding out for something new.

The Hannah Arendt Haus

The Hannah Arendt Haus in Hannover is not Hannah Arendt's childhood home, but a small community library housed in a room on the first floor of an old school, now a citizens' center, in the Nordstadt district of the city. The autumn light filtering through the trees and visible through the tall windows on the day I visited in September 2019 cast the same warmth it would have done when Arendt was born in October 1906. The custodian, Walter Koch, had written to welcome me and had made it clear that it was Hannah Arendt the radical who lived in this house:

> You are welcome to Hannah Arendt Library, Hannover. It is not a place to venerate personalities but to try to undermine European and German "closed shops." We try to follow stories of flight, of new beginning and of resistance . . . Naturally we are also inspired by books, essays like "We

Refugees" or *On Revolution* . . . and are glad to live in the tradition of Elizabeth Eckford's struggle.

The first thing Walter pointed out to me as I entered the room was the worn path on the floorboards, trodden into the wood by the regular pacing of long-dead teachers.

The Hannah Arendt Haus is a library made up of books that migrants and refugees have brought with them to Hannover or which have been sent on from their homes. Thanks to the historically close relationship between Germany and Iran, Iranians have the biggest collection. There are shelves filled with volumes from China, Vietnam, Iraq, Afghanistan, and Kurdistan. Books deposited by Palestinians sit next to those left by Israeli dissidents, some of whose older hardbacks may well have returned to Germany having fled with their previous owners during the Holocaust. A few years ago, the man who runs the Greek workers' co-operative upstairs presented Walter with a volume that told of his own family's expulsion from Turkey in 1923. Walter supplemented the Turkish collection with some lavishly illustrated volumes on the Ottoman Empire from his grandfather's library.

The Hannah Arendt Haus is a library of survival. Separately, each collection conserves a small piece of national tradition, culture, and history. But the books are there in the first place because of political, economic, and now, environmental catastrophes. Violence, seen and unseen, fast and slow, blew these volumes off their former bookshelves and into the Hannah Arendt Haus. It is a library of, and for, the modern uprooted.

The mood of the Hannah Arendt Haus is the opposite of that of the lonely scholars and readers who inhabit "The Library of Babel" in Argentine writer Jorge Luis Borges's famous short story first published in 1941, the year that Arendt left Europe for the United States. "The Library of Babel" contains the infinity of the universe, all knowledge is there; all that has been thought and written. Yet, no matter how hard they search among the books, for all their theories, all their intellectual endeavor, the citizens can find no explanation as to why they live as they do, in hexagonal libraries, following traditions and rules that appear to have come from nowhere and make little sense, until they die and their bodies are gently pushed out into space by their friends.

Hannah Arendt would say that the readers were looking in the wrong place to start with. What really makes life in the library meaningful is what goes on between the people, and between their books, themselves. Nobody knows the meaning of the *storybook of mankind,* but without it life would be unbearable (*HC* 184). The human world is built on little more than the necessities and hazards of living, speaking, and being human together. The little more, of course, is also everything there is. It is on this precious ground, Hannah Arendt believed, recognizing both our powerlessness and our courage, our banality and our splendor, that we are free to start something new in the world.

An air of fragility permeates the Hannah Arendt Haus. But the warm light and Walter's orderly shelves hold, rather than disguise, the sense of lives suddenly and unexpectedly thrown in the air, and the library is a quiet not a sad place. I asked Walter about its history—how had the library begun? He began to tell me how during the early 1990s he and other activists wanted to open an alternative venue to access the scientific knowledge that was then available only behind the walls of nearby Leibniz University. So much was happening so quickly, particularly with climate science and with nuclear, genetic, and information technology, it was important that ordinary citizens have the means to understand and respond to a rapidly changing world situation. But then he stopped and asked: Did I know about Gotthold Lessing? And had I ever been to Hamburg?

I did and I had, and so had Hannah Arendt. In 1959 she had gone to Hamburg to receive the Lessing Prize. Her address on accepting the prize, "On Humanity in Dark Times," was a significant event. Germany was no longer in the grip of the denial that had so disturbed her in 1949. The country was growing wealthy again. The reparations agreement with Israel had been signed in 1952. Two years after her visit, the Eichmann trial would kickstart Germany's eventual reckoning with the Holocaust.

The lecture started well. She reminded her audience of Lessing's insistence on the importance of free movement to enlightened thought. If there is no free movement, there can be no free thinking, she said. This was a quiet reference to those then imprisoned behind the border with East Germany just a few miles away. The stage was set for a comfortable reaffirmation of liberal and Enlightenment values.

But then she changed tack. I am of course, she said, in speaking of freedom also speaking to you as a Jewish woman who was once forced to leave this country. *I so explicitly stress my membership in the group of Jews expelled from Germany at a relatively early age, because I wish to anticipate certain misunderstandings which can arise only too easily when one speaks of humanity*.[1] The misunderstanding she wished to correct was the idea that any shared humanity her audience might have been congratulating themselves on by this point, somehow stood outside of the politics and history in which everyone in the room in 1959 was implicated.

This was some characteristically stark truth telling. Arendt was polite, patient, and learned in her explanations but unsparing in her conclusions. She was bringing reality back to Germany. Humanity can be neither wished nor willed into existence, she told her audience. Pleading humanity did no good for the Jews of Europe. Humanity, such as it is, is what we make of it together when faced with the facts. *We humanize what is going on in the world and in ourselves only by speaking of it, and in the course of speaking it we learn to be human,* she said, in one of her most beautiful sentences.[2]

She closed her lecture by evoking Lessing's play about religious and ethnic tolerance *Nathan the Wise* (1779) which, as she probably knew, was the first play to be performed in Germany after the war. Set in Jerusalem during the Third Crusade, the wise Jew, Nathan (modeled on Lessing's friend Moses Mendelssohn), befriends Saladin, the equally wise Muslim sultan, and one of the famous Christian knights, Young Templar. In the middle of a bitter and protracted religious war, the three deeply devout men set out a vision for pluralism. They keep their faiths and their truths but grant one another the right to speak those beliefs. "Let each man say what he deems truth, and let truth itself be commended unto God!" Amen to that.

It is not big abstract ideas about humanity that will defeat totalitarianism, Arendt concluded in her lecture. A genuinely plural politics requires the kinds of friends who not only grant one another their own truths, but who know exactly what they are up against politically and historically when they do so. For a German and a Jew under the Third Reich *it would scarcely have been a sign of humanness for the friends to have said: Are we not both human beings? It would have been a mere evasion of reality and the world common to both at* *that time: they would <u>not have been resisting the world as it was</u>.*[3] Resist the world as it is—it is hard to imagine a better summary of Hannah Arendt's lesson, nor one more relevant to us now.

Working in the Berlin State Library (formerly the Prussian State Archives) in the 1990s, Walter had come across an Arabic translation of *Nathan the Wise*. It was dated 1932, so the book had probably arrived there just one year ahead of Hannah Arendt's clandestine visits with Kurt Blumenfeld. A Hebrew edition had been published in 1866 but it wasn't widely known that the play had been translated into Arabic.

It was a little later that the Hannah Arendt Haus started to take shape in Hannover, and Walter met Hamied Al-Iriani, a scientist and scholar from Yemen. The sudden end of the Cold War in Europe had had direct consequences for Yemen. Soviet subsidies to the south of the country ended. Yemen became one country, igniting the civil wars funded by foreign powers that incrementally led to the catastrophe unfolding with dull and desperate horror today. In 2007 Hamied took a photocopy of the Arabic translation of the play with him back to the country and produced the first contemporary performance of *Nathan the Wise* in Arabic in Sana'a. Walter was there at the premiere. A trilingual production of *Nathan the Wise* is currently being planned in Palestine.

But where is the Yemeni collection of books? I asked at the end of my visit. I had been scanning the shelves, clocking the nationalities, drawing a crooked timeline of wars and mass displacements since the 1990s in my head. "Oh, there isn't one," Walter replied cheerfully. We—pointing at himself and Hamied, who had joined us for tea—are that library.

I like to think that Hannah Arendt would be smiling broadly at the thought that a house in her name was dedicated to stories of flight, new beginnings, and resistance. There you are, she might say, tapping her finger on the table in front of her in the bar where the lost angels of history hang out, right there, miracles happening under your noses even as the earth burns, the authoritarians and populists make new mischief out of the lonely hearts, and conventional politics seems as impotent and foolish as it ever did in my time. Now pay attention and get on with the work of resisting the sorry reality that you find yourselves in. And for goodness' sake—a puff of smoke, raising a glass of Campari—have some fun!

Hannah Arendt, 1975.

Acknowledgments

This book began with a conversation I had about Hannah Arendt with Krista Tippett for her radio show, *On Being,* in 2017. Donald Trump had been elected the year before. Across the world, an aggressive nationalist populism had surfaced. The response to our episode persuaded me that the time was right for a new creative and critical conversation with the woman who set her mind to destroying totalitarian thinking and learned to love the world more as a result. Thank you to Krista, her listeners, and to my agent, Zoë Waldie, who showed me how to turn that conversation into a book.

Thanks to The Hannah Arendt Bluecher Literary Trust for permission to quote from Arendt's archive at the Library of Congress, and to the archivists whose patient digitalization of her papers was completed at just the right time. The Hannah Arendt Collection at the Stevenson Library at Bard Library was an invaluable resource. I am indebted throughout to Elisabeth Young-Bruehl's defining biography *Hannah Arendt: For Love of the World.*

I could not have written this book without the work of Arendt's scholars and critics. Thank you Kathryn Sophia Belle, Seyla Benhabib, Roger Berkowitz, Judith Butler, Samantha Rose Ellis, Bonnie Honig, Martin Jay, Kathleen B. Jones, Jerome Kohn, John Macready, Patchen Markell, Roy Tsao, Dana Villa, and Susannah Young-ah Gottlieb. Many friends, colleagues, and some very kind strangers accompanied me as I retraced Arendt's biographical and intellectual journeys. Thank you Lisa Appignanesi, Jenni Barclay, Anika Carpenter, Niamh Coghlan, Sara Connolly, Hannah Dawson, Christian Dries, Robert Eaglestone, Lara Feigel, Kate Fitzpatrick, Diana Al-Halabi, Sari Hanafi, Hamied Al-Iriani, Lucas Johnson, Hussein Kassim, Walter Koch, Vivienne Koorland, Rima Majed, Itamar Mann, Anna-Louise Milne, Hasan Patel, Yousif M. Qasmiyeh, Jacqueline Rose, Amanda Rubin, Richard Saltoun, Philippe Sands, Marty Schain, Christopher Smith, Andrew Steggall, Danae Stratou, the late Georgios Varoufakis, and Yanis Varoufakis. *Mes amis et voisins de Cenne Monestiés: vous représentez le meilleur de la condition humaine.* Thank you to the Leverhulme Trust for the Major Research Fellowship, which gave me time to write and research, and to Andrzej Gasiorek, Fiona de Londras, Liese Perrin, and Nando Sigona, and my colleagues at the University of Birmingham for providing such a supportive and creative context in which to do so.

My truly brilliant editors, Bea Hemming and Parisa Ebrahimi, were always several steps further ahead of this book than its author. Thank you to Jenny Dean and all at Random House in the UK and the US for their expert book-wrangling.

Hannah Arendt teaches us that thought happens between private and public life, between tradition and experience, and frequently, and perhaps most preciously, between friends. My friend Sarah Churchwell thought with, beside, and sometimes against me throughout the writing of this book, which simply would not be what it is without her generous intelligence.

My four walls are three people: Shaun Hargreaves Heap, Joe Heap, and Mizzy Heap, who tolerated various kinds of absences when I hit a wall in the middle of writing this book, and then picked me up when I literally hit a wall while finishing it. Joe's best friend, and our friend, Laurie Herring, died tragically in May 2021. Laurie's last Instagram post showed him smoking outside an old British red telephone box. Underneath he had quoted Hannah Arendt, channeling Kant: *Nobody has the right to obey!* We miss him.

Works by Hannah Arendt

Love and Saint Augustine, eds. Joanna Vecchiarelli Scott and Judith Chelius
    Stark (1929; Chicago: University of Chicago Press, 1996).

" 'The Rights of Man': What Are They?," *The Modern Review* 3:1 (1949):
    4–37.

The Origins of Totalitarianism (1951; New York: Schocken Books, 2004).

The Human Condition (1958; Chicago: University of Chicago Press, 1998).

Rahel Varnhagen: The Life of a Jewish Woman, translated by Clara and Richard
    Winston (1958; New York: Harcourt Brace Jovanovich, 1974).

Between Past and Future: Eight Exercises in Political Thought (1961; Harmonds-
    worth: Penguin, 1993).

On Revolution (1963; New York: Viking Press, 1965).

Eichmann in Jerusalem: A Report on the Banality of Evil (1963; Harmondsworth:
    Penguin, 1994).

Men in Dark Times (1968; New York: Harvest/Harcourt Brace & Co., 1983).

On Violence (1969; London: Allen Lane, 1970).

Crises in the Republic (New York: Harvest/Harcourt Brace & Co., 1972).

The Life of the Mind (New York: Harvest Harcourt Inc., 1978).

Essays in Understanding, 1930–1954: Formation, Exile and Totalitarianism, ed. Jerome Kohn (New York: Schocken Books, 1994).

Responsibility and Judgment, ed. Jerome Kohn (New York: Schocken Books, 2003).

Denktagebuch: 1950–1973, eds. Ursula Ludz and Ingeborg Nordmann (Munich: Piper, 2003).

The Promise of Politics, ed. Jerome Kohn (New York: Schocken Books, 2005).

The Jewish Writings, ed. Jerome Kohn and Ron H. Feldman (New York: Schocken Books, 2007).

Reflections on Literature and Culture, ed. Susannah Young-ah Gottlieb (Stanford: Stanford University Press, 2007).

Thinking Without a Banister: Essays in Understanding 1953–1975, ed. Jerome Kohn (New York: Schocken Books, 2018).

LETTERS

Within Four Walls: The Correspondence Between Hannah Arendt and Heinrich Blücher 1936–1968, eds. Lotte Kohler and Peter Constantine (New York: Harcourt, 1996).

Letters 1925–1975: Hannah Arendt and Martin Heidegger, ed. Ursula Ludz, translated by Andrew Shields (New York: Harcourt, 2003).

Hannah Arendt, Karl Jaspers Correspondence 1926–1969, eds. Lotte Kohler and Hans Saner (New York: Harcourt Brace & Co., 1992).

Between Friends: The Correspondence of Hannah Arendt and Mary McCarthy 1949–1975, ed. Carol Brightman (London: Secker & Warburg, 1995).

The Correspondence of Hannah Arendt and Gershom Scholem, ed. Marie Knott, translated by Anthony David (Chicago: University of Chicago Press, 2017).

Notes

THINKING WHAT WE ARE DOING

1. Masha Gessen, *The Future Is History: How Totalitarianism Reclaimed Russia* (London: Granta Books, 2017).
2. Hannah Arendt, "Concern with Politics in Recent European Political Thought" (1954), *EU,* 444.
3. Mary McCarthy, "Saying Good-bye to Hannah," *The New York Review of Books,* January 26, 1976.
4. Arendt, "We Refugees," *JW,* 264–65.
5. McCarthy, "Saying Good-bye to Hannah."
6. Hannah Arendt to Professor Sacher, October 25, 1967, Hannah Arendt Archive, Library of Congress (HAA).

CHAPTER ONE: WHERE DO WE BEGIN?

1. "On Hannah Arendt: 'Truth and Politics' with Martin Jay," Richard Saltoun Gallery, December 16, 2021, youtube.com/watch?v=Kc6SNI bfx7A, accessed March 6, 2023.

2. Quoted in Elisabeth Young-Bruehl, *Hannah Arendt: For Love of the World* (New Haven: Yale University Press, 1982), 13.

3. Arendt, "On Humanity in Dark Times: Thoughts About Lessing," *MDT,* 8.

CHAPTER TWO: HOW TO THINK

1. Joachim Fest, "Das Mädchen aus der Fremde," in *Der Spiegel,* September 13, 2004, 142–46.

2. Arendt, "What Is *Existenz* Philosophy?" *Partisan Review* 13, no. 1, Winter, 1946, 41.

3. Arendt, "As If Speaking to a Brick Wall: A Conversation with Joachim Fest," *TWB,* 279.

4. Arendt, "As If Speaking to a Brick Wall," 285.

5. Arendt, "Thinking and Moral Considerations," *RJ,* 184.

6. Arendt, " 'What Remains? The Language Remains': A Conversation with Günter Gaus," *EU,* 20.

7. Arendt, "What Remains?" 11.

8. Rudy Koshar, *Social Life, Local Politics and Nazism: Marburg, 1880–1935* (Chapel Hill/London: University of North Carolina Press, 1986), 283.

9. Philip Oltermann, "Hanau Attack Gunman Railed Against Ethnic Minorities On-line," *The Guardian,* February 20, 2020.

10. Arendt, "Heidegger at Eighty," *TWB,* 420.

11. Arendt, "What Is *Existenz* Philosophy?" 35.

12. Jean-Paul Sartre, "The Root of the Chestnut Tree," *Partisan Review* 13, no. 1, Winter, 1946, 25–33.

13. Arendt, "Concern with Politics in Recent European Thought," 439.

14. Elżbieta Ettinger, *Hannah Arendt/Martin Heidegger* (New Haven: Yale University Press, 1995), 96.

15. Arendt, "What Is *Existenz* Philosophy?" 50.

16. Arendt, "What Is *Existenz* Philosophy?" 51.

17. Reprinted as "Heidegger the Fox," *EU,* 361–62.

18. Arendt, "What Is *Existenz* Philosophy?" 52.

19. Arendt, "What Is *Existenz* Philosophy?" 59.

20. Ettinger, *Hannah Arendt/Martin Heidegger,* 26–28.
21. For more about Günther Anders, who is long overdue a wider readership, see the Günther Anders Society website: guenther-anders-gesellschaft .org/gesellschaft.

CHAPTER THREE: HOW TO THINK LIKE A REFUGEE

1. Yousif M. Qasmiyeh, *Writing the Camp* (Talgarreg: Broken Sleep Books, 2021).
2. See Elena Fiddian-Qasmiyeh and Yousif M. Qasmiyeh, "Refugee Solidarity in Death and Dying," *Refugee Hosts,* refugeehosts.org/2017/05/23/ refugee-refugee-solidarity-in-death-and-dying/.
3. missingmigrants.iom.int/region/mediterranean, accessed April 28, 2022.
4. Young-Bruehl, *Hannah Arendt,* 158.
5. Arendt, "Guests from No-Man's Land" (1944), *JW,* 211.
6. Jonathon Catlin, "Hannah Arendt and the Twentieth Century," May 2020, literaturwissenschaft-berlin.de/hannah-arendt-and-the-twentieth -century-dhm/, accessed August 15, 2020.
7. Arendt, "What Remains?" 5.
8. Arendt, "What Remains?" 11–12.
9. Young-Bruehl, *Hannah Arendt,* 105.
10. Bettina Stangneth, *Eichmann Before Jerusalem: The Unexamined Life of a Mass Murderer* (London: The Bodley Head, 2014), 37.
11. Young-Bruehl, *Hannah Arendt,* 106.
12. Robert Lowell to Hannah Arendt, January 9, 1961, HAA.
13. Hannah Arendt and Günther Stern, *"Rilke's Duino Elegies," Reflections on Literature and Culture,* ed. Susannah Young-Ah Gottlieb (Stanford: Stanford University Press, 2007), 1–23.
14. Arendt, "The Concept of History," *BPF,* 51.
15. Simone Weil, "The *Iliad* or *The Poem of Force*" (1945 [1941]), trans. Mary McCarthy, *Simone Weil: An Anthology,* ed. Siân Miles (London: Penguin, 2005), 211.
16. Arendt, "The Concept of History," 58.
17. Young-Bruehl, *Hannah Arendt,* 275–76.

18. Arendt, "Stefan Zweig: Jews in the World of Yesterday" (1943), *JW,* 326.
19. Arendt, "What Remains?" 20.
20. Arendt, "Some Young People Are Going Home," *JW,* 37.
21. See Raef Zreik, "When Does a Settler Become a Native?" *Constellations* 23, no. 3, 2016, 354–64.
22. Elena Fiddian-Qasmiyeh, "Responding to Precarity: Baddawi Camp in the Era of Covid-19," *Journal of Palestine Studies* 49, no. 4, 2020, 27–35.
23. Arendt, "We Refugees," 271.
24. Arendt, "We Refugees," 274.

CHAPTER FOUR: HOW TO LOVE

1. Arthur Koestler, *The Scum of the Earth* (New York: Macmillan, 1941), 275.
2. Lisa Fittko, *Escape Through the Pyrenees,* trans. David Koblick (Chicago: Northwestern University Press, 2000), 66.
3. John Berryman, "New Year's Eve," *Partisan Review* 15, no. 4, 1968, 456–57.
4. McCarthy, "Saying Good-bye to Hannah."
5. "About New York: The West Side Intellectuals," *The New York Times,* February 6, 1974.
6. Alfred Kazin, *New York Jew* (London: Secker & Warburg, 1978), 71.
7. See Margaret Miles, "Volo ut sis: Arendt and Augustine," *Dialog: A Journal of Theology,* 41, no. 3 (2002), 221–24; R. Coyne, *Heidegger's Confessions: The Remains of Saint Augustine in Being and Time and Beyond,* Chicago: University of Chicago Press, 2015, 67. Thanks to Christopher Smith and Kate Kirkpatrick for expert guidance on Augustine on this point.
8. Martin Heidegger to Elisabeth Blochmann, January 11, 1928, *Martin Heidegger/Elisabeth Blochmann: Briefwechsel, 1918–1969,* ed. Joachim W. Storck (Marbach am Neckar: Deutsche Schillergesellschaft, 1990), 23.
9. Heidegger to Elisabeth Blochmann, *Martin Heidegger/Elisabeth Blochmann: Briefwechsel,* September 12, 1929, 33. Translated by Ian Alexander Moore, "A Letter from Martin Heidegger to Elisabeth Blochmann," *A Review of Metaphysics: A Philosophical Quarterly,* Vol LXXII, no. 3, 287, March 2019, 560.

10. Arendt, *Denktagebuch: 1950–1973,* eds. Ursula Ludz and Ingeborg Nordmann (Munich: Piper, 2003), 204.

11. Arendt, *Denktagebuch,* XVI.372ff.

12. Ian Sansom, "The Right Poem for the Wrong Time: W.H. Auden's September, 1, 1939," *The Guardian,* August 31, 2019.

13. Arendt, "Remembering Wystan H. Auden, Who Died in the Night of
Twenty-eight of September, 1973," *Reflections on Literature and Culture,*
294.

14. Hannah Arendt to W. H. Auden, February 14, 1960, HAA.

15. W. H. Auden, "Thinking What We Are Doing," *Encounter,* June 1959, 72.

16. Reproduced in and translated by Young-Bruehl, *Hannah Arendt,* 485–89.

17. James Baldwin, "Letter from a Region in My Mind," *The New Yorker,*
November 9, 1962.

18. James Baldwin, *Go Tell It on the Mountain* (1953), (London: Penguin,
1991), 28.

19. Hannah Arendt to William Shawn, November 21, 1962, HAA.

20. Baldwin, "Letter from a Region in My Mind," 26–28.

21. Hannah Arendt to James Baldwin, November 21, 1962, HAA.

22. Interview with Eva Auchincloss and Nancy Lynch, 1969, *Conversations
with James Baldwin,* eds. Fred L. Standley and Louise H. Pratt (Jackson:
University of Mississippi Press, 1989), 75.

CHAPTER FIVE: HOW TO THINK—AND HOW
NOT TO THINK—ABOUT RACE

1. *The Times Literary Supplement,* August 18, 1961.

2. Arendt, "A Reply to Eric Voegelin," *EU,* 404–405.

3. Arendt, "A Reply to Eric Voegelin," 403.

4. *Time,* "Elon Musk: Person of the Year, 2021," December 31, 2021.

5. George Orwell, "Review of Clarence K. Streit's *Union Now*" (July 1939)
in *George Orwell: Orwell and Politics,* ed. Peter Davison (Harmondsworth:
Penguin, 2001), 66–70.

6. Aimé Césaire, *Discours sur colonialisme* (Paris: Présence Africaine, 2000), 14.

7. Vladimir Putin, "On the Historical Unity of Russians and Ukrainians,"

July 21, 2021, en.kremlin.ru/events/president/news/66181, accessed November 13, 2022.

8. Arendt, "Reflections on Little Rock," *RJ,* 196–97.

9. W. E. B. Du Bois, *The World and Africa: An Inquiry into the Part Which Africa Has Played in World History* (1946), ed. Henry Louis Gates, Jr., with introduction by Mahmood Mamdani (Oxford: Oxford University Press, 2007), 63.

10. Quoted in David Margolick, "Through a Lens, Darkly," *Vanity Fair,* September 24, 2007.

11. Arendt, "Reflections on Little Rock," *RJ,* 204

12. Daisy Bates, *The Long Shadow of Little Rock: A Memoir* (Fayetteville: University of Arkansas Press, 1962), 62.

13. Chimamanda Ngozi Adichie, "Freedom of Speech," BBC Radio 4 Reith Lecture, December 2022, bbc.co.uk/programs/m001fmtz, accessed December 12, 2022.

14. Arendt, "Reflections on Little Rock," *RJ,* 193.

15. Arendt, "A Reply to Critics," *Dissent,* Spring 1959.

16. Bates, *Long Shadow of Little Rock,* 69–71.

17. Arendt, "Reflections on Little Rock," *Dissent,* Spring 1959.

18. Fred Moten, *The Universal Machine: Consent Not to Be a Single Being* (Durham, NC: Duke University Press, 2018), 85.

19. Robert Penn Warren, *Who Speaks for the Negro?* (New York: Random House, 1965). The full transcripts of Ellison's interview with Penn Warren are available in the archival collection of the Jean and Alexander Heard Library, University of Vanderbilt, whospeaks.library.vanderbilt.edu/interview/ralph-ellison, accessed March 11, 2023.

20. Ralph Ellison, "The World and the Jug," *Shadow and Act* (London: Secker & Warburg, 1967).

21. Hannah Arendt to Ralph Ellison, July 29, 1965, HAA.

CHAPTER SIX: HOW NOT TO THINK

1. As described in Nicole Eaton's excellent *German Blood, Slavic Soil: How Nazi Königsberg Became Soviet Kaliningrad* (Ithaca, NY: Cornell University Press, 2023), 253.

2. Jonathan Derbyshire, "The Mere Thought of Kant Stirs Russian Nationalism," *Financial Times,* December 7, 2018.

3. Young-Bruehl, *Hannah Arendt,* 196–97.

4. Arendt, "Truth and Politics," *BPF,* 258.

5. Arendt, "The Image of Hell," *EU,* 198.

6. Arendt, "A Reply to Eric Voegelin," 404.

7. Stangneth, *Eichmann Before Jerusalem,* 79.

8. Arendt, "No Longer and Not Yet," *RLC,* 125.

9. Arendt, "The Aftermath of Nazi Rule: A Report from Germany," *EU,* 249.

10. Young-Bruehl, *Hannah Arendt,* 187.

11. Arendt, "The Aftermath of Nazi Rule," 254.

12. For this background, see Victor Farias, *Heidegger and Nazism,* trans. Paul Burrell (Philadelphia: Temple University Press, 1993) and Thomas Sheehan, "Heidegger and the Nazis," *The New York Review of Books,* June 16, 1988.

13. Quoted in Farias, *Heidegger and Nazism,* 233.

14. Arendt, "On Organized Guilt and Universal Responsibility," *EU,* 121–32.

15. Stangneth, *Eichmann Before Jerusalem,* 67.

16. David Reisman to Hannah Arendt, August 28, 1949, HAA.

17. McCarthy, "Saying Good-bye to Hannah."

18. Dwight Macdonald, *The New Leader,* May 14, 1951; *The Listener,* January 31, 1951; *Manas,* January 14, 1954.

19. Young-Bruehl, *Hannah Arendt,* 273.

20. Young-Bruehl, *Hannah Arendt,* 238.

21. Arendt, "Karl Marx and the Tradition of Political Thought," *Hannah Arendt: The Modern Challenge to Tradition/Fragmente eines Buchs,* eds. Barbara Hahn and James McFarland (Göttingen: Wallstein Verlag, 2018), 249.

22. Arendt, University of California, Berkeley, "Contemporary Issues," undergraduate seminar, 1955, HAA.

CHAPTER SEVEN: WHAT ARE WE DOING?

1. Richard Neer, *The Emergence of the Classical Style in Greek Sculpture* (Chicago: University of Chicago Press, 2010), 186.

2. Arendt, "Thinking and Moral Considerations," 173.

3. Arendt, "Walter Benjamin: 1892–1940," *MDT,* 204.

4. Yanis Varoufakis, "Greece's Deadly Wild Fires Were Caused by 30 Years of Political Failure," *The Guardian,* August 29, 2021.

5. Karl Marx, "Debates on the Law Concerning the Theft of Wood. Proceedings of the Sixth Rhine Province Assembly." October 1842. First published in the supplement to *Rheinische Zeitung,* no. 298, supplement, October 25, 1842.

6. I owe the details of the hairdressing and the typewriter to Amanda Rubin. See Rubin's forthcoming documentary on Charlotte Beradt's life and work, *The Third Reich of Dreams.*

7. Martin Heidegger, *Early Greek Thinking,* trans. David Farrell Krell and Frank A. Capuzzi (New York: Harper & Row, 1975), 78.

8. P. Gardner, "Furtwängler's Excavations in Aegina," *The Classical Review,* July 1906, 20, no. 6, 327–30.

9. William J. Diebold, "The Politics of Derestoration: The Aegina Pediments and the German Confrontation with the Past," *Art Journal,* Summer, 1995, 54, no. 2, 60–66.

10. Martin Heidegger, "The Origin of the Work of Art" (1936), *Poetry, Language, Thought,* trans. Albert Hofstader (New York: Harper & Row, 1971), 44.

11. Ettinger, *Hannah Arendt/Martin Heidegger,* 114.

12. Mary McCarthy, "Philosophy at Work," *The New Yorker,* October 19, 1958, 198.

13. Arendt, "The Crisis in Culture," *BPF,* 211–12.

14. Rachel Carson, "Silent Spring—I," *The New Yorker,* June 9, 1962.

15. Arendt, "Home to Roost," *RJ,* 262.

16. Baldwin, "Letter from a Region in My Mind."

17. Alexandre Koyré to Hannah Arendt, July 13, 1957, HAA.

18. Elizabeth Bishop to Hannah Arendt, January 22, 1975; Hannah Arendt to Elizabeth Bishop, February 5, 1975, HAA.

19. Poems quoted here: "Brazil, January 1, 1502," "Questions of Travel," and "Squatter's Children," *Poems: The Centenary Edition* (London: Chatto and Windus, 2011).

9. From the transcripts of the Eichmann Trial, nizkor.com/hweb/people/e/ eichmann-adolf/transcripts/AQ, accessed June 26, 2022.

10. Hannah Arendt to Sigmund Neumann, June 5, 1961, HAA.

11. Arendt, "As If Speaking to a Brick Wall," 279.

12. Louis Althusser, *Machiavelli and Us,* trans. Gregory Elliot, ed. François Matheron (London: Verso, 2001), 6.

13. Stangneth, *Eichmann Before Jerusalem,* 419.

14. As beautifully recounted in the film *Hatalyan (The Hangman)*. Netalie Braun, dir., Torch films, 2010, torchfilms.com/products/the-hangman, accessed March 11, 2023.

15. Lowell, "On Hannah Arendt," 3.

16. Arendt, "What Remains," 16.

17. Arendt, "Thinking and Moral Considerations," 160.

18. Arendt, "Personal Responsibility Under Dictatorship," 45.

19. Arendt, "Personal Responsibility," 45.

CHAPTER TEN: WHAT IS FREEDOM?

1. Arendt, "Remembering W.H. Auden," *TWB,* 532.

2. Henry Raymont, "Violence as a Weapon of Dissent Is Debated in Forum in 'Village,'" *The New York Times,* December 17, 1967.

3. Arendt, "Thinking and Moral Considerations," 177.

4. Arendt, "Thinking and Moral Considerations," 167.

5. Samantha Rose Hill, *Hannah Arendt* (London: Reaktion Books, 2021), 199.

6. Hans Morgenthau to Hannah Arendt, undated postcard, HAA.

7. Arendt, "Heidegger at Eighty," 430.

8. Jacqueline Rose, *On Violence, and On Violence Against Women* (London: Verso, 2020).

9. Arendt, "Active Patience" (1941), *JW,* 139–142.

10. Raquel Varela, *A People's History of the Portuguese Revolution* (London: Pluto Press, 2019).

11. Young-Bruehl, *Hannah Arendt,* 466.

12. Arendt, "Sonning Prize Acceptance Speech," April 18, 1975, HAA.

13. Hannah Arendt to J. Glenn Gray, August 13, 1973, HAA.

14. Arendt, "Home to Roost," 267.

15. Arendt, "Home to Roost," 267.

16. Craig R. Whitney, "Law: Is It Dead or 'Breathing Hard?' " *The New York Times,* May 1, 1970.

17. Arendt, "Home to Roost," 263.

18. Arendt, "Truth and Politics," 252.

19. Arendt, "Truth and Politics," 264.

20. Joe Biden to Hannah Arendt, May 27, 1975, HAA.

21. Hannah Arendt to William Cole (Alfred A. Knopf Inc.), December 16, 1952, HAA.

THE HANNAH ARENDT HAUS

1. Arendt, "On Humanity in Dark Times," 17.

2. Arendt, "On Humanity in Dark Times," 25.

3. Arendt, "On Humanity in Dark Times," 23.

Index

Note: Page numbers in *italics* refer to photographs and illustrations.

Latvia, 160
Lawrence, T. E., 78
Lebanon. *See* Beirut, Lebanon;
   Baddawi Camp
Lebanese revolution, *thawra,* 227,
   236–37, 239, 240
Lefort, Claude, 173
Leibniz University, 305
Lenin, Vladimir, 167, 237
Lessing, Gotthold Ephraim, 31–32
Lessing Prize, Arendt's address on
   accepting, 306–8
"Letter from a Region in My Mind"
   (Baldwin), 123–24, 220–21
"The Library of Babel" (Borges),
   304–5
Liebhold, Eva, 107
Liebknecht, Karl, 49, 231
Life (magazine), 261
life of the mind, 25
The Life of the Mind (Arendt), 24, 46,
   221, 279, 284
Life? or Theater? (Salomon), 107
Linden-Limmer. *See* Hannover,
   Germany
Lisbon, Portugal, 101
Lithuania, 42, 160
Little Rock Nine, 142–44, 146,
   149–53
Locke, John, 292
loneliness, 182–84
Lonely Crowd, The (Riesman), 183
Lorch, Grace, 144
Lourdes, France, 69, 104, 105
love
   Arendt's problem with, 116
   as charity, 121–22
   collective human story and, 118
   duplicity of, 109

finding, 127
God's love, 116, 117
as guarantee of plurality, 128–29
at heart of human existence, 109
Heidegger on, 113–14
as meaning of being, 117, 125
moral reason for, 119
as a paradox, 109
poetry and, 120
politics and, 128–29
as singular, 118
as state of grace, 113, 124–25
as worldless, 120–21
Love and Saint Augustine (Arendt),
   63, 75
Lowell, Robert, 85–87, 110,
   221–22, 259–60, 284
Luxemburg, Rosa, 49, 229–32, *230,*
   233–34, 240
lying, 295–96

M. Carey Thomas Award for
   Distinguished American
   Women, 301–2
Macdonald, Dwight, 110, 186
Machiavelli, Niccolò, 9, 21, 229,
   272
Madison, James, 241
Magnes, Judah, 96, 261
Majed, Rima, 240
Malcom X, 294, 297
"The Man-Moth" (Bishop), 224–25
Manomet village, 181
Marburg, Germany, 47–48, 50–55,
   65–66
Marseilles, France, 69, 70, 95
Marx, Karl, 9, 93, 161, 187, 206–7,
   229
mass displacement, 72

ABOUT THE AUTHOR

Lyndsey Stonebridge is a professor of humanities and human rights at the University of Birmingham (UK). Her previous books include *Placeless People: Writing, Rights, and Refugees* (2018), which was the winner of the Modernist Studies Association Book Prize in 2019 and a Choice Outstanding Academic Title in the same year, and *The Judicial Imagination: Writing After Nuremberg* (2011), which won the British Academy Rose Mary Crawshay Prize for English Literature in 2016. Her essay collection, *Writing and Righting: Literature in the Age of Human Rights,* was published in 2020. She is a regular media commentator and broadcaster. She lives in London.

A B O U T   T H E   T Y P E

This book was set in Bembo, a typeface based on an old-style Roman face that was used for Cardinal Pietro Bembo's tract *De Aetna* in 1495. Bembo was cut by Francesco Griffo (1450– 1518) in the early sixteenth century for Italian Renaissance printer and publisher Aldus Manutius (1449–1515). The Lanston Monotype Company of Philadelphia brought the well-proportioned letterforms of Bembo to the United States in the 1930s.